Instructional Supervision for Physical Education

Michael W. Metzler, PhD
Virginia Polytechnic Institute and State University

Human Kinetics Books
Champaign, Illinois

> **For my teacher, Allan**

Library of Congress Cataloging-in-Publication Data

Metzler, Michael W., 1952-
   Instructional supervision for physical education / by Michael W.
Metzler.
     p.   cm.
   Bibliography: p.
   Includes index.
   ISBN 0-87322-254-7
   1. Physical education teachers--Training of--United States.
   2. School supervision--United States.   I. Title.
   GV365.M47   1990
   613.7'07--dc20   89-7461
                                        CIP

ISBN: 0-87322-254-7

Developmental Editors: Jan Progen, EdD, and Christine Drews
Production Director: Ernie Noa
Copyeditor: Julie Anderson
Assistant Editors: Robert King, Timothy Ryan, Holly Gilly, and Valerie Hall
Proofreader: Gregory W. Teague
Typesetter: Angela K. Snyder
Text Design: Keith Blomberg
Text Layout: Denise Lowry
Cover Design: C.J. Petlick
Printer: Braun-Brumfield, Inc.

Printed in the United States of America

10 9 8 7 6 5 4 3 2 1

Human Kinetics Books
A Division of Human Kinetics Publishers, Inc.
Box 5076, Champaign, IL 61825-5076
1-800-DIAL-HKP
1-800-334-3665 (in Illinois)

Contents

Preface

As I write this, *Instructional Supervision for Physical Education* is nearing completion. At this same time I have just read with great interest several articles and news features that address important concerns about the quality of public school physical education programs today and about how we can justify their inclusion in the school day. I felt that nearly every page presented a different perspective of what is wrong with American physical education. The opinion of most of the authors is that our profession has a sorry and unrealized legacy, despite the regular, grandiose claims we make for our place in education. We stand on an eroding base of support for new and continuing physical education programs. That base is crumbling as much from our own rhetoric and proselytizing as it is from social, economic, and curricular reform forces.

The authors offered many solutions to this crisis and suggested roads to salvation for American public school physical education. Some of the ideas amount to little more than "business as usual" with a few new twists. Some represent viable and exciting options to consider for physical education programs. I believe we must resist any effort that simply repackages the same low-impact programs under the guise of public relations or even worse just declares that we have something to offer children, self-evidenced through our literature and place in history. Any curricular area that provides nothing more than a self-evident logic in this age of accountability will surely lose its place in the school day!

I firmly believe two things about American public school physical education and its chances for survival and prosperity from now until the turn of the century. First, we must make a difference in the lives of those children who are now in schools and who will one day decide the value of our programs in their children's schools. In order to make this difference we must demonstrate the ability to help children reach programmatic goals in meaningful ways and with noticeable maintenance across their lifetimes. It seems all too obvious that we have not been able to do that for past generations of students, who now as parents question the worth of our programs.

My second conviction is that the best way for physical education to make a difference with children is to make a difference with teachers. We should not fool ourselves into thinking that the grave contextual problems confronting American physical education will be relieved soon; these problems include time limitations, overcrowded classes, heterogenous ability grouping, teacher isolation, and restrictive equipment and facility resources. We need to find ways to help teachers be the best they can while working within these constraints.

However, a great effort is needed to overcome the contextual constraints, and quick improvements are not guaranteed. It is more likely that we can find success and make a difference to students by first helping their teachers acquire and improve instructional skills on a regular basis. The most meaningful differences teachers can make to children is to help them learn motor skills, work toward improved fitness, and develop lasting positive attitudes toward our subject matter. The best way to accomplish this is to ensure they are instructed by competent, effective teachers.

This book is about helping teachers become more effective in their physical education programs. *Instructional Supervision for Physical Education* is meant to serve as a reference and resource for those who take on the important job of teaching teachers. It can be useful for methods course instructors, student teaching supervisors, clinical supervision trainers, and school administrators who interact with physical education teachers (including both classroom teachers who instruct physical education and physical education specialists).

While some excellent books serve as resources for physical education teaching, this one has been written to guide the processes of physical education supervision. It is a resource for immediate ideas to improve existing supervision practice and can be a major source for planning new supervisory programs. However, this is not just a resource text meant to be placed on a shelf and opened only for advice!

This book goes beyond the narrow perception of supervision as a university-based effort directed to student teachers. Rather, the book guides supervisory practice as it takes place in many different teaching situations and with teachers at different stages of development. Supervision is defined to include any direct and intentional strategy for helping teachers become more effective. Those efforts can occur at various times and places and can be carried out by various people. My intentions were to write a book *for* supervisors, not about supervision as a profession.

It is intended to be a place to look for a viewpoint on physical education supervision across many applications and to provide the means for guiding practice within that perspective. The primary purpose of this book is to improve supervision wherever it happens and by whomever does it for the sake of helping physical educators become better instructors.

This book demonstrates that teaching instructional skills to teachers is remarkably similar to teaching sport skills to children. The concept of supervision-as-teaching makes a great deal of sense to me and has served me well in my own practice. I hope it does the same for you as a reader and as a professional assuming responsibility for helping some of the most important people in students' lives—their physical education teachers. If we are to have school programs that make a difference, we must first have quality teaching in them.

Michael W. Metzler

Acknowledgments

This book would not have been possible without the contributions of many people along the way. Special thanks go to Alice Niles, who helped edit my original thoughts into coherent copy.

Others who took the time to listen to my ideas along the way include George Graham, Melissa Parker, and Sue Magliaro. I am especially thankful to Melissa Parker for her help with the section on clinical supervision. Equally important help was given by Cheryl Close, Kathy Eddleman, Glenn Reif, Laura Treanor, and Wendy Mustain in the field testing of various observation instruments developed at Virginia Tech for this book. These last five people played a key role in the development of the supervisory model used in the book—thanks! I would also like to acknowledge the Human Kinetics Publishing staff; this book was surely made better by their meticulous attention to the major ideas and editing of the original manuscript.

And even though I'm sure she wasn't aware of her contribution, my wife, Sue, deserves many thanks for giving an erratic and moody first-time author the support and freedom to pursue this long-awaited project.

PART I

The Supervision Process for Physical Education

Teaching supervision can occur in different situations, be conducted by different people, and include a wide variety of activities. It occurs when one person helps another person become a better teacher. Supervision traditionally implies that the helper is a university faculty member, the teacher is a student teacher, the time is the formal student teaching term, and the place is a school.

The first chapter in this part focuses on teaching supervision as it is currently practiced that way as part of a teacher training program. Shifting from that narrow perspective, the chapter considers *instructional supervision* as a set of complex processes in which the helper works within accepted guidelines and functions to effectively supervise a teacher's pedagogical development. We can make a direct comparison between learning commonly recognized sport skills and acquiring skills for effective teaching; this comparison allows instructional supervision for the improvement of teaching skills to be guided by integrated decision-making, communication, analytic practices, and prescriptive practices.

Throughout this book, effective teaching is regarded simply as achieving the intended outcomes of instruction. This point of view does not attempt to prioritize one outcome over another (e.g., fitness before motor skills, or sportsmanship ahead of strategy), but rather examines *how well* the teacher is able to promote student achievement of *any* stated goal. The closer a teacher comes to meeting intended learning outcomes for students, the more effective he or she is, regardless of the specific nature of that outcome. Similarly, effective supervision is viewed as the ability to promote intended outcomes related to the teacher's performance.

The second chapter presents two concepts important throughout the entire book. The first is a definition of instructional supervision. This definition helps to limit the scope of supervision to decisions and actions that enhance the acquisition and maintenance of effective teaching skills. While allowing that the supervisor's job includes a diverse set of responsibilities, this book focuses mainly on that portion of the job that helps teachers acquire and maintain effective teaching skills.

Supervisory efforts to help teachers with their instructional skills occur simultaneously within many contexts. One of the most critical contextual factors is the teacher's own stage of development. The latter part of the second chapter describes five stages of teacher development and discusses how supervisors must consider each teacher's place on that developmental continuum in order to better assist the teacher.

Chapter 3 presents the Physical Education Instructional Supervision (PEIS) Model. This model, designed to guide the establishment of a supervision program in physical education, outlines procedures for conducting supervisory decision making, observations, analyses, and interactions with teachers. The model has three unique characteristics. It is intended for supervision in physical education; it can be used in all supervisory situations from micro teaching to in-service teaching; and it considers each teacher's own stage of development as an integral part of the instructional improvement effort.

Even when provided with a model for supervising physical education teaching, supervisors need to decide just what to observe and analyze during lessons. Chapter 4 lists effective teaching and learning behaviors on which physical education supervisors can focus their observations. Following that list are suggestions for determining how to make valid observations of those behaviors for supervisory analyses. Here another major construct of this book is introduced— supervision for improved teaching skills is best accomplished under a thoughtful plan of systematic observation. After selecting effective teaching and learning processes to monitor, a supervisor can select the best way to observe those processes in a systematic approach.

Chapter 5 presents observational systems designed exclusively for supervising physical education instruction. As designing and field testing observational systems are long and complex tasks, the samples of existing systems are provided ready to use. Each system can monitor one or more of the effective teaching and learning processes presented in chapter 4. The descriptions include the purpose of each system, category definitions, instructions for use, and examples of completed observations.

The observation systems described in chapter 5 provide a supervisor with an abundance of data-based information on selected teaching and learning processes. But only having that information is not sufficient; the supervisor must be able to analyze the data, relate the observed performance to intended instructional outcomes, communicate those results to the teacher, and identify necessary prescriptive action. Those interactive processes are presented in chapter 6. At some point in time supervisors will need to have specific plans available for helping teachers improve instructional skills. Several indirect and direct strategies for that purpose are presented in chapter 7, illustrating the practice of "teaching teachers."

Part I attempts to provide an overall approach to instructional supervision in physical education. This approach is based on the assumptions that effective teaching can be considered a set of skills (albeit myriad and complex) and that systematic supervision offers the best way to assist teachers with acquiring and maintaining those skills. This book views supervision as a special kind of teaching and asserts that we can approach the teaching of teachers in much the same way we help someone learn sport skills and strategies. Although good teaching involves much more than effective instructional skills, the perspective presented in this book allows a supervisor to use familiar sport teaching approaches in the supervisory process. This is one of the major themes expressed throughout Part I.

Chapter 1

Current Supervision and a View Toward Improvement

It is helpful to outline the difference between studying about supervision and learning how to supervise. For many years we have discussed, analyzed, and often criticized the conduct of teaching supervision in American education. These efforts have shed much light on this important function; but only talking about supervision has little potential for improving it. We need to use those insights to lead us to better supervisory practice, helping all teachers become more effective. This chapter briefly outlines a few of the major weaknesses in supervision as it is commonly practiced today and identifies specific areas where it can be improved. Three assumptions about how to view supervision are provided, setting the stage for the rest of Part I. It is these assumptions that form the foundation for how supervision will be defined and operationalized throughout this book.

Supervision Today

To examine the current conduct of teaching supervision is to find differences between words and action at every turn. Most departments or colleges that prepare new teachers will acknowledge that supervision is vitally important, yet set aside scant resources for it. Directors of student teaching will express a need for experienced, dedicated, and well-trained personnel to do this important job, yet the supervisor is likely to be an overburdened junior faculty member, a disinterested senior faculty member, or a graduate student who can devote little time to the job. Even marginally effective supervision requires a regular schedule of meetings and observations, yet allocations of time and travel resources make this modest goal unreachable.

Although practiced in a setting away from the university, supervision of student teachers is really teaching. Its central function is to assist a learner (the student teacher) in the acquisition of new content (the relevant skills, attitudes, and dispositions for effective instruction). Supervision is the process of helping a student teacher proceed from his or her present skill level to the skill level needed to capably carry out the many complex decisions and behaviors of teaching physical education.

Deficiencies in Supervision

Like any other teaching task, supervision works best within the framework of an overall plan that includes frequent assessment of its purposes, activities, and outcomes. Such a plan implies that several people work in concert to help teachers throughout their developmental continuum. Unfortunately, today's supervisor more often works alone than as an integral member of a complete team of teacher trainers. Student teachers readily acknowledge the key role played by the supervisor during that point in their development (Acheson & Gall, 1987). Yet while some studies show supervision as a positive factor in that field experience, many others characterize the effects of supervision to be at best dubious and at worst negative (see Thies-Sprinthall, 1980).

Locke (1979) described the ideal "noble triad" of student teacher, cooperating teacher, and supervisor as a group bonded together for the singular benefit of the novice teacher. In reality, it can be transformed into a "Devil's Triangle" in which the supervisor is sometimes at odds with the others due to the necessary detachment from the day-to-day dynamics of helping a young person learn to teach. The university-based supervisor, a member of a teacher training faculty, can become caught squarely between the ideals of the academy and the pragmatic compromises faced each day by new teachers who want nothing more than to learn quickly what works in the real world of teaching. Too often, the supervisor is on the front line of battle, directly in the crossfire between the university's sometimes lofty agenda for teacher training and the public schools' need for teachers with survival skills.

For these and many other reasons, university-based student teaching supervision has never held the esteem that even begins to equal the importance regularly attested to it. In fact, that kind of supervision has received more negative commentary than any other part of the teacher training enterprise. Mosher and Purpel's (1972) classic description of supervision as the "reluctant profession" has received few serious rebuttals to its scathing characterization of this important function.

Goldhammer (1969) identified three major deficiencies in supervision: (a) Most techniques used by supervisors are educationally invalid and stem more from personal experience than from what we know about how people learn; (b) supervisors lack training in providing emotional support for those learning the difficult tasks of teaching; and (c) by failing to exemplify in action what they promote in word, supervisors practice under double standards. In other words, they fail to equate the necessary processes of teaching teachers with accepted processes for teaching other groups of learners. Cogan (1973) adds this about supervisors' attempts to help teachers when those actions prove miseducative:

> Such regressions have too often transformed the history of attempts to improve instruction into a history of potentially useful educational innovations enfeebled and finally defeated by the failure to provide the teacher with the professional support required for the tasks of innovation. (p. xi)

The message seems clear—supervision has failed to look upon itself as a teaching process, one in which the supervisor helps the teacher learn the many and complex tasks, skills, and decisions necessary for effective instruction in schools. That single failure can be viewed as the major error that leads to many other problems now inherent in supervisory practice.

Supervision in Physical Education

While supervision of physical education teachers has received little attention by itself, the evidence we do have suggests that its effectiveness is no greater than that of supervision in general. Locke (1979) states, "At the outset you can rest assured that the program supervisor plays no negative role. This is because the college supervisor plays no significant role at all" (p. 6). Supervision in physical education suffers from all the systemic problems mentioned earlier and seems to reproduce many of the same dubious effects as its counterparts in other areas of education.

Teacher education, including supervision, has not shown the capability to promote a transfer of instructional practices learned at the university (Locke, 1983; Templin, 1979), to prevent student teachers from reverting to previous custodial outlooks on teaching (Templin, 1979, 1981), or to foster demonstrable professional socialization outcomes among student teachers (Lawson, 1983, 1986). The references cited do not mention supervision directly or attempt to blame it for these inadequacies; in fact, supervision in these depictions is conspicuous mostly by its absence! If supervision did exert a tangible influence, surely it would be recognizable. These outcomes for physical education supervision coincide with what we know about the low impact of teacher education and student teaching supervision in other subject areas (Zeichner & Tabachnick, 1981).

Not only does physical education supervision fail to show any break from the dysfunctional pattern of supervision in general, many supervisors in our field are in that role for the wrong reasons. This is due in part to tradition ("If someone has teaching experience, he or she must be qualified to supervise") and in part to the same low priority given to supervision nearly everywhere. The faculty group from which physical education supervisors are drawn shows an alarming degree of disparity (Metzler & Freedman, 1985).

- Most supervisors have public school teaching experience but usually not recent experience. Some have no public school teaching experience at all.
- Almost all have other teaching duties in the program (nearly 20% also coach intercollegiate teams).
- Very few have an advanced degree that could be construed as supervisory training.
- Fewer than 10% have their own agenda for researching an area related to teacher education.

Physical education supervisors identify themselves as such because of their job duties, not because of a common training and professional disposition. The traditional university-based model for student teacher supervision has many negative aspects; in physical education this model appears to have little potential to consistently help teachers improve their instructional skills.

Toward Better Supervision

Supervision as it has just been described suffers from two separate but related problems. The first problem is that the university-based model used almost exclusively for student teacher supervision doesn't work and isn't likely to ever work within the present structure of preprofessional teacher training. This assertion is based in part upon the abundant literature on the ineffectiveness of university supervision, offering little substantiation for a positive and consistent impact from the ways supervision is practiced today. Furthermore, supervision is often viewed as something separate and apart from the rest of the teacher training program, even to the extent that in some programs supervision is provided by personnel other than physical education faculty! It can become even more separated by how little it relates to other components of the program; supervisors cannot effectively link pre-student-teaching experiences with events in the real world of schools, leaving that difficult task for the novice teacher to sort out alone.

If supervision is to be effective, it must be delivered in the right place at the right time; this is rarely possible when its delivery depends entirely upon one person. The campus-based supervisor cannot realistically be expected to be available each time a student teacher needs pertinent insights and courses of action. Thus, different people at different times must fulfill the role of supervisor. For example, the best supervisor for on-campus peer teaching most likely is the methods course instructor who designed the simulated teaching episode. The assigned cooperating teacher is probably the best supervisor for student teaching, because of the frequent opportunities to observe and a familiarity with the context of lessons.

The second problem is that educators have seldom attempted to outline just how supervision should work. Mosher and Purpel's (1972) label of "reluctant profession'' originated largely from the lack of research, procedural, and content bases for supervision, not from supervisors' lack of interest in their own effectiveness. In many cases supervisors simply did not know what they were supposed to do within some stated framework of practice; thus supervision was guided much more by an individual supervisor's feel for what should be done rather than intentional, systematic decisions and actions.

Fortunately, the focus of supervision—what a supervisor might choose to monitor during instruction—has become more evident in recent years. Research on teaching effectiveness in classroom and physical education settings has identified several key teaching and learning processes that can lead to increased student achievement of intended outcomes. Some of these processes are now accepted as preferred instructional practice in physical education; they include increased student time on task, clear statements of task structure and accountability, relevant and specific performance feedback, reduced management time, and meaningful teacher-student interaction. Supervisors can now promote these and many other pedagogical practices as desirable goals and monitor teachers' ability to appropriately demonstrate them during instructional episodes.

Reiterating criticisms will not improve the practice of instructional supervision within physical education. Providing a perspective for supervision, formulating new and effective strategies for its conduct, and offering assistance to those who perform supervisory roles is more likely to lead to better practice.

Supervision as a Process, Not a Person

Almost without exception, teacher supervision is considered the domain of one person—the university supervisor from a teacher training program—and is practiced at one point in time, during the formal student teaching term. (Some school divisions designate a curriculum supervisor, but most often that person directs supervision only as a portion of his or her overall administrative responsibilities.) This common outlook on supervision narrowly defines that role and assumes that no other persons can or should carry out this function in teacher training. It also assumes that focused teaching supervision can or should take place only once during a teacher's career, ignoring the reality that teachers need varying amounts of assistance at every stage of their development as effective physical educators. Learning to teach better involves a highly dynamic set of events that we cannot expect to happen at predetermined, convenient times; supervisors must strive to be in the right place at the right time, continuing to help teachers when and where assistance is needed.

University supervisors probably have the most experience in helping teachers improve their instructional skills; however, experience should not be mistaken for training. In a survey of teacher training faculty in physical education, Metzler and Freedman (1985) found that supervisors seldom had formal coursework or other training in the practice of their roles, an alarming finding about a group who identified themselves as teacher trainers!

Many of the reasons for present supervisory ineffectiveness stem from a reliance on one person for its practice. To be more effective, supervision must break not only from this reliance on one person but also from its narrow model of delivery. A broader perspective would allow supervision to occur in many more contexts, be intended for all physical education teachers, and be practiced under certain procedures by many different people.

Assumptions About Supervision

What supervision should include and how it should be practiced in physical education can be viewed in many ways. While recognizing those diverse approaches, this book proposes that supervision is most effective when it proceeds from a logical set of related assumptions about teaching and the improvement of instruction. These assumptions stem from my own viewpoint that effective teaching is a set of complex decision and action skills, and that the most critical function of supervision is to assist teachers in the acquisition and maintenance of those skills.

Assumption 1: Teaching Is a Skill

The age-old debate whether teaching is an art or a science ignores one important characteristic necessary to both concepts: Regardless of the source of a teacher's intent (art or science), the teacher must have the skills to carry out the decisions and actions needed to fulfill that intent. Necessary skills include decision making (e.g., deciding that students will benefit from viewing a demonstration of the bunker shot in golf) as well as physical abilities (e.g., demonstrating the shot for them).

When effective teaching is considered a set of skills, the learning of them then becomes similar to learning skills in sport and fitness activities.

- It is possible (and desirable) to identify a finite set of skills necessary for certain applications. Just as a baseball outfielder does not need to learn infield skills, a secondary physical education teacher does not need to learn strategies typical of elementary physical education.
- It is possible to design environments that foster the improvement of teaching skills. Teachers can improve, and that improvement can be pursued through a properly planned series of practice, simulations, and actual instructional experiences.
- An individual teacher's skills can be monitored through systematic observation. Just as a coach can record and refer to game statistics, a supervisor can compile objective data on effective teaching performance. When

properly recorded and analyzed, those data can serve as valid indicators of selected teaching skills.

- By monitoring a teacher over time, a supervisor can identify changes in teaching skills. This is similar to a coach monitoring changes in an individual's skill throughout a season. These changes can be used to assess improvement in teaching skills and the effectiveness of supervision itself.

Assumption 2: Supervision Is Teaching

Sport skills can be learned, and they can be learned better through teaching. This logic also applies to the learning of instructional skills in physical education and the role of supervision in that process. Supervision is actually a special type of teaching; it is similar to instructing students how to throw, catch, steal third base, make a lay up, or plan a game strategy. Teachers, like students, must progress through a variety of learning activities that take into account their present skill levels, the present context, and past experiences, advancing them toward reasonable learning outcomes. Teachers, like students, can benefit greatly from receiving accurate, relevant, and constructive feedback about their current performance, along with strategies for reaching stated instructional goals.

Supervision and teaching share other similarities. Teachers must be keenly aware of the instructional context—factors about students, content, schools, and themselves that influence teaching practice and effectiveness. Supervisors must also consider contextual factors as they interact with and observe individual teachers. Good teaching is thought to be context specific; so too is good supervision.

Supervision, like teaching, must provide learners with certain analytical, supportive, diagnostic, prescriptive, and evaluative processes. Learning is more likely to take place when learners are meaningfully engaged with the subject matter, assigned tasks commensurate with previous learning experiences, and given timely and accurate feedback about performance. These processes must be presented in a logical and well-planned pattern to be most effective; that these processes are in place and working is more important than who delivers them. If several kinds of persons can be trained as supervisors (i.e., teachers of teachers) and can carry out well-grounded supervisory processes, then supervision has a greater chance to help physical educators improve their instructional skills.

Assumption 3: Systematic Observation Enhances Supervision

The final assumption upon which this book is based concerns the role of systematic observation of teaching skills in physical education. If teaching itself can be viewed as a series of intentional decisions and actions, so too can supervision. Supervisory decisions and actions are more effective when based on valid and objective information; such information is best compiled by the use of systematic observation instruments designed specifically for monitoring physical education instruction.

The use of systematically gathered teaching data is much like a football coach's use of game statistics. Each statistic is selected for its potential to influence the outcome of the game (e.g., time of possession, turnovers, penalties assessed). Because this influence is widely recognized, each statistic is identified for monitoring prior to the game and is measured objectively by a trained scorekeeper. At halftime, the coach reviews the statistics and relates them individually (or in some combination) to the game score at that point. The coach then uses the statistics to identify performance areas in need of improvement or maintenance in the remaining half.

A supervisor does not have a tangible outcome indicator comparable to a game score but can still deploy systematic observation techniques to monitor a teacher's ability to instruct effectively. This type of observation can verify the acquisition of teaching skills, the degree to which they have been improved, or the need for further development. Viewing teaching as a set of demonstrable skills and viewing supervision as a means for facilitating acquisition of those skills greatly depends on the use of systematic observation techniques; without this third component, the others would be much less meaningful for effective supervisory practice.

Summary

Teaching supervision today is in need of many improvements. Some of those needs stem from the narrow supervisory practice within student teaching and the resulting dependency upon one kind of supervisor. Other needs surface from the lack of resources devoted to supervision despite its acknowledged importance. Finally, supervision suffers from inadequate conceptualizations of what it is about, who should conduct it, and where it should happen.

This chapter offers some assumptions that can help formulate a perspective or approach for instructional supervision in our field. If we equate the relationship between supervisors and teachers to the relationship between teachers and students, the role, purpose, and procedures of supervision become much more apparent.

Chapter 2

Instructional Supervision Within Stages of Teacher Development

Traditional teaching supervision is based entirely on the assumption that supervision is a role assumed by only one kind of person, practiced at only one point in time, and intended for only one type of teacher. That description does not recognize teachers' needs for supervisory assistance at many other times and from many other people. Supervision defined only in terms of student teaching by necessity must encompass a variety of tasks unrelated to helping teachers improve instructional skills. Supervisors in that capacity often serve as liaisons with the public schools, as counselors for their young charges, as a parental figure, or as a consultant to schools.

Instructional Supervision: Limited Role and Expanded Applications

This book views instructional supervision quite differently, limiting instructional supervision to those decisions and processes undertaken for the main purpose of improving teachers' pedagogical skills. Supervision at times must take on a broader meaning but those other parts of the job of supervision are not addressed here. While the role of instructional supervision is limited in this book, its applications are expanded considerably to include all physical education teachers who attempt to increase their skills. This might take place early or late in a teacher's career, in settings ranging from methods course teaching laboratories to public school classrooms.

A singular focus on the processes of instructional supervision can improve physical education instruction in any setting conducted by any teacher who intends to help students learn motor skills, attitudes, or sport knowledge. The content of instructional supervision becomes those decisions and actions taken by the supervisor and teacher to improve teaching; the lesson content decided by the teacher many times will not be a central concern.

This book defines instructional supervision as any systematic and intentional activity intended for improving teaching skills in physical education. This definition has four features:

- Instructional supervision is a systematic process that is most effectively carried out using certain recognized processes and available strategies for teaching/learning.
- Instructional supervision is an intentional process and is most effective when performed within a framework of known guidelines, stated objectives, and observable outcomes.
- Instructional supervision must limit itself to the development and maintenance of effective teaching skills, which are those decisions and actions carried out by teachers that contribute to increased student learning of motor skills, attitudes, and knowledge.
- Instructional supervision in physical education has its own unique set of processes for helping teachers along a developmental continuum.

Regarding the final point, ample evidence supports the notion that good teaching is context specific. While it is possible to apply generalizations from classroom teaching to some physical education supervisory functions, subject matter and contextual differences between the classroom and the gymnasium require that many supervisory practices be developed exclusively for physical education teachers. For example, the many different learning environments used in physical education (as opposed to the single classroom in which most other teachers work) require instructional supervisors to consider the impact of changing environments on the teacher's ability to meet expressed outcomes.

The importance of contextual specificity can be extended to every situation in which supervision is practiced, right down to working with one teacher, in one school, during one instructional unit. Each supervisor must constantly be aware of existing and potential factors that can influence how well a teacher achieves his or her intended goals. While a supervisor can generalize to some extent about teachers who share certain contextual factors (e.g., rural teachers, teacher/coaches, or secondary teachers), the supervisor must always consider each teacher's unique context, skills, attitudes, and stage of development.

The Role of Teacher Developmental Stages in Supervision

Physical education teachers find themselves in different stages of skill development for instructional effectiveness. As teachers must always be sensitive to students' skill levels, supervisors must consider teachers' current skills as well as the context in which each teacher applies those skills. To ignore a teacher's experiences and abilities limits the potential effectiveness of instructional supervision. Supervisors will not always know the exact abilities of every teacher but can be familiar with general characteristics within several defined stages of instructional skill development.

Classifications of Teacher Development

This book uses four stages of teacher development, which are similar to Feiman-Nemser's (1983). They are shown, along with a fifth category, below.

STAGES OF TEACHER DEVELOPMENT

- **Preservice**
- **Student teaching**
- **Induction**
- **Veteran**
- **(Classroom teacher as physical educator)**

Feiman-Nemser's pretraining stage is deleted due to its relative immunity from any formal supervisory attempts to help teachers improve instruction prior to entering a training program. The preservice stage includes all undergraduate and preprofessional program experiences leading up to the student teaching term. The student teaching stage encompasses that time actually designated as the culminating field experience in schools. The induction stage retains Feiman-Nemser's original place but is defined by attainment of teacher competencies and professional dispositions, not merely by passing of time. Once teachers pass through the induction stage, they enter the veteran stage and remain until they leave the teaching force.

A fifth type of physical educator (who does not maintain a temporally-defined stage on the developmental continuum) is considered in this classification scheme—the classroom teacher who has responsibility for conducting elementary physical education programs, either alone or with supplemental instruction. The classroom teacher as physical educator is a combination of the previously described stages and the special circumstances that find him or her providing physical education programming.

Teachers within each stage are likely to share many of the same concerns, attitudes, experiences, and instructional skill abilities. Thus, they will require similar needs from instructional supervision. Teachers from different stages are likely to have different supervisory needs; supervising these teachers the same way, ignoring each one's developmental stage, will certainly prove ineffective.

Preservice Stage

The preservice teaching stage begins with the very first experience in a preprofessional teacher certification program. Prospective physical educators no doubt learn about teaching before this time through previous experience as students in school programs (Lawson, 1983). However, because the developmental process of learning how to teach is the most important feature of this stage, the formal training program will be used to mark the onset of this stage. The preservice stage ends when the formal student teaching term begins.

The preservice stage usually entails courses in arts and sciences, physical education/sport theory, skill acquisition, and teaching methods, along with a few limited-scope field and laboratory teaching episodes. These episodes commonly take the form of micro teaching (teaching small groups of children for a short time), or peer teaching (teaching fellow preservice teachers); they can occur on campus and in schools. Almost every teacher training program provides field experiences so preservice teachers can learn about, practice, and improve instructional skills prior to student teaching in schools. Within these preservice teaching experiences instructional supervision plays its largest role for the preservice stage.

The intentionally limited instructional contexts typical of this stage offer preservice teachers several opportunities to focus on and practice a similarly limited set of teaching skills in a safe environment. The frequency and simplicity of these teaching episodes allow preservice teachers to concentrate on developing a few skills (perhaps even one) at a time and to receive systematic and highly individualized feedback about their performance. These episodes can be videotaped for later review by the supervisor (methods course instructor) and teacher. These reviews can be used to make insightful comments, link performance data with class events, and foster teacher reflection (Cruickshank & Applegate, 1981). Micro- and peer-teaching laboratories have become integral parts of most teacher training programs today, offering valuable opportunities to develop effective supervisory processes.

Supervision for Preservice Teachers

Preservice teachers initially need a comfortable, manageable context in which to practice and develop a working repertoire of basic teaching skills. Such practice time is relatively short within preservice training programs but it is important, as overburdening teachers at this stage with too many complex decisions and high expectations can result in failure, insecurity, or an inadequate set of skills to carry into the next developmental stage. The most effective supervision for preservice teachers (a) limits the number and complexity of expected teaching skills, (b) provides analyses that focus on practical strategies for skill demonstration, and (c) begins to promote maintenance effects as student teaching approaches.

For instance, at Virginia Tech we often design teaching experiences in which preservice teachers instruct 8 to 10 of their peers. We carefully outline the instructional environment (e.g., how much time they have, how much space they have, what equipment is available). The teachers are expected to plan and implement the lesson while focusing on just two or three instructional skills. For example, they try to reduce the number of managerial minutes, provide clear and correct demonstrations, and avoid the use of distracting verbal patterns (e.g., "uhs," "okays," "you guys"). All of the skills practiced in these lessons are expected to be shown later during the student teaching placement; if it is important in methods classes, it will remain important throughout their time in our program.

Supervisory monitoring must be highly focused on the limited set of preferred instructional skills sought in the preprofessional program. These are the instructional practices viewed by the program faculty as being the most important ones for their students to acquire and demonstrate. This requires the use of a variety of single-focus observation systems at several points within the program to monitor students' progress on those skills. Because preservice teaching experiences represent the first such opportunities to practice and exhibit these preferred skills, supervisors should provide ample time to review each episode with teachers for diagnosis, prescriptions for improvement, formative evaluation, and support. As Siedentop (1983) points out, a general feeling of discomfort characterizes this initial stage of practicing teaching skills with peers and students; supervision needs to address this problem and help preservice teachers overcome it before they enter the more complex world of student teaching. Effective supervision for the preservice stage should feature frequent, direct interaction between the university staff and novice teachers.

Student Teaching Stage

The formal student teaching term is characterized by transition. At this time teachers must begin to formulate strategies for transferring skills learned at the university into the daily world of school programs. Teachers should have acquired a wide repertoire of effective instructional skills through simulation and lead-up experiences within the preservice stage. Finding strategies that help transfer those skills from limited contexts to intact classes within a full teaching day is the difficult task for supervisors and teachers in this stage.

Supervision for Student Teachers

Instructional supervision has focused almost entirely on the student teaching stage, and at this stage the failures of traditional supervision are most obvious.

Possibly a more logical sequence of preparatory teaching experiences and a supervision plan designed to better facilitate the transition into student teaching could overcome these problems.

Part of past failures at this stage come from a false assumption that all student teachers can and should display complex skills right from the start of the term. The desired transition from preservice teacher to competent student teacher does not automatically occur by just placing a new teacher in a classroom. Supervision for student teaching should begin where it left off in the preservice stage—by focusing on a limited set of skills with reduced performance expectations. This suggests that early instructional monitoring uses single-focus observation systems, gradually progressing to multiple-focus analyses of teaching skills.

Supervisors can reinforce this gradually expanded focus by initially using a simple observation instrument that monitors one teaching skill (e.g., a teacher's pattern of instructional information). During a golf lesson, for instance, the supervisor could record statements made about proper grip, stance, and swing pattern, as well as feedback provided by the teacher. As the term progresses, the supervisor could expand the number of teaching skills to monitor, working toward a more detailed and comprehensive analysis of the teacher. The mentioned golf analysis might then include instructional information, time management, behavior management, student engagement patterns, and content development.

Possibly the most important criterion for effective supervision at this stage is its frequency. Clinical supervisors (specially trained cooperating teachers), who observe student teachers during every class period, can provide frequent instructional assistance more effectively than any other kind of supervisory personnel. In fact, the unique arrangement between clinical supervisor and student teacher, carried out during this culminating field teaching experience, offers supervision its greatest potential for success, despite common perceptions to the contrary.

Student teachers need ideas about what decisions and practices work best with intact classes of students in actual field settings. They also need immediate feedback on the effectiveness of their instructional strategies. The regular monitoring of teaching skills in this new setting, followed by specific and timely feedback and ultimately leading to new and refined instructional strategies, should characterize the chain of supervisory events within this stage.

Induction Stage

Until just a few years ago, formal teacher training (along with active supervision) often ceased when teachers left undergraduate programs for full-time positions in schools. While in many ways formal teacher preparation does end with initial certification, many educators agree that not only do teachers continue to learn throughout their careers but their first years on the job are the most critical. The induction stage of teacher development is the stage between the end of student teaching and the beginning of the teacher's more complete formulation of professional attitudes and skills; this stage usually spans two or three years. During these years, teachers learn many more things about teaching and about being teachers—knowledge beyond the scope of preprofessional teacher training programs. Teachers learn what it is like to work within our school system; they learn about students and the unique characteristics of particular age groups, social groups, and community demographics; and they also learn about other teachers. Most importantly, teachers learn to formulate ideas and practices related to their instruction that they will likely carry with them throughout their careers.

During the induction years teachers learn how to teach in ways that allow them to withstand the physical demands, professional socialization stress, and emotional rigors of their jobs; they learn to function at a level that adequately balances their willingness to perform their jobs well with their ability to do their jobs well. Teaching after the induction years rarely resembles the kind of teaching promoted and practiced within the preservice and student teaching stages. Many effective teaching skills seem to get lost in the series of transitions from preservice to student teaching to induction; those that do remain are often subject to a gradual "washing out" through the induction years (Zeichner & Tabachnick, 1981).

Supervision for Induction Teachers

Supervision for the induction stage must work on two problems at once. The first involves reducing a teacher's tendency in the early period of induction to rely on simplistic teaching strategies that work at the expense of educational goals and sound pedagogy. The second problem involves providing support mechanisms for new teachers to help them resist forces that can easily impede their instructional skill development, darken their outlook, and ultimately reduce their desire to continue within the profession.

Induction stage teachers need both peer and administrative supervision at this time. Mentoring programs that pair experienced, master teachers with new teachers are a promising way to provide instructional supervision and professional support during the induction years. Several states now have such assistance programs for the induction stage, and some states and school districts have mandated formal mentoring programs in response to the growing need to help new teachers by providing regular instructional supervision in this crucial stage. Despite this attention on developing innovative ideas to support induction teachers, delivering effective instructional supervision for this stage remains problematic because it is not the sole and direct responsibility of any single group of individuals.

Veteran Stage

A teacher who has demonstrated the ability to effectively and regularly perform the many complex tasks of teaching enters the veteran stage. Entry into this stage is marked more by performance than by the mere passage of time.

Supervision for Veteran Teachers

Supervision faces its most difficult task in trying to help experienced teachers improve their instruction. Experienced teachers are likely to have deeply ingrained instructional patterns and sometimes little incentive for working on new teaching skills. Not only might these teachers resist attempts to improve their teaching, they will also likely react to the source of those attempts (e.g., they may feel that university professors cannot relate, new teachers are too green, and administrators do not know the content area). Thus peer supervision and self-supervision are the most viable instructional improvement strategies for veteran teachers.

Effective supervision for veteran teachers considers that these teachers already possess a deeply imbedded repertoire of skills and managerial routines; starting from scratch will most likely fail. Instead, supervision should try to build on veteran teachers' existing strengths, interacting with those teachers to constructively refine and recast their known assets into effective teaching practices. The experience these teachers possess should enhance the supervisory process, not inhibit it. Experienced teachers like to become better instructors, just like other teachers; however, they often show more sensitivity to the manner in which supervision is provided for them. For example, if Don has been using the same techniques for teaching the volleyball serve for 10 years, it will likely not work if the supervisor begins by telling him he is teaching the serve wrong. Instead, the supervisor should point out correct aspects of his approach, and then try to update the deficiencies with examples of more currently accepted techniques.

Classroom Teachers as Physical Educators

It is disquieting that many teachers who conduct elementary physical education programs do not consider it their primary teaching task and further have neither certification nor sufficient preparation to design or implement sound physical education programs for young children. They are the elementary classroom teachers who carry out physical education programming each week either completely on their own or as supplemental instruction for certified specialists. These teachers represent a sort of hidden teaching force that operates almost daily on one of two agendas: They either do not wish to promote physical education, or they do wish to have good programs but do not possess the time, resources, knowledge, or energy to make their physical education lessons worthwhile learning experiences for children. If the former attitude prevails and the administration does not strongly advocate sound physical education programming, no amount of instructional supervision will help. However, if teachers and administrators wish to have an effective physical education program, then supervision can play a key role.

Supervision for Classroom Teachers as Physical Educators

As with veteran physical education teachers, supervisors should not ignore what classroom teachers already know about good teaching but should help these teachers find ways to transfer effective classroom practices into the gym. Because much of what we know about effective teaching has evolved from research in classrooms, it makes sense to start from this point. Effective classroom practices like reducing management time and providing instructional feedback will look a bit different when moved into the gym; however, the reasons why teachers should use these techniques and the strategies for implementing them remain the same.

For example, classroom teachers usually establish routines for ending one activity and beginning another. Those routines are familiar to both teacher and students and are implemented for efficiency and control. The teacher should carry those same routines into physical education teaching, making adjustments only for the different kind of teaching space used (i.e., gym or field). Supervision, most likely from principals, should provide ways to help classroom teachers manifest the same skills in a different instructional setting and within physical education curricula. When it is approached in this manner, principals will likely discover that they know more about physical education instruction and supervision than they previously thought!

Summary

This chapter has provided two constructs important to instructional supervision in physical education. The first is a definition of supervision that calls for a direct focus on the acquisition of effective teaching skills; it leaves no room for eclectic supervision that attempts to be all things to all teachers. Certainly, supervisors must perform other functions besides those which improve teaching skills; however, those functions have a lower priority.

The second part of this chapter addressed the influence of a teacher's developmental stage on supervision. If effective supervision is context specific, then one of the most important features of any context has to be the teacher. Teachers, like other learners, acquire skills in progressive, incremental steps; supervision must consider a teacher's skill level and proceed from that point with each individual teacher. The recognition of characteristics shared by teachers at each of the five developmental stages is an instrumental feature of effective supervision for physical education.

Chapter 3

A Model for Physical Education Instructional Supervision

If a single word could characterize supervision in physical education today, it would be *unsystematic*. Physical education supervision currently refers almost exclusively to university-based supervision during student teaching (Locke, 1979). However, few university-based supervisors have any formal training in teaching analysis and supervision (Metzler & Freedman, 1985). Supervisors typically assume these responsibilities as an afterthought to their teacher training job roles or other duties in various parts of the department. Fewer than 10% consider supervision as their primary or total responsibility (Metzler & Freedman, 1985). In many cases, teaching experience is the primary qualification, regardless of whether the supervisor is a graduate student, a faculty member, or a school district administrator. This observation is not meant to minimize the importance of teaching experience for supervision; rather, it merely suggests that teaching experience alone does not provide sufficient background for effective supervision in physical education.

Allocating too little time for supervision and using mostly untrained personnel result in a lack of recognized supervisory systems to guide the process of helping teachers become better instructors.

Much of the supervision practiced in physical education today is based solely on individual knowledge and preference. Lacking formal training in both teaching analysis and supervisory processes, many supervisors mirror practices they saw when they were student teachers. Just as novices tend to teach as they have been taught, many supervise as they have been supervised, resulting in unsystematic, ineffective supervision, or sometimes no supervision at all.

The detachment and isolation in which supervisors often practice hinder the development of timely and effective strategies for helping teachers, strategies that could become the basis for a general set of procedures shared by supervisors. The need for such a model is apparent; a physical education supervision model would effectively improve teachers' skills across grade levels, stages of development, and instructional contexts.

Many general models of supervision exist. Boyan and Copeland (1978), Goldhammer (1969), Hoy and Forsyth (1986), and Acheson and Gall (1987) describe various models for effective supervision, presumably designed for all teaching situations and all content areas. Closer review, however, reveals that these models focus on more common classroom teaching applications. Assumptions in these models about the contexts of teaching, the definition of effective teaching, identification of the teacher and supervisor, the evidence to be gathered about teaching, and the processes for improving teaching all derive from the teaching and learning of classroom subjects. Because of their origins and intended applications, these models are probably unsuited for supervision in physical education. Furthermore, the models tend to ignore the importance of the teacher's developmental stage in the supervisory process, a consideration just now coming into the forefront of instructional improvement efforts (Feiman-Nemser & Floden, 1986).

Improved supervisory practice in physical education requires models that reflect the unique problems of helping physical education teachers. Not only is our content different from other subjects in schools, so too are the contexts in which physical educators learn and apply their instructional skills—from university methods laboratories to school programs. Physical educators often operate under some of the most restrictive and debilitating conditions in our educational system (Griffin & Locke, 1986; Lambdin, 1986). The unique contextual features of most physical education instruction require similarly unique approaches for supervision; if effective teaching is highly context-specific, it stands to reason that effective supervision must be, too.

In addition, some models fail to consistently recognize the importance of not only measuring teacher performance, but also recording student learning. Effective teaching implies an impact on student learning. Effective teaching skills cannot be identified without referring to student learning, either by measuring outcomes directly or by identifying situations likely to lead to increased learning. Therefore, effective teaching processes cannot be separated from effective learning processes; thus, a new term, *teaching/learning*, is used throughout to highlight that interrelationship.

This chapter outlines one physical education instructional supervision model that can apply to all stages of teacher development and focus on a variety of effective teaching practices. It is called the Physical Education Instructional Supervision (PEIS) Model. The PEIS Model operates on two levels, program and implementation, which address different aspects of effective supervisory practice.

THE PEIS MODEL:
PROGRAM LEVEL

The *program level* represents the overall set of supervision processes available for instructional skill improvement in a given situation. Those processes result from the unique resources and circumstances in which each supervision program must practice. Thus, many different programs can exist under this model. Factors such as available resources, trained personnel, departmental priority for supervision, access to teachers, and the number of teachers needing supervision at one time will determine the exact combinations possible. The nature of these combinations and the manner in which they are employed determine the overall supervisory program in place at a given time. A schematic of the PEIS Model Program Level is shown in Figure 3.1. The dotted box around *available supervisory processes* indicates that the program must not only move across the continuum of teacher developmental stages but must also operate under different combinations of guidelines, functions, and personnel.

Physical Education Instructional Supervision Model: Program Level

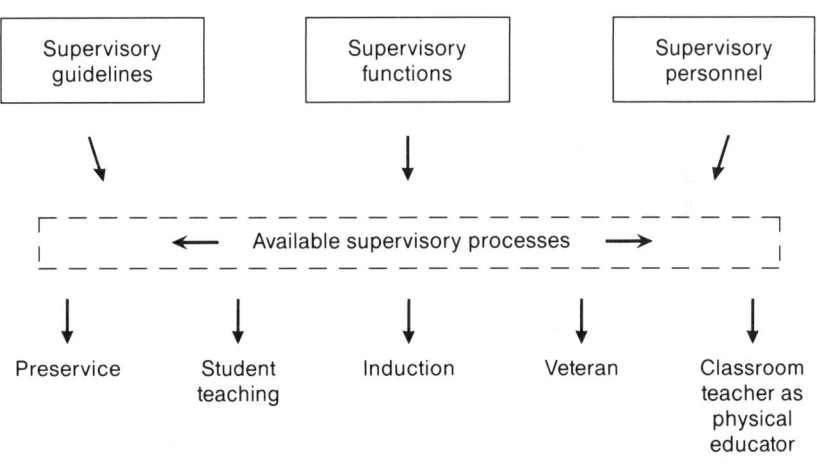

Figure 3.1.   The PEIS program level contains variables in guidelines, functions, and personnel that may be combined depending on the developmental stage of the teacher to create the overall supervisory program.

Supervisory Guidelines

Supervisors traditionally have approached their instructional improvement strategies without a well-established set of common guidelines. In the absence of recognized standards and procedures, supervisors must plan and carry out this complex and demanding role relying almost entirely upon a loosely communicated set of routines and expectations. If instructional supervision is to result in a consistently positive influence on teachers, it must rely more on some widely accepted guidelines for practice. Once such a set of *supervisory guidelines* has been proposed, supervisors can then test each guideline's usefulness and effectiveness in simulated teaching and field settings. Potentially, this kind of validation activity can lead to the acceptance of some guidelines across many applications in physical education.

The eight guidelines presented in the box below can serve as the foundation of a supervisory program in which many people work together in similar ways to help teachers improve instructional skills. The intent here is to view these guidelines as potential goals and to recognize that they may occasionally be modified or discarded due to programmatic or situational constraints, such as limited personnel, time, or travel resources, or the inability to provide systematic observations of teaching in a timely manner. However, an instructional supervision program that strives to implement all the guidelines at a reasonable and sustained level stands a much greater chance to succeed at helping teachers improve.

GUIDELINES FOR
EFFECTIVE SUPERVISION

- **Frequent**
- **Systematic**
- **Consistent across time, settings, teachers, and personnel**
- **Focused on relevant teaching skills**
- **Related to training and developmental goals**
- **Directed to provide accurate, timely, relevant, and objective performance feedback**
- **Diagnostic *and* prescriptive**
- **Goal oriented**

Frequent Supervision

Like students learning motor skills, teachers need to receive appropriate and timely help to reach proficiency. Students cannot be expected to benefit from instructional processes delivered long after a class has ended. Neither can teachers be expected to steadily improve their skills with supervisory processes delivered long after a teaching episode has ended. Supervision should be available when teachers practice their skills; supervisors should monitor teachers regularly and provide performance analysis and feedback immediately following a teaching episode.

The implications for this guideline are clear: We must find ways to provide supervisory processes when they can help a teacher the most—at or near the same time the teacher is practicing instructional skills. Because teachers practice those skills at various times and in different settings, supervision must be carried out by more than one person.

Systematic Supervision

Supervision is most effective when practiced systematically according to a preconceived plan consisting of logical and sequential components. Each component of the system should work to facilitate the efficient completion of the supervisory process. Systematic supervision has several positive features:

- It provides an overall scheme for program implementation.
- It clearly delineates each person's role in the program.
- It provides for more efficient monitoring of a teacher's progress.
- It allows for better evaluation of program outcomes and effectiveness.

A supervisory system can work in two ways. First, it can serve as a blueprint for supervision across the entire spectrum of a teacher's developmental stages. This encompassing plan can outline specific supervisory strategies and practices for a variety of teachers, stages of development, and contexts; it can be more sensitive to an individual teacher's needs. Second, a supervisory system can facilitate the monitoring of teaching skills by collecting supervisory information and providing performance feedback about observed teaching/learning activities.

When supervisory processes originate within such a two-part system, several trained persons can perform different functions at different times. Supervisors then become members of a supervisory team, working together toward the same system goals using the same procedures. A supervisory team for the preservice stage can comprise all faculty who teach methods courses or supervise student teachers. Teams for other situations and stages can include a school's physical education staff, designated building administrators, and the physical education coordinator from the central office.

Consistent Supervision Across Time, Settings, Teachers, and Personnel

Using a system structure for supervision increases opportunities to provide consistent processes regardless of time, settings, teachers, and supervisory personnel. This is important when a supervision program or team is responsible for working with many teachers simultaneously.

Consistency in monitoring certain performance areas helps individual teachers bridge the gap between skills acquired in simulation experiences and those needed for field-based settings. Supervisory consistency also is useful in repeated observations of individual teachers, as it provides a dimension of continuity when focusing on particular performance aspects over time. Finally, consistency among supervisory personnel allows the program to extend itself past the "one teacher-one supervisor" approach, so that any member of the supervisory team can comfortably and effectively work with any teacher.

Supervision Focused on Relevant Teaching Skills

Instructional supervision for physical education includes an effort to limit the number and kinds of focal points for helping teachers. Not all teachers need improvement on every instructional skill, and not all of what supervisors observe is relevant to improved teaching. Supervisors should first focus on those performance aspects needing immediate improvement while simultaneously noting the complex contextual factors under which a teacher functions, especially those that can reduce the potential for effective teaching (Griffin & Locke, 1986; Lambdin, 1986). Factors like overcrowded classes, inadequate equipment and facilities, insufficient administrative support, and understaffing are common conditions for physical educators in schools today, yet they are outside the realm of supervisory interventions.

An effective supervisor will help the teacher to concentrate on the most important (and remediable) instructional needs first, typically those most directly related to student learning. Under such prioritization, the first question is not, "What does this teacher need to do to improve?" but rather, "What is the impact of present teaching and contextual patterns on student learning?" The answer to this question is followed by, "What can this teacher *in this context*, do (or not do) to increase students' opportunities to learn?"

Another reason to focus on relevant and effective instructional skills is that most teachers improve when given proper supervision. Teachers who are dedicated to improving their instructional skills and who are provided with proper assistance are likely to realize noticeable differences in their teaching, differences that are positive and that can be maintained over long periods of time.

Idiosyncratic teaching behavior patterns and personal characteristics are resistant to even the best supervision. Supervision rarely can alter a teacher's perceptions, improve attitudes, or foster positive professional outlooks—at least not within the constraints of typical supervisory practice. Many of these characteristics relate to a teacher's personality and are immune to the kinds of interventions possible within instructional supervision. Thus, the realities of working with teachers in schools suggest that supervision should focus on relevant teaching processes rather than a teacher's personal characteristics.

A supervisor who focuses on relevant teaching skills should take care not to overload the teacher with instructions. Just as it is difficult for a novice golfer to remember several cues during a swing (e.g., "keep your head down; eyes on the ball; easy backswing; go all the way to the top; watch your weight shift; bring the club through the ball"), it is difficult for novice teachers to successfully execute several complex instructional decisions and actions without proper preparatory experiences. It is unreasonable to expect a preservice physical educator to simultaneously monitor students' skill attempts, provide detailed feedback information, maintain efficient class management, and make multiple on-the-spot decisions in his or her first methods course! Supervision must be sensitive to the novice's needs and should attempt to develop a teaching repertoire gradually. However, skilled and experienced teachers can perform several complex functions at once and should be receptive to more demanding instructional performance monitoring.

Supervision Related to Training and Developmental Goals

Designing a complete system for physical education instructional supervision represents one important task; matching the system with the needs of the teacher being supervised represents an entirely different one. Both the system and its appropriateness for individual teachers are important. Like other complex skills, teaching is learned over time and involves prior experiences and performances. A supervisor who views the acquisition of teaching skills without regard to developmental stages may expect too much or too little from a teacher at any given time. Expecting too much can threaten a teacher's sense of efficacy (Dembo & Gibson, 1985) and possibly hinder improvement. Expecting too little robs a teacher of an opportunity to apply teaching skills in a professionally challenging way, possibly inhibiting further refinement of those skills. When supervision approaches learning to teach as a developmental process, with different foci within each stage, it can establish expectations accordingly.

Preservice Supervision

Teaching in an on-campus micro-class should have a limited set of goals; supervision for these preservice teachers should focus directly on selected skills. Comments about "the real world," and statements beginning with, "Once you get actual students. . ." should not be part of the supervisory process at this stage.

Student Teaching Supervision

Supervision for student teaching should help interns transfer skills acquired in more limited experiences to intact classes within regular school routines. To date, supervision has failed to promote this transfer (Locke, 1979, 1983).

All teacher training programs emphasize certain preferred pedagogical skills and teacher characteristics in the preservice years. Supervisors should continue to monitor these selected skills as the setting changes from micro teaching on campus to student teaching in schools. Undoubtedly, these preferred skills will manifest themselves in different ways with larger classes and more diverse student groups. However, supervision should strive to help student teachers learn new ways to apply previously learned skills.

Induction Supervision

Instructional supervision for physical education should strive to help new teachers find ways to apply their skills within the daily context of public schools. Supervision at that time should focus on ways to help teachers avoid "washout" (Zeichner & Tabachnick, 1981) of their skills, which can lead to the development of traditional and often ineffective instructional patterns.

Veteran Supervision

Supervision for veteran teachers should work within existing skill repertoires. It should not attempt major overhauls that might threaten teachers, making them resist supervisory efforts. At this advanced stage, teachers probably need fine tuning and skill upgrading rather than totally fresh approaches to performing routine teaching tasks.

Sharing Expectations of Supervision

Teachers should be aware of their supervisor's short-term and long-term expectations. The supervisor should consider the teacher's stage of development and the context of the observed lesson when working with the teacher to identify and implement the supervisory plan. For example, in a simulated teaching lesson as a part of a methods course it is appropriate for the instructor (supervisor) to unilaterally establish the performance foci and acceptable practice; the impact of contextual factors is quite limited. In school settings, the teacher and supervisor should share the information and decisions necessary to make supervision work better; in most cases the teacher will know the context best and will be the best person to initiate supervisory plans. A supervisor using different supervisory priorities for the various stages of development should explore ways to communicate expectations clearly to the teacher. An effective supervisory system requires clear channels of communication and must provide ways for teachers to have input into the system.

Supervision Directed to Provide Accurate, Timely, Relevant, and Objective Performance Feedback

To learn more efficiently, and with fewer failures, students need feedback regularly after learning trials. Not only should teachers provide feedback in sufficient amounts, the feedback should be accurate, relevant, delivered at the appropriate time, and based on some objective measurement. Feedback that does not meet these criteria can confuse and hinder a learner, reducing chances of success on the next trial. Likewise, the feedback that teachers receive should occur within a framework that reflects the notion of teacher as learner.

Teachers can benefit more when supervisory feedback is

- based on reliable and accurate performance information,
- directed toward relevant teaching skills of immediate concern,
- provided soon after the observed teaching episode, and
- based on objective monitoring of performance.

A supervisor's personal impressions of a teacher's performance do not comprise an adequate basis for description and analysis. An effective supervisory system requires the collection and analysis of critical teaching/learning process performance data, which is used in postobservation conferences as the basis of diagnostic/prescriptive comments communicated to the teacher.

Diagnostic *and* Prescriptive Supervision

Supervision is *not* the same as evaluation—that process of determining whether a teacher is good, bad, or worthy of advancement or retention. Teacher evaluation has its own purposes, functions, and standards for conduct, which rarely match those of instructional supervision (McGreal, 1988). Instructional supervision is a helping process, intended to improve teachers' pedagogical skills sytematically. It is derived from practices effective in analyzing instructional performance, diagnosing skills needing improvement, and communicating prescriptive efforts to benefit teachers. To identify a specific weakness correctly and then leave the teacher to his or her own devices for remediation is insufficient for instructional supervision.

Effective supervisors practice much like physicians, making deliberate and careful diagnoses and offering commonly accepted remedies or prescriptions. While a complete and definitive list of established symptoms and remedies does not exist for teaching physical education, supervisors can now refer to an emerging body of literature for suggestions and guidance. Hawkins, Wiegand, and Landin (1985) have devised a strategy for using research-based "collective wisdom" that supervisors can pass on to teachers who show certain common patterns of ineffective teaching. For example, if a teacher shows a pattern of having students with high rates of misbehavior and low rates of engagement, the supervisor could offer the general suggestion to revise learning tasks to make them more difficult; one common source of student misbehavior is boredom with tasks that are too easy.

Supervisors can improve their own practice by keeping abreast of new developments in research on effective teaching and learning how to translate those findings into prescriptive courses of action for teachers. Sometimes a supervisor can call upon his or her own experiences to assist in this role, relating an actual incident to increase a teacher's understanding. While not a necessary condition for effective practice, field-based experience with physical education instruction can enhance supervisory effectiveness.

Goal-Oriented Supervision

Good teaching is context specific (Brophy & Evertson, 1978) thus disallowing direct and totally replicative process-product outcomes. However, recent research on effective teaching has allowed for the determination of some generally important teaching/learning processes. Increased amount of student time on task, the accrual of relevant and successful practice time, the delivery of timely and specific feedback, the reduction of management time, and other teaching/learning processes are considered indicators of effective teaching (Brophy & Good, 1986; Metzler, 1989; Waxman & Walberg, 1982). Furthermore, these aspects of teaching and learning are monitored easily with direct observation techniques.

If certain patterns of teaching are found to be more effective than others and can be recorded reliably, supervisors can then establish setting-specific goals for teaching performance. Mosher and Purpel (1972) coined the phrase "reluctant profession" because they found that supervisors have few ways to verify that what they consider key teaching skills or characteristics really do make a difference! While research on teaching has not yet identified a complete battery of effective teaching skills, sufficient evidence now exists to support an expanding core of teaching/learning behaviors that can make a difference in student achievement. Supervisors can translate those desired teaching practices into sets of expectations and observable performance goals for teachers.

To establish functional goals for teaching performance, the supervisor must first identify a teacher's current level on selected skills, which is accomplished by taking baseline measures in a typical classroom setting. After identifying ineffective teaching patterns, supervisors can then work with teachers to outline systematic and sequential plans for improvement. A teacher's stage of development will influence those plans, and supervisors can learn just how many goals and which specific goals a teacher can generally attain in each stage. Goals should be set (mutually, when feasible) to reflect each teacher's school and program setting; they should be context specific. If a supervisor establishes reliable baseline measures of relevant aspects of performance and considers a teacher's unique setting, then performance goals become more meaningful and attainable, and it becomes more reasonable to hold a teacher accountable for reaching established goals.

Supervisory Functions

Supervisors make and act upon many decisions as they work directly with teachers before, during, and after instructional episodes. Hopefully, these actions are guided by the supervisory system in place. Preparatory decisions, exploratory discussions, on-site observations, and personal interactions performed to improve teaching skills are called *supervisory functions*. These functions can be completed as part of the various laboratory and field-based episodes in which physical education teachers practice to improve their instructional skills. Although supervisors carry out these functions on a person-to-person basis within different contexts, an overall systematic effort can promote a more consistent kind of supervision. Performing supervisory functions without the guidance of an overall system or plan will limit the impact those functions have on instructional improvement.

Six key functions for effective supervision are outlined in the box below. These functions can be implemented regardless of how many of the previous supervisory guidelines a particular program is able to develop and maintain. These functions represent suggestions for implementing supervisory processes directly with teachers; the functions consist of decisions, communications, and actions to be carried out before, during, and after an observed teaching episode.

FUNCTIONS FOR EFFECTIVE SUPERVISION

- **Brief teacher prior to observation**
- **Determine teacher's intent for the lesson**
- **Interfere only for safety purposes**
- **Collect systematic data on instructional processes**
- **Provide immediate and relevant performance feedback**
- **Provide a written record for the teacher**

Brief Teacher Prior to Observation

Teachers should be familiar with the supervisory system under which they will practice; they should know the supervisory personnel, techniques used to monitor their upcoming lesson, and the specific teaching/learning behaviors under focus. When appropriate, the supervisor and teacher should discuss and agree upon the performance expectations for the lesson (formative) or for the entire supervisory program (summative).

Prior to an observation the supervisor and teacher should identify instructional areas in need of improvement, the ways they will be monitored, and performance expectations. A supervisor may review a teacher's past performances and recall previously observed episodes, which will allow both the supervisor and teacher to put the upcoming observation into better perspective by placing it into an ongoing stream of events.

A supervisor should also provide suggestions during the briefing for reaching targeted teaching goals. This strategy helps the teacher avoid trial-and-error learning and communicates to the teacher that supervision is a helping process, not a trap!

Determine Teacher's Intent for the Lesson

No two classes are identical; each teaching episode has its own features that the supervisor must learn in order to properly consider the influence of context on the lesson. Supervisors must first know what teachers are attempting to accomplish in observed lessons. Just as supervisors should communicate their intentions to teachers prior to observations, teachers should have the same opportunity to make their plans known to supervisors. This can be done informally by asking the teacher to generally describe the upcoming lesson (and context) or more formally by reviewing the teacher's written lesson plans.

The supervisor should try to clarify any parts of a lesson plan that are not clear. Sometimes, reviewing past lesson plans for the class under observation can offer a better perspective on the upcoming lesson. If the supervisor feels that something on the plan is not likely to work, he or she should advise the teacher and offer alternatives before the class begins; again, pointing out potential mistakes prevents a trial-and-error approach to learning teaching skills. Carrying out good plans is often difficult enough; planning deficiencies in a supervised lesson can only place unneeded tension on a teacher and promote failure.

The preclass briefing also allows the teacher to provide the supervisor with a detailed description of the class. Information about the number of students, their grade level, previous experience with the content of the lesson, and potential interruptions helps the supervisor to know more about the class before observing it.

Knowing the teacher's intent and the key contextual characteristics of the class allows the supervisor to determine an appropriate monitoring strategy for the upcoming observation. The supervisor must focus on particular aspects, deciding with the teacher *before the lesson begins*, when feasible, which areas of performance will be monitored and the criterion goals for each aspect.

The preclass briefing should prepare both the teacher and the supervisor for the upcoming teaching episode, fostering a cooperative atmosphere during the entire supervisory process.

Interfere Only for Safety Purposes

A supervisor should remain out of the teacher's way once a lesson has started. Unless teacher or student safety is threatened, the supervisor should not interfere with an observed class. Stepping in might undermine the teacher's plans as well as risk damaging his or her confidence. Student teachers work particularly hard to earn acceptance by students, cooperating teachers, and colleagues; halting class to correct a student teacher's performance could undermine those efforts.

The only exception to this rule might occur in micro-teaching labs, when the instructor/supervisor wishes to make a point to the entire group. Even then, care should be taken to avoid damaging the teacher's self-confidence during what Siedentop (1983) has termed "the initial discomfort stage" (p. 13). Occasionally it helps to stop the lab lesson to call all students' attention to an important aspect of the teaching, while at other times the instructor/supervisor should confer privately with the teacher after the lesson.

Collect Systematic Data
on Instructional Processes

As mentioned earlier, supervisors can monitor a growing list of effective teaching practices. Many reliable instruments have been designed to collect objective measures of those practices, some specifically for monitoring physical education teaching skills (Darst, Mancini, & Zakrajsek, 1989). The supervisory process should focus on providing the teacher with an accurate picture of performance related to items outlined in the preclass briefing. For example, if the rate and nature of certain kinds of instructional feedback have been identified as a focus prior to the lesson, then the supervisor ought to provide the teacher with specific and objective information about that aspect of the performance, rather than a subjective estimation. Instead of saying, "It seemed like you gave enough feedback during that lesson," the supervisor could report, "Your overall feedback rate was 2.2 per minute. That's pretty high for this kind of lesson. Seventy-five percent of those feedbacks had a specific content, while only 25% did not; I like that balance."

Systematic supervisory data collection for monitoring effective teaching/learning processes has several unique characteristics. *First*, when many different aspects of teaching are under focus, the supervisor should provide the teacher with comprehensive information. Effective physical education lessons are comprised of many elements; instructional supervision should attempt to monitor them systematically.

When teachers have become familiar with the program's set of preferred instructional skills, they should expect supervisory monitoring and performance feedback on those aspects of observed lessons. For example, a university program might establish that the following instructional processes are important for preservice teachers to demonstrate:

- Using class time efficiently
- Giving clear and concise directions
- Providing timely and specific cues
- Demonstrating tasks properly
- Addressing students by first name
- Planning proper task orientation for learning activities
- Maximizing student Academic Learning Time accrual

Of course, each program can identify its own set of preferred teaching skills and characteristics, which will differ from the ones cited. However, if certain features of instruction are deemed essential, supervisors should seek ways to provide teachers with systematic performance information related to those features.

Second, supervisors should learn and employ a variety of data collection techniques. Event recording, duration recording, time sampling, and PLACHECK recording yield particularly useful data on physical education teacher/learning processes (see chapters 4 and 5). Using one technique at a time most effectively focuses on an isolated performance aspect and can be a good strategy for observing preservice teachers in micro and peer laboratory settings. Other observational techniques work best when used simultaneously or in combination with a sampling scheme in the same lesson. This maximizes the strengths of each single technique and provides a comprehensive picture of teaching practice in physical education. Several systems for observing physical education teaching and learning are shown in chapter 5.

Third, supervisors should recognize the difference between data collection for research purposes and data collection intended for monitoring and improving instruction. Teaching research data are collected to answer a small set of well-defined questions that may or may not relate to effective teaching. Those data conform to rigorous procedures and exacting standards. The observation systems used for research are complex, involving intensive and limited focus during teaching lessons. Supervisory data are collected to serve as judgmental aids in making decisions about how well teachers meet stated performance goals. Typically, supervisors need to monitor several aspects of teaching in a single lesson, which requires more flexible observation systems and broader sampling strategies. This need for broad observation sometimes means sacrificing the ability to concentrate on one aspect of instruction.

Fourth, supervisors cannot easily observe and measure all aspects of effective physical education teaching with objective instruments. Some of these aspects include planning, ongoing decision making, enthusiasm, and "withitness"

(Kounin, 1970). Behavior checklists and rating scales sometimes yield better information about these areas of performance. However, use of such techniques ought to be limited, and they should be used to supplement objective data.

Fifth, supervisors can round out an observation by writing notes that add meaning to data or that recall other events from the lesson. Reporting anecdotal notes and critical incidents helps to bring the whole lesson together, providing the teacher with a much clearer picture. This more complete description of the lesson can also help teachers understand the relationships between noted in-class events and the observational data. For example: "Remember when you stopped the whole class to remind them how to toss the ball to their partners? Because of that, the students' success rate went from 25% all the way up to 65%. That was a timely piece of information for them."

Provide Immediate and Relevant Performance Feedback

The observational portion of the supervisory process can provide three kinds of information for supervisors and teachers: objective data, checks or ratings on key facets of the lesson, and anecdotal notes. These three sources should formulate a comprehensive and coherent picture of performance in observed lessons as it relates to intended outcomes. Like other learners, teachers must have this information as soon after the teaching episode (the learning trial) as possible. Sometimes, it will not be possible to communicate with a teacher right away; physical education teachers, particularly in elementary schools, are likely to have several consecutive classes with no time between them. In such cases, the supervisor should attempt to meet with the teacher as soon as possible.

Making the data collection process complicated enough to require long delays for analysis and feedback reduces its effectiveness with teachers. Performance feedback ought to be immediately available and should come directly from the sources used in the observation (i.e., raw data should not have to be radically manipulated by the supervisor).

Supervisory feedback is most effective when it relates to aspects of teaching/learning discussed in the preclass briefing and when it is placed within the context of the total instructional assistance program. That is, performance feedback must relate both to the intended purpose of the observed lesson and to the teacher's current developmental needs. Specific feedback regarding certain parts of the lesson is most effective (e.g., "You had only 8% management time in that lesson, an acceptable amount for a class like that"). General feedback (e.g., "It went well," or "You seemed comfortable") provides teachers with virtually no useful information or future goals for improving instruction.

The importance of performance feedback in learning motor skills is universally recognized; it is equally important in the learning of teaching skills. The following characteristics comprise effective instructional performance feedback:

- It is delivered immediately after the skills are practiced.
- It reflects the immediate focus of the teaching episode goals.
- It contains specific comments and examples.
- It is stated in terms the teacher can understand.
- When negative feedback is necessary, it is coupled with prescriptive suggestions for helping the teacher improve on the next try.

Provide a Written Record for the Teacher

The supervisor should provide the teacher with a copy of the observational data, subjective ratings, and notes taken during the teaching episode. This practice has several advantages. It provides the teacher with the sources of the postobservation comments; the teacher can see the array of information used by the supervisor. It also provides the teacher with a complete record of the lesson in case some key items cannot be covered in the conference. And it allows the teacher an opportunity to make a more thorough review of the record at a later time and to analyze the data for additional insights.

Supervisory Personnel

Depending on one university faculty person to perform most supervisory functions limits the effectiveness of the entire supervisory process. Others must take an active role in helping teachers improve instructional skills. Several kinds of personnel can be oriented to the goals of a supervisory program and can learn to provide effective supervisory functions within the program. Such an approach provides teachers with consistent and effective supervision, regardless of teaching context and stage of development. The box on page 39 lists five different kinds of personnel who can supervise physical education teachers. The degree to which these personnel work as an integrated team is the most important indicator of the quality and effectiveness of instructional supervision.

Clinical Teacher As Supervisor

Most educators believe that novice teachers learn instructional skills best in settings that most closely approximate the environment for professional practice (Acheson & Gall, 1987; Goldhammer, 1969). Indeed, every profession emphasizes the importance of a field or clinical assignment during which students gain extensive, closely monitored experience in the "real world." For

---

PERSONNEL FOR
EFFECTIVE SUPERVISION

- **Clinical teacher (cooperating teacher)**
- **Peer**
- **Teacher as self-supervisor**
- **University personnel**
- **Principal**

---

teacher training, interns are usually called *student teachers* and are assigned to work with certified physical educators in school programs. The term *clinical teacher* accurately denotes these teachers' ability to provide frequent and direct supervision for student teachers. (The terms *clinical teacher* and *clinical supervisor* are used interchangeably in this book.) When properly selected, compensated, and trained, clinical supervisors undoubtedly provide the most effective supervisory assistance to student teachers.

Past problems with clinical teachers have stemmed mostly from failure to supply them with supervisory skills enabling them to be more effective in their roles. While clinical supervision models are plentiful, proven ways to implement them are not.

Another problem with implementing clinical supervision programs has been a general reluctance by university staffs to reassign responsibility for formal supervision to clinical personnel. If clinical supervisors are made familiar with the goals of a teacher training program, and if they learn the proper techniques for providing supervisory functions, no reason exists not to give them an expanded or complete role in that process. No other person has a similar opportunity to monitor and improve student teachers' instructional skills in field settings.

Peer As Supervisor

In many cases several teachers can work on instructional improvement at the same time, especially if all are in the same developmental stage. Several student teaching programs in physical education now place two or more student teachers in the same school (Verabioff, 1983), and most programs have lead-up experiences in which groups of students practice similar skills simultaneously. Teachers who work cooperatively in the same developmental stage may provide each other with a limited number of supervisory functions; this arrangement probably cannot facilitate all of the functions discussed earlier.

Many physical educators support the practice of training preservice and student teachers to systematically monitor class teaching/learning events, conduct data analyses, and help each other establish goals for improved teaching skills (Siedentop, 1981). If this interactive approach can work with preservice and student teachers, it should also work for in-service and veteran teachers who are provided with the proper training in analytical techniques and prescriptive goal setting. Peer supervision benefits both the teachers who practice skills and those who monitor and analyze that practice. The observers can learn both from what they see and from the suggestions they formulate for their peers. The practicing teachers benefit from receiving supervisory information that is delivered from the perspective of another person who shares a similar developmental stage and teaching context.

Teacher As Self-Supervisor

Often, physical education teachers cannot rely on another person to help them improve instruction. This is true especially for in-service elementary physical educators, who usually are the only such teacher in their school. While not a common practice, self-supervision is an option for these teachers. This can be accomplished with the aid of a stop watch for recording time, a compact tape recorder for conducting analyses of verbal interactions, or a video camera for providing more complex supervisory functions. Several helpful strategies for self-supervision were devised at Ohio State in the late 1970s (Siedentop, 1981) and might prove even more useful today, given recent developments in audio and video technologies.

Teachers probably cannot provide themselves with the full range of supervisory functions, but they can achieve noticeable results on a limited set of teaching skills. The process of outlining focal areas, self-monitoring performance, and formulating honest progress assessments epitomizes the idea of autonomous professional development. Self-help is often the very best kind!

University Personnel As Supervisors

Training and experience probably make university supervisors the most qualified to deliver supervisory functions. Unfortunately, they can rarely be with teachers at the most critical times for providing assistance—when teachers are practicing instructional skills in schools. Time and distance constraints usually cause university supervisors to violate the critical criterion regarding frequency of services to student teachers. Others, either a clinical supervisor, a peer supervisor, or a self-directed teacher, can provide services much more regularly and offer greater chances for effectiveness.

University supervisors can have an impact in other ways, such as guiding on-campus teaching skill development activities and prestudent teaching practicums. In lead-up teaching laboratories, the university faculty person can provide all supervisory functions well within suggested guidelines. These on-campus supervisors are usually able to videotape teaching episodes for multiple and detailed analyses and then share their critical viewings with preservice teachers. These same benefits are available for micro teaching episodes completed prior to student teaching. Viewing these episodes together allows the supervisor and the preservice teacher opportunities to discuss the episodes at length. Similar interaction during student teaching is usually not possible, given the limited time and personnel resources in most programs. A more effective plan for student teaching supervision would involve sharing or giving over all responsibility to a trained clinical supervisor.

Giving up some or all supervisory functions to clinical personnel should not diminish the overall role played by trained and experienced university personnel. Rather, it should be viewed as an opportunity to take on an even greater role—that of leading the entire supervision component of a teacher training program (Parker, 1986a; 1986b). Expanded responsibilities in this leadership role could include

- designing the overall instructional monitoring and improvement system within each stage of teacher development,
- establishing and monitoring preservice teaching laboratory performance goals for micro and peer teaching,
- providing training for others on the supervisory team, and
- actively directing the training of clinical personnel who work with student teachers.

Because university faculty often cannot provide direct supervision for teachers in schools does not mean that their expertise should be ignored or wasted. Instead, those persons ought to head up the program's entire supervisory team effort and work in this new capacity to help teachers at all stages become better instructors.

Principal As Supervisor

Current literature on effective schools indicates that the building principal should be the key leader for instructional improvement (Manasse, 1985). The principal has the ability to set expectations for teaching and to hold teachers accountable for their instructional practices. However, the principal or another administrative staff member often observes teachers solely for the purpose of evaluation for continued certification, retention, or promotion rather than for providing instructional supervision functions.

Direct and purposeful assistance occurs even less frequently for physical education teachers, as some administrators don't know how to observe effective teaching in the gym (Faucette & Graham, 1986; Ratliffe, 1986). Administrators who do not know how to monitor key teaching skills for physical education instruction are likely to opt for a kind of general "eyeballing," considering safety, fun, student compliance to rules, and discipline. Just as clinical supervisors can be trained to provide supervisory functions for student teachers, so too can principals and other administrators learn to identify and monitor effective physical education instruction.

Some school districts employ curriculum supervisors who take on many different roles and responsibilities. Typically, these people have few opportunities to actively work with teachers toward instructional skill improvement. Even though curriculum supervisors comprise a potentially valuable resource group for delivering instructional supervision processes, they often have the same limitation as the university supervisor—too few chances to observe teachers in class and to implement ongoing assistance efforts. Training curriculum supervisors to work directly with building principals in supervising physical educators on a more regular basis would surely increase the effectiveness of instructional supervision in many schools.

Determining Available Supervisory Processes

The lists of supervisory guidelines, functions, and personnel offer only suggestions for designing the overall supervision program. Each program must weigh its own ability to adequately use these suggestions; some programs may need to eliminate several due to situational constraints. The schematic in Figure 3.2 illustrates how this assessment results in a specific set of supervisory processes available to one program. Those features in each category that are available or achievable become part of an overall program; those that are not can be identified as future components to be added.

THE PEIS MODEL:
IMPLEMENTATION LEVEL

The *implementation level* of the PEIS Model focuses on the direct processes to be applied when supervisors actively monitor and interact with teachers for instructional skill development. This level guides the questions to be asked, the decisions to be made, and the actions to be taken as one supervisor interacts with one teacher. It is the time when the *available supervisory processes* of the program level are converted into courses of action—when the real work of teaching teachers occurs.

Three stages comprise the delivery level of the PEIS Model: preteaching, observation, and postteaching. These stages represent the three distinct times when supervisors make decisions, observe instruction, and communicate with teachers for the purpose of improving performance. The implementation level of the PEIS Model is a cyclical set of interactions; the results of previous observations impact upon decisions to be made in subsequent preteaching,

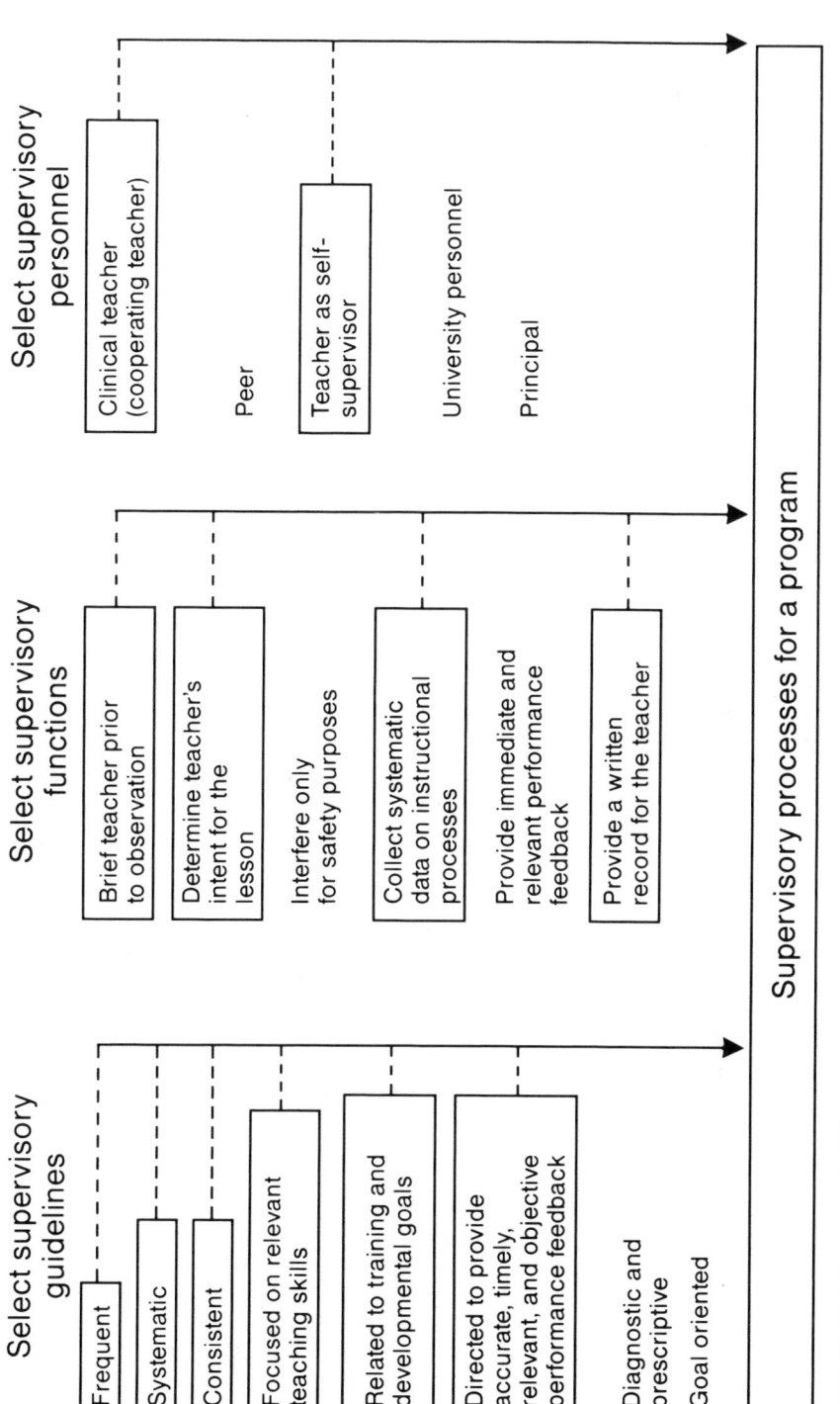

Figure 3.2. An example of the design of one supervisory program.

Physical Education Instructional Supervision Model: Implementation Level

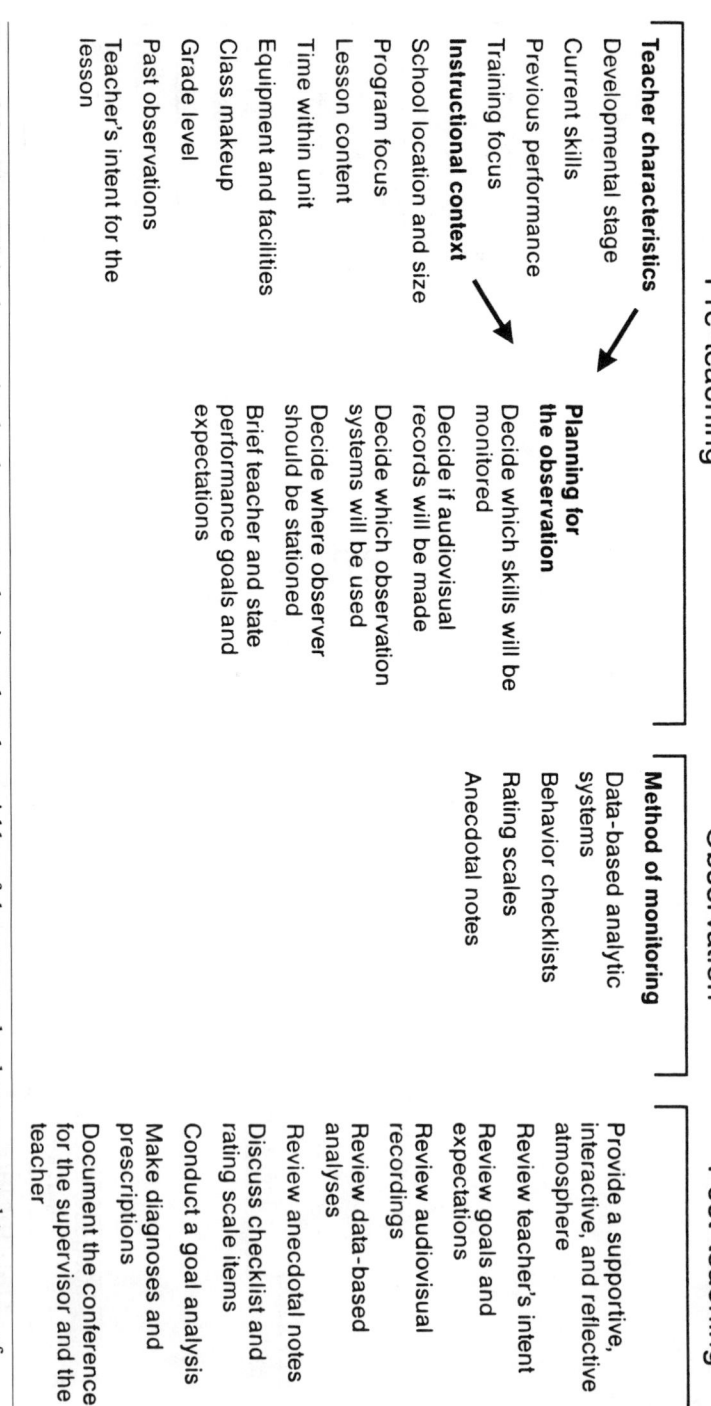

Pre-teaching		Observation	Post-teaching
Teacher characteristics		**Method of monitoring**	Provide a supportive, interactive, and reflective atmosphere
Developmental stage		Data-based analytic systems	
Current skills		Behavior checklists	Review teacher's intent
Previous performance		Rating scales	Review goals and expectations
Training focus	**Planning for the observation**	Anecdotal notes	
Instructional context	Decide which skills will be monitored		Review audiovisual recordings
School location and size	Decide if audiovisual records will be made		Review data-based analyses
Program focus	Decide which observation systems will be used		Review anecdotal notes
Lesson content	Decide where observer should be stationed		Discuss checklist and rating scale items
Time within unit	Brief teacher and state performance goals and expectations		Conduct a goal analysis
Equipment and facilities			Make diagnoses and prescriptions
Class makeup			Document the conference for the supervisor and the teacher
Grade level			
Past observations			
Teacher's intent for the lesson			

Figure 3.3.　The PEIS implementation level represents the time when the variables of the program level are converted to courses of action.

observation, and postteaching stages. A schematic of the PEIS Model implementation level is shown in Figure 3.3.

Preteaching Stage

A supervisor must gather a variety of information prior to observing each teaching episode. Only when both supervisor and teacher are properly informed and when adequate interaction has taken place can the subsequent observation and feedback strategies be effective. Thus, the preteaching stage comprises a series of interactions between supervisor and teacher that allow supervisors to identify many subtle contextual features of the teaching to be observed.

When observing in campus teaching laboratories, supervisors will be familiar with much of the preteaching information, and special research will be unnecessary. For experiences in the field, supervisors must gather preobservation information centering on two aspects: *teacher characteristics* and *instructional context*. The information is then used in planning for the observation and eventually as the frame of reference guiding the postteaching conference.

Teacher Characteristics

Effective supervision begins with knowledge of the teacher being observed. Important questions must be addressed prior to the observation: What is the teacher's current *developmental stage*? Is he or she a student teacher, a new teacher, or a classroom teacher? What *current skills* does the teacher have? What is the teacher's *previous performance* record, if this is not the first observation? Finally, what has been the teacher's *training focus* (i.e., what has been emphasized or de-emphasized in training that should be apparent in his or her teaching)?

Standard practice rarely marks good physical education teaching; what might pass for acceptable instruction for a teacher at one stage might reflect underdeveloped skills for a teacher in another stage. Effective supervision should always consider the individual teacher to be observed in order to make more reasonable performance expectations.

Instructional Context

Good teaching is context specific, and the contexts for teaching physical education vary greatly across schools, teachers, classes, programs, and communities. A series of concurrent *contributing* and *inhibiting* factors, the sum of which largely determines context, can work to influence each teacher's instructional effectiveness. Conducting supervisory processes with little regard for context is a disservice to teachers. To understand teaching more fully, a supervisor must be aware of the many nuances related to conditions under which teaching takes place. The pertinent considerations for this part of the PEIS Model become the following:

- *Where is the school located?* Inner city, suburban, and rural schools are distinctly different from one another.

- *How large is the school?*

- *In what kind of physical education program does the teacher work?* Is it elective, fully coeducational, skill focused, or recreational? The nature of the program can determine how teachers and students approach their responsibilities in classes.

- *What is the content of the lesson to be observed?* In physical education, the lesson content often determines acceptable teaching processes and performance expectations central to making decisions for instructional supervision.

- Related to content, *what is the time within the unit for the observed lesson?* Knowledge of previous coverage and the sequencing of content is important in providing perspective on the upcoming lesson. For example, teaching objectives and behavior on the first day of a soccer unit will most likely differ from objectives and behavior in the final set of classes.

- *How much and what kind of equipment and facilities are available for teaching the lesson?* Due to teachers' heavy reliance on equipment and facilities, proper amounts and varieties of them are crucial for effective physical education instruction. This reliance on equipment and facilities is probably more important for physical education than other content areas in the school.

- *What is the class makeup?* Class size, numbers of boys versus girls, student skill level, and other characteristics work together to influence the kind of teaching supervisors are likely to observe.

- *What is the class grade level?* Or, how many different grade levels are represented in the class? Many good teaching practices in the gym are grade level and age specific. Teaching second graders differs greatly from teaching tenth graders, even when teaching the same content.

- If this is not a teacher's first observation, *what has his or her past performance indicated to the supervisor?* Reviewing previous observational data, notes, and postteaching conferences helps the supervisor focus on certain aspects in the upcoming observation and can serve to remind the teacher of known strengths and weaknesses.

- Finally, *what is the teacher's intent for the upcoming lesson?* It is impossible to understand teaching and learning processes without relating them to what was attempted in the class. This can be done formally by reviewing lesson plans or informally through discussion in the preobservation conference.

Planning for Observation

After the supervisor has gathered adequate information on teacher characteristics and instructional context, he or she can make specific plans for the lesson observation. If teachers' developmental stages, characteristics, and instructional contexts can vary, so too should observational strategies. No single observation strategy can work well in every situation; thus, the supervisor must make important decisions to prepare for the observation:

- *Which effective teaching skills or instructional processes will be monitored in the lesson?* One person cannot systematically observe everything in a physical education class; decisions must be made to limit the scope of the observation to a few key performance and process indicators discussed in the preteaching conference. When working with micro-teaching experiences, one might even restrict the focus to a single aspect of performance (e.g., reducing the amount of class time spent in transition).

- *Will audiovisual recordings be made of the teaching?* One way to expand the analytic focus of an observation is to make a permanent record of it. Besides allowing for multiple playbacks and analyses by supervisors, recordings can be reviewed later by teachers themselves. This offers a powerful tool for improving performance.

- *Which observational systems will be used to monitor selected teaching skills?* Having identified one or a few specific foci for the observation, a supervisor can then select appropriate instruments for monitoring teacher and/or student class processes. Chapter 5 illustrates a variety of useful instruments designed for physical education instructional supervision. If a supervisor has decided to concentrate on certain aspects of teaching, then he or she should be able to make objective and reliable measurements of them.

- *Where is the best place for stationing during the lesson?* Even though most physical education facilities are large rooms or fields, supervisors can inadvertently intrude upon the class, distracting the teacher and the students. The preteaching conference should include questions about which parts of the field or facility the class will use and where might be a good spot to observe from. Supervisors should always maintain one rule relative to stationing: Stay within sight and hearing distance of the teacher or students being monitored. Stationing should emphasize gaining access to the teaching/learning behaviors to be monitored, without being intrusive at the same time. If the class will use only a small area, the supervisor can remain in one place; if a large area is used, the supervisor must be prepared to move about to stay with the target individuals. Also, anticipating paths for student activity and projected objects is a practical and safe supervisory skill!

- *What are the instructional performance goals and expectations?* Each supervisory observation should monitor one or more teaching performance goals. These goals can focus on teacher behavior, student behavior, or both. Because supervision should help teachers improve skills, teachers should clearly understand the parameters of the observation. The supervisor, aware of both the context and the teacher's intent for the lesson, formulates expectations for effective teaching in the episode.

- *The teacher should know those expectations and should be given supervisory assistance about how to meet them in a briefing prior to the teaching episode.* Much of the effectiveness of the PEIS Model depends upon teacher and supervisor interaction prior to the observed lesson.

Observation Stage

The observation stage verifies whether performance expectations decided and communicated in the preteaching stage were met by the teacher during the lesson. This stage provides an opportunity to gather information that will serve as the basis of the postteaching conference and support supervisory decisions about the teaching. Because not everything that might happen in a physical education class can be monitored, supervisory observations should be limited to those performance parameters identified in the preteaching conference. In some cases monitoring additional performance areas during an observation becomes possible, but the first objective should be to gather specific performance information on parameters identified before the lesson.

The observation stage is characterized by a process in which the supervisor seeks the best way to gather performance information on the selected teaching/ learning behaviors. Sources of performance monitoring typically used in physical education include

- data-based analytic systems,
- behavior checklists,
- rating scales, and
- anecdotal notes.

All four techniques have their own particular strengths and limitations for supervisory use. Supervisory personnel should become familiar with several samples of each and know which are most appropriate for particular monitoring applications.

Some data-based analytic instrument should always be used as the primary source of supervisory information, with anecdotal notes, checklists, and scales used strictly as supplemental sources. Chapter 5 illustrates a variety of supervisory monitoring systems and provides directions for use and guidelines for application. The primary criterion for selecting an observation system is the degree to which it can validly measure processes indicative of the teacher's intentions for the lesson. Once valid measures have been taken, they can be used by the supervisor as judgmental aids in ascertaining how well the teacher met his or her goals.

Data-Based Analytic Systems

Research conducted over the past 15 years on teaching has benefited supervisory practice in physical education in two ways. The first is the emergence of a commonly accepted set of teacher and student process behaviors that contribute to effective teaching. While a complete list of effective teaching practices has not yet been identified, current research suggests that students learn more when teachers conduct classes in a businesslike atmosphere; use appropriate rates and kinds of instructional feedback; provide maximum engaged time with relevant subject matter; plan instructional activities that allow students a reasonable opportunity to succeed at the task; allow students adequate opportunities to learn; and use a set of strategies called *direct instruction* in their classes (Brophy & Good, 1986; Rosenshine, 1979; Walberg, 1986).

Other practices thought to be related to effective teaching in physical education have not yet received a similar level of research-based support as those in general education. However, existing evidence and pedagogical logic indicate that physical education students learn more when teachers clearly communicate task structure to students (Tousignant & Siedentop, 1983); provide students with increased rates of academic learning time (relevant and successful motor engagement for physical education skills [Metzler, 1983]); overtly monitor student activity (Landin, Hawkins, & Wiegand, 1986); use efficient and innovative teaching devices (McKenzie, Clark, & McKenzie, 1984); and maintain a smooth flow between instructional activities (Siedentop, 1983). Supervisors who use these research findings and pedagogical logic can select from a wide variety of effective teaching practices to identify appropriate teaching/learning performance parameters. Chapter 4 provides a list of such processes.

The second benefit from research in classrooms and gymnasiums has been the rapid development of techniques for observing and measuring effective teaching/learning processes. Literally dozens of instruments have been designed for systematically observing events in physical education instruction (such as the instruments outlined by Darst, Mancini, & Zakrajsek [1989]). Many of these systems were developed for research on sophisticated and highly specific teaching/learning behaviors and require modification for best use by supervisors.

Data-based analytic systems have several advantages.

Advantages

- Objective records are produced on predefined categories of teaching and learning processes.

- Systems allow reliability across time, teachers, and observers.
- Observers are able to focus directly on relevant teaching performance behaviors rather than on their own impressions.
- Systems result in tangible, permanent records of performance.
- Data can be used to establish baseline levels of performance, determine interim goals for teaching skills, and monitor changes in performance over time.
- Adaptation of observation techniques allows teachers to self-monitor performance when no supervisor is present.
- The selection of a particular observation system clearly communicates a priority for certain teaching skills within each episode.

Data-based analytic systems do have some shortcomings, but these are negligible in comparison to the benefits above.

Disadvantages

- Learning how to select and properly use observation systems takes time, which is a limited resource for most supervisors.
- Systems with a single or limited focus suffer from observational tunnel vision, as they monitor only a few teaching/learning processes at the expense of many others. However, multiple-focus systems designed exclusively for physical education supervision do not have this limitation.
- Most systems monitor only those teaching/learning processes that are related to motor skill performance outcomes. Valid and reliable systems are needed for monitoring processes thought to increase student learning in the affective and cognitive domains.

Behavior Checklists and Rating Scales

Behavior checklists contain descriptions of effective teaching practices that teachers are expected to demonstrate. A checklist can also contain descriptions of student learning processes that teachers are expected to promote during the observed lesson. Each item on the list is reviewed following an observation, with the supervisor indicating whether it was exhibited in the episode. Examples of checklist items include: ''Teacher provided a verbal explanation of the lesson objectives'' (Yes/No); ''Students were allowed to pursue skills according to their own ability level'' (Yes/No); and ''Teacher provided a question-and-answer time at the end of class'' (Yes/No). Checklist items tend to have relatively low inference levels, making them easy and attractive for supervisors to use; however, they are not sensitive to the qualitative or quantitative match between teaching behavior merely demonstrated and that which is appropriately demonstrated.

Rating scales are similar to behavior checklists in that they contain descriptions of desired teaching/learning process behaviors and characteristics. Rating scales are able to address the quality of observed processes by including an evaluative dimension to each reviewed item. The typical evaluative scales are designed for either numerical evaluations (e.g., 1 to 5, with 5 being the highest rating), or verbal evaluations (e.g., poor, fair, good, outstanding). When using a scale, a supervisor observes the lesson and then rates the teacher on each item from a predominantly subjective viewpoint.

Behavior checklists and rating scales are the most commonly used methods for monitoring teaching performance in physical education and in other subject areas. Nearly every teacher training program uses checklists and scales to evaluate teachers on performance parameters deemed important by the staff, and school systems use checklists and rating scales almost exclusively to make decisions on teacher tenure, promotion, and retention. Behavior checklists and rating scales have several potentially useful applications.

Advantages

- They can monitor aspects of teaching performance not amenable to direct and efficient measurement by supervisors (e.g., decision-making skills, enthusiasm, and classroom control).
- They can provide supervisory monitoring and evaluation on global performance aspects of teaching that entail several overlapping parts (e.g., task structure, discipline, and class climate).
- They can round out a supervisory observation by monitoring performance features not defined in the preteaching briefing.

Behavior checklists and rating scales should be used only to supplement systematic data-based observation, due to the following limitations.

Disadvantages

- They do not actually monitor teaching performance, but rather a supervisor's individual impressions of effective teaching and learning processes.
- Inclusion of items on checklists and scales is typically quite arbitrary, determined mainly by personal preference; categories rarely reflect valid constructs of effective teaching and learning processes.
- Observers' ratings are generally not reliable across time, teachers, and supervisory personnel.
- Rating scale measurements have an acknowledged low correlation with effective teaching/learning processes; that is, rated items do not commonly reflect actual performance during lessons.

Anecdotal Notes

Supervisors typically make extensive notes while observing physical education lessons. Most notes originate from critical incidents that happen in class, incidents that the supervisor feels are either positive or negative and need to be reviewed with the teacher. Taking generous and relevant notes should be an integral part of the supervisory observation. However, like checklists and rating scales, notes should only supplement a primary data-based observation system. Anecdotal note taking has the same limitations as the use of checklists and rating scales plus an additional one: Note taking requires no *a priori* decisions to be made about the observation; the supervisor simply waits until an event strikes him or her as important and then takes notes about it.

Anecdotal notes also tend to record only obvious events. If an event caught the attention of the supervisor, it probably did not escape the teacher either. Postteaching suggestions based solely on notes would then merely offer redundant information of negligible value for the teacher.

Postteaching Conference Stage

The postteaching conference is the most critical stage in the supervisory process. While the observation stage provides the necessary information and evidence on monitored teaching/learning processes, the resulting exchange between supervisor and teacher is central in helping to improve instructional skills; it is the key time for the supervisor to interact with the teacher for improving instruction. The conference is a discussion about the degree to which goals were met in the observed episode. The conference should not only highlight deficiencies in performance, but should also provide teachers with information about positive aspects of the performance. The conference should help reduce the potentially negative impact of a bad performance as well as reinforce positive teaching skill demonstrations.

The postteaching conference should be conducted as close to the teaching episode as possible, preferably immediately afterward. As when teaching students motor skills, the impact of feedback decreases as the amount of time between the performance and the presentation of feedback increases. This is one reason why unmodified research-based observation systems are not always useful for supervision; many of them require much time to collate, analyze, and communicate results to teachers.

The PEIS Model provides 10 components for the postteaching conference stage.

Provide a Supportive, Interactive, and Reflective Conference Atmosphere

The supervisor should consider the conference atmosphere as the key facilitator of the model's effectiveness. All teachers are sensitive to the manner in which they receive information, feedback, and evaluations about their instructional skills; therefore, supervisors should carefully plan their approach to these conferences. The overall atmosphere of the postteaching conference is established by three related factors: support, interaction, and reflection.

Supervisors should work with teachers to help them view the entire supervisory process, especially the postteaching conference, as supportive. Instructional supervision cannot help teachers improve pedagogical skills when the tone of the conference is overwhelmingly negative. The tone of the conference should be businesslike yet supportive of teachers' attempts to improve. Comprehensive, incisive observation and pertinent suggestions for improvement provide teachers with effective and welcome support.

Planned and uninhibited interaction between teachers, supervisors, and cooperating teachers promotes a constructive atmosphere for the conference. A mentoring relationship is much more conducive to this process than one based on superiority. Teachers should have the opportunity to express their ideas and opinions freely during conferences with supervisors; such communication helps them become full partners in the supervisory process. Teacher-initiated interaction can also facilitate progress along the developmental continuum by encouraging teachers to be more analytical and independent in their instructional decisions and actions.

Reflection—the careful use of questions that require teachers to consider thoughtful answers—can be a valuable strategy for effective supervisory conferences. Reflection can both impart information (implied through the question) and help teachers become more aware of events that have occurred in teaching episodes. Reflective supervision and teaching (Cruickshank & Applegate, 1981; Gitlin, Ogawa, & Rose, 1984) offer a systematic way to help teachers recall immediate past events from a class and consider alternative solutions for future events. Chapter 7 discusses reflective teaching as a formal supervisory strategy.

Review Teacher's Intentions

By restating intentions discussed in the preteaching conference, supervisors can immediately outline the parameters for the postteaching conference. This determines the focus of the conference for both teacher and supervisor, assuring the teacher that no new expectations will be introduced after the observation. The supervisor should then ascertain whether the teacher encountered any unanticipated problems or interferences that might have adversely affected his or her ability to teach the lesson as planned. Some events can alter the context of the teaching environment to the extent that the teacher cannot carry plans through successfully. Typical problems include a large number of tardy students, changes in the school routine that affect class time or attendance, injuries during class, equipment failure, severe behavior problems, safety considerations, and announcements over the intercom.

Review Goals and Expectations

Objective measures of performance that were established during the preteaching conference should be reviewed at the start of the postteaching conference (e.g., using less than 10% management time, having an overall feedback rate of 2.5 per minute, using students' first names at least 30 times). If the observation focused on processes less amenable to objective measurement, more subjective statements about effective teaching should be reviewed (e.g., "I saw that you were trying to get your students divided into evenly matched teams for the tournament; that's good" or "Remember that you were going to pay more attention to the lower-skilled students in this class").

Review Audio or Video Records

Many on-campus micro- or peer-teaching laboratories include making audio or video records. Because the teacher and instructor/supervisor are both on campus, they can review these tapes after a lesson. If it is a short teaching episode, the supervisor and teacher should view or hear the entire tape before examining certain segments in depth. A longer episode might necessitate a single uninterrupted review. This immediate review helps the teacher see or hear the episode just as the supervisor did. It then serves as the reference for many of the comments in the postteaching conference.

If the tape is made from lessons conducted in schools, the teacher and supervisor usually are unable to view the tape together right away. In this case, it is best to complete the postteaching conference without reviewing the tape first. When the teacher does view the tape, he or she should have the supervisory record of the lesson on hand for the review and should be encouraged to make personal observations from the tape.

Taping teachers in schools and reviewing the tapes are not simple tasks; teachers rarely have the necessary free time during the school day to review entire lessons. One solution is to tape the whole lesson but replay only certain segments during the postteaching conference. The segments could be selected to correspond with parts of the lesson or aspects of performance identified in the preteaching conference and to illustrate the teacher's effectiveness in those areas. When time and logistics cannot allow for even this condensed kind of review, recordings should probably not be used, as they may reduce or interfere with more direct interactions between teacher and supervisor.

Review Data-Based Analyses

Typically, teachers are quite curious about their performance relative to goals established for each monitored lesson. Supervisors should quickly collate their observational information and present an itemized and uninterrupted report of the data in a matter-of-fact tone. This prevents teachers from making premature self-evaluations based on the manner used to communicate one item or another; some teachers attempt to read into the delivery of the data rather than understand the specific results of the observation.

Next, the supervisor should review each part of the performance data record, highlighting evidence that illustrates obvious strengths and weaknesses. Once again, the supervisor should point out both positive and negative performance aspects. More importantly, supervisors should be able to account for items in the supervisory record by identifying particular plans, decisions, and processes that directly influenced the resulting data. Coupling in-class teaching and learning processes with data-based outcomes reinforces the relationship between the two (i.e., what teachers and students do in class has a real impact on effective teaching/learning processes; in fact, they are often the same). For example, a supervisor might point out to a teacher that insufficient information was given to students about how to do a task, resulting in the students taking over 10 minutes to become on-task.

The supervisor can illustrate this relationship by showing objectively how the results of contrasting decision and instructional behavior patterns affect student opportunity to learn; sometimes the contrast can originate from differences of opinions between teacher and supervisor. One particularly effective strategy for supervising student and in-service teachers involves reteaching a lesson (with similar content and students) while incorporating suggested changes in decisions or processes. The resulting data from the two lessons can then be compared directly to see how effective the changes were. This strategy has two benefits: Teachers implement the suggestions under direct supervision, and they realize tangible results verified by the data comparisons.

Review Anecdotal Notes

Notes taken during an observation provide valuable information for the supervisory conference. Detailed, insightful notes can stimulate discussion of points not apparent in the data. Notes can capture important events from the teaching episode not directly monitored with systematic observation. These events are usually unanticipated but are significant enough to review with teachers. In many cases, these incidents become pertinent points for reflection during the conference by serving as key references for the observed teacher (e.g., "Remember when you . . . ? That's just what I meant when we spoke before class."). The best notes are functional, clearly reminding the supervisor of a class event without elongated descriptions to detract from other parts of the observation. Making some notes next to related data entries helps to recall the exact time of the event, once again illustrating the relationship between class events and teaching/learning process data.

Discuss Checklists and Scales

Basing the total content of a supervisory conference on checklists and rating scales is both inadequate and difficult; they should be used only as supplements to data-based information. With behavior checklists, the observer merely indicates the presence or absence of a listed teaching or learning process, without sufficient consideration of whether the behavior should have been present or absent in that lesson. In addition, checklists don't show whether the behavior was demonstrated at the correct times or in the correct manner.

Rating scales do not show whether a rated item of teaching actually improves over time. Advancing from a 6 to an 8 on "Maintaining class control" cannot really indicate if there was actually more control by the teacher, nor does it describe a quantified amount of actual improvement; it merely means that the supervisor perceived that the teacher improved in that aspect of teaching.

Rating scales should be used for aspects of teaching performance that are of interest to supervisors and teachers but are not easily measureable (e.g., enthusiasm, monitoring, class climate, control, and student rapport). But rating scales should not serve as the basis of a supervisor's diagnoses and prescriptions for improving teaching skills; if a teacher needs to improve in a certain area, systematic observations should be used to monitor, diagnose, prescribe, and document the attainment of that particular skill. For example, if a supervisor wants to document improvement on an item defined as "Promoting proper student behavior in class," the supervisor should identify behaviors related to that construct and monitor improvement by noting changes in those behaviors, not by merely making a more positive indication on the rating scale.

I suggest that numeric rather than word descriptors comprise the rating scale and that the scale be wide, with at least 8 or 10 points separating the lowest and highest ratings. A wide scale allows supervisors more flexibility in discriminating between perceived levels of performance; the difference between an 8 and 9 on a 1-10 scale is probably more sensitive to performance than is the difference between a 1 and 2 on a 1-3 scale. Numeric descriptors remove the potential impact of words like "poor," "fair," "unacceptable," and "excellent." These words are highly evaluative and offer no useful prescriptions for better teaching; teachers can sometimes interpret these terms out of context or categorize their total performance on the basis of just a few words.

Conduct a Goal Analysis

After the supervisor and teacher have examined all of the information gathered during the observation, they can review this information as it relates to goals established during the preteaching conference. In most cases, this goal review will occur throughout the conference as each part of the observational record is presented and discussed.

If no major contextual changes occurred during the lesson, then the teacher should expect to account for performance aspects in the postteaching conference; that is, the observation record should corroborate the teacher's reaching of his or her goals. However, reviewing goals should not be primarily evaluative; rather, the goals should provide interim performance indicators for teaching skill proficiency. For every goal attained, the supervisor should offer reasons why the teacher achieved it. For example, a supervisor might tell a teacher that her overall feedback rate was high because she drew upon a list of potential feedback statements that she compiled before the class began. Similarly, for every goal not reached the supervisor should offer explanations along with suggestions for improvement.

Make Diagnoses and Prescriptions

Teaching/learning process goals analyses identify performance areas in which the teacher was or was not successful. However, effective supervision must go further than merely matching intended teaching processes with observed outcomes. Supervision must be able to provide teachers with accurate and relevant diagnoses of classroom events relative to intended outcomes; supervision must diagnose areas in need of improvement and be prepared to offer tangible and context-specific prescriptions for their remedy. Informing a teacher that he or she has not adequately met predetermined performance expectations is only part of effective supervision; another part comes from suggesting ways the teacher can improve his or her instructional skills and providing the means for documenting the efficacy of those suggestions. Teachers must see that supervisory suggestions can result in noticeable changes in teaching/learning processes.

Hawkins, Wiegand, and Landin (1985) have suggested the use of "collective wisdom" for diagnosing areas of needed improvement and prescribing sound pedagogical alternatives to physical education teachers. Chapter 6 describes that strategy in greater detail.

The final step in the goal analysis process for instructional supervision is the setting of new performance goals for teachers to attain in subsequent lessons. These new goals can serve as guidelines for monitoring instructional processes in the absence of regular supervision.

Document the Observation and Conference for Supervisor and Teacher

Keeping detailed records of systematic data gathering, instructional goals, suggestions for improvement, and other information pertinent to a teacher's ongoing supervisory program can help maintain continuity from one observation to the next. Making an observation without regard to others made prior or failing to use current supervisory information as the basis for future observations are ineffective methods. Both teachers and supervisors should have some documentation of completed observations in order to make the delivery of supervisory processes more open and interactive.

Summary

The PEIS Model is designed to be practical and cyclical. It is practical because it allows each supervisory program to use its own guidelines, functions, and personnel. It is cyclical because the information gathered in the observation stage and the outcomes of the postteaching discussion become part of the next preteaching conference (considered under the teacher characteristics section). Examinations of previous observational data and notes facilitates setting performance goals and expectations for future supervised or unsupervised teaching. The PEIS Model is dynamic, as it recognizes the importance of both teaching context and developmental stages; the model can help supervisors identify the right process for the right time. The PEIS Model is also nondirective, allowing for a variety and innovative sequencing of events and directions to be followed by supervisors and teachers. It provides an outline for supervisory decision making, allowing supervisors and teachers several options for completing a particular component. The model emphasizes that processes be completed well while allowing for personal variations by individual supervisors as they carry out the decisions and processes for their own unique settings and applications. In this way, the context of supervision, like the context of teaching, becomes an integral part of the entire delivery process for effective physical education instructional supervision.

The PEIS Model offers a plan for the conduct of instructional supervision in physical education. While the encompassing model is theoretical, every component is based upon already existing practice. In fact, the PEIS Model is quite similar to the more formal clinical supervision models of Goldhammer (1969) and Acheson and Gall (1987) but is applied here to supervisory practice in any kind of physical education teaching episode.

Even though the PEIS Model can provide a general plan, specific applications and best uses will come from individuals and supervisory teams as they decide which program level components are at their disposal and experiment with various implementation level features. The model should be applied differently when used for a prestudent teaching practicum, for example, than when used for working with an induction teacher during his or her second month on the job. This flexibility allows supervisors to use the model in many different ways as they practice their role of teaching teachers.

Chapter 4

Monitoring Physical Education Teaching/Learning Processes

In the past supervisors developed their own priorities for selecting important teaching skills to monitor and analyze. Individual supervisors were also left to verify that those skills were in fact acquired. What were considered critical aspects of teaching were often personal preferences for how teachers should look and proceed. Little research evidence supported one person's priorities over another's, resulting in varied and dubious rationales for selecting key teaching skills for supervisory observation. In effect, supervisors had little information to draw on as they worked with teachers for instructional skill improvement.

Research on effective teaching, beginning in earnest during the mid-1970s, has largely reduced this dilemma for instructional supervision. The primary goal of research on effective teaching is the identification of variables related to more and faster student learning. Research has found that effective teaching encompasses a complex set of variables, some of which are not within a teacher's domain to control and exhibit. Many of these factors are based on the context of the school setting (e.g., student socioeconomic status, class size, allocated time for a subject matter, and student entry skill level). Teachers cannot change these factors but must consider them in nearly every decision and action. However, the majority of effective teaching practices are under control of the teacher, and those behaviors can influence student achievement significantly.

Our knowledge base on effective teaching is not yet complete; any listing of effective teaching/learning processes and abilities cannot be fully authoritative, exhaustive, or absolute. However, items on any such list all have one important feature in common—each has been derived from research on effective teaching and not from supervisors' personal preferences.

The value of identifying practices related to effective teaching is apparent; those practices provide viewpoints from which to discuss, monitor, analyze, reflect upon, and improve teaching in physical education. Support and validation of those viewpoints are based primarily in research, not on personal perceptions.

Establishing supervisory focal points on effective teaching practices can advance physical education teaching skills on a broad basis. If many supervisors can agree that certain features of instruction are important for teachers to demonstrate, then more teachers will strive toward the same processes and expectations, allowing supervisors to acknowledge and promote a common set of effective practices. The notion of a common set of effective teaching practices does not mean all teachers should teach alike; each teacher can exhibit unique planning and implementation skills in a variety of ways while working toward the same instructional process goals. This is based upon an assumption that supervisors can find ways to monitor those creative variations in physical education. For example, if a teacher is trying to use a logical sequence for a third grade throwing skill theme lesson (Graham, Holt/Hale, & Parker, 1987), he or she could use many instructional tasks within each of four content development categories (Rink, 1985). The supervisor must also learn the various categories of content development, become acquainted with the throwing skill theme, and be able to systematically monitor how well the teacher met his or her goals for that lesson.

Effective Teaching/Learning Processes for Physical Education

Effective teaching is based on decisions and instructional behaviors, carried out by students and teachers, that lead to more and faster student learning. Supervisors must have the skills to monitor both sources of effective processes; however, supervisors should keep the observational focus on *student* process behaviors as much as possible. Effective instructional practices are more likely to emerge by monitoring student behavior, as the real test of effective teaching comes from the ability to get students into meaningful contact with the subject matter. For example, to observe a teacher's ability to design instruction for maximum participation, a supervisor must monitor student trial and engagement rates within class activities, not just note how many minutes the teacher allocates for skill practice.

Teachers tend to plan and implement lessons based on whole-class activities, while student achievement is based on individual learning activity within the class structure (Metzler, 1989). Supervisors must recognize and look to the best source of evidence for various effective teaching/learning processes in the gym. Sometimes that means monitoring the teacher; at other times it means monitoring students.

As mentioned earlier, a generally recognized set of effective teaching/ learning practices that indicate effective instruction now exists. Based on one's own interpretation of available research evidence on effective teaching/learning, it is possible to devise a finite list of such practices to serve as the basis for supervisory observation and instructional improvement efforts. I propose that the 14 effective teaching/learning processes found below comprise a list for physical education instructional supervision. (I recognize that other indicators of effective teaching that receive support in the research literature may not be included here.) Depending on the context of the teaching episode, the teacher's developmental state, and stated lesson objectives, one or more items from this list could be monitored by a supervisor during an observed lesson.

Effective Teaching/Learning Process Indicators for Physical Education

Time management

Resource management

Behavior management and task accountability

Task relevance and structure

Engagement and success rates

Instructional cueing

Performance feedback

Class climate

Planning

Verbal and nonverbal interaction

Use of questions

Content development

Regular evaluation of student progress

Establishment of a safe learning environment

Each of the first 13 aspects listed has received some support in the effective teaching/learning literature (Walberg, 1986). When properly demonstrated by teachers and students, these practices can lead to increased achievement of intended learning outcomes. The final item, establishment of a safe learning environment, is a necessary precondition for many activities commonly taught in school physical education programs. However, we currently have no empirical support for its role in effective teaching.

Time Management

In the early 1980s, much of the research on effective teaching focused on teacher and student use of class time. Indeed, many of the differences in effectiveness of teachers are thought to be based on how well class time is managed for instruction. This research resulted in many constructs of time; one such construct is *functional curriculum time*, time in which students are meaningfully engaged with the lesson content. Effective teaching provides students with increased amounts of functional curriculum time and reduced amounts of noncontent (nonengaged) time.

Other categories of time management are pertinent for physical education instruction:

- Allocated time (class time apportioned for learning activities)
- Management time (time taken up with clerical and preparatory tasks like calling roll and setting up equipment)
- Waiting time (time between opportunities to participate)
- Transition time (time spent moving to and between class activities)
- Demonstration time (time spent showing students how to perform skills)
- Instructional time (time spent providing students with cues and feedback)
- Engaged time (actual time for participation)
- Academic learning time (time spent in relevant participation with regular student success)

Effective teachers are keenly aware of how they plan class time and are even more aware of how students actually spend time in class. Most teachers perceive time from a whole-class perspective when they plan lessons and observe class events, not realizing individual students spend their time quite differently from others, even within the same class activity. For example, a teacher might allocate 35 minutes of a class for practicing tennis serves, but typical tennis activities like retrieving balls, warming up, moving to the various courts, and waiting one's turn could reduce those 35 minutes to less than 10 minutes of actual practice time for some students.

Resource Management

Resource management involves the selection, design, and deployment of materials, equipment, facilities, fields, and audiovisual aids for improved teaching. (Time is also a resource.) Physical education instruction is especially dependent upon equipment and facilities for student achievement; students cannot learn many of the sport skills in physical education without the proper kinds of equipment and adequate fields or courts.

Effective teachers identify, plan for, and use a variety of resources for maximum student participation and benefit. Effective use of material resources provides for increased engagement (by decreasing waiting time) and enhances the quality of student engagement through task-intrinsic feedback (e.g., targets and mechanical aids) to promote higher success rates.

Behavior Management and Task Accountability

Effective teachers project a businesslike atmosphere in their classes, both by planning for preventive management and by carrying out interactive management programs (Siedentop, 1983). Preventive management involves taking steps to reduce the potential for behavior problems, such as establishing class rules and using behavior contracts with students. Interactive management decisions are made during class when preventive measures are not sufficient. In a sense, behavior management is time management—increasing the amount of functional curriculum time while reducing noncontent time of a specific nature. Being ''businesslike'' means showing students that class time is learning time and that deviations from learning tasks are neither expected nor tolerated. This also means that students should be properly informed of desired behavior and participation expectations and held accountable through teacher monitoring, feedback, and contingency programs.

Task accountability involves outlining the specific procedures and expectations for assigned learning tasks in class and supplying sufficient information about how the class can best use their time within that task. One common example is the use of task signs posted at the several stations of a fitness circuit. Each card explains what exercise is to be done at the station and communicates the reasons for doing the exercise, the proper techniques for maximum benefit, and the number of trials students should complete. Clear communication leaves students certain about tasks and expectations, giving them more reason to remain engaged.

Task Relevance and Structure

Relevant learning tasks have an obvious relation to short- or long-term instructional outcomes, regardless of which outcomes are intended. Relevancy is determined by the degree to which tasks might lead students to the intended learning goal. This relationship is usually quite apparent to experienced observers. Effective teachers analyze task components and help students progress through them sequentially, always striving to have students working toward immediate or distant goals. Task structure refers to a teacher's ability to design relevant tasks and keep students engaged in learning activities (Tousignant & Siedentop, 1983). A relevant learning task without proper structure can lead to reduced effectiveness and outcomes; structure is decided before class and is enhanced by in-class monitoring and by strategies for keeping students on task during practice times.

Engagement and Success Rates

In order to learn, students must interact with the subject matter; that is, they must be engaged in it. Vicarious learning strategies (mental practice,

Sybervision, and mere observation) have come in and out of vogue but have not been proven more effective than meaningful, active engagement for acquiring motor skills. Student achievement in physical education is based primarily upon active engagement in tasks that are appropriate for them. This means the teacher must take into account each student's developmental characteristics, past experiences, and proficiency when designing current learning tasks. Tasks that are too easy may bore students; tasks that are too difficult may frustrate students. Both can promote student withdrawal from the task, inhibiting achievement.

The importance of engagement and appropriate success rates holds for learning outcomes in the cognitive domain as well. If the intent is to teach tennis rules, for example, students must somehow interact (be engaged) with that material through verbal explanations, written descriptions, or some audiovisual medium. And, that material must be presented on a level students can comprehend. In that example, comprehension (i.e., understanding the stated concepts), is related to success rate.

Instructional Cueing

Students need two kinds of information about in-class learning tasks: information about what a task looks like when performed correctly (i.e., a model) and information about how to prepare for and pursue the task efficiently. Both kinds of information are provided by the teacher through *instructional cues*, which have many forms: verbal, visual, written, audio, and live demonstrations.

Effective teachers clearly communicate not only what, where, and when student engagement will take place, they also provide pertinent advice and strategies for completing tasks. These cues must be transmitted in terms students can comprehend. Advice and strategies can be given before engagement, during practice, and in preparation for upcoming trials to increase student achievement. Effective use of cues involves these three distinct teaching skills:

1. The ability to provide students with clear and concise information.
2. The ability to provide accurate information that will facilitate learning progress.
3. The ability to present pertinent cues in a logical and proper order, based upon student readiness, task analysis sequencing, and prior learning.

Thus, the proper cues for a third grade kicking task might include these:

- Selecting words describing the kick that are within the students' vocabulary. The teacher should speak slowly and periodically ask, "Do you know what that means?"
- Deciding what the students need to know and carefully defining and explaining the importance of each action. Information should be accurate

and descriptive; verbal and nonverbal cues (e.g., pointing) are helpful for young learners.

- Giving students cues about the kick in a functional order. "Take a long step with your nonkicking foot, plant it near the ball, kick with your instep (remember, that's where you tie your shoes), then follow through by taking an extra step forward." Young learners can become confused if a cue is inserted after the initial description because the teacher omitted it the first time. Even advanced learners find this annoying and disruptive.

Performance Feedback

That learning motor skills requires appropriate feedback, given in adequate amounts at the proper time, is undisputed. Students cannot acquire proficiency without knowing the adequacy of completed trials. Effective teachers provide high rates of both task-intrinsic and augmented feedback. *Task-intrinsic feedback* occurs when a student knows the outcome of performance directly (e.g., an arrow hits a certain ring on the target, the bar remains in place after a high jump, the kicked ball goes through the uprights, etc.). *Augmented feedback* is information delivered by the teacher or another person in the class. It may be related to outcome ("You threw seven strikes and three balls in that sequence") or to process ("The three balls occurred when you did not follow through completely, causing those pitches to be high"). Both types can help students learn motor skills, attitudes, and physical education knowledge.

Effective teachers provide students with high rates of specific feedback, which is delivered as soon after the skill trials as possible. It is also advantageous to deliver feedback in *chains*, making continuous comments to one student until the desired performance is attained.

Teachers can also provide students with feedback on behavior and adherence to planned task structure. Just as students must know performance outcomes, they need to be told how well they are doing relative to sportsmanship, effort, class management, and staying on task.

Class Climate

Physical educators have long believed that students who enjoy physical education class, their teacher, and physical education activities will be more likely to participate and learn. Siedentop (1983) calls these *subject matter approach tendencies* (p. 151). Attitudes toward physical education depend largely on the climate of the gym—the way it "feels" to be in class each day. Effective teachers are sensitive to the climate of their classes and actively attempt to improve it. Improvement can come from being more friendly, accepting students' opinions, planning for interesting lessons, sharing decision making with students, showing enthusiasm, and providing students with real opportunities to learn and achieve in physical education.

Planning

Whether through explicit written plans or personal decision-making patterns, effective teachers plan adequately for lessons. They have a clear picture of what they wish to accomplish in a class and how they will accomplish this efficiently and productively. The sparse research evidence we have about planning priorities suggests that physical educators are likely to focus on managerial and content matters, not on specific instructional processes and outcomes (Housner & Griffey, 1985; Placek, 1984). Effective planning involves reflection upon completed lessons and noting things to remember or adjust the next time that lesson is taught.

Supervisors can monitor teachers' planning decisions in two ways—either by closely reviewing and discussing plans prior to class or by monitoring indicators of good planning as the lesson progresses. For example, if a teacher has planned to allow students adequate opportunity to ask questions after an introductory demonstration, the supervisor can examine the teacher's planned lead-in and interactions for that segment or monitor the amount of time actually provided for such questions, along with recording the teacher-student interactions during that part of class. Both strategies can provide the supervisor with information related to teacher planning.

Verbal and Nonverbal Interaction

We probably know more about teacher-student interaction in physical education than any other aspect of teaching in the gym. Research on interaction analysis (Mancini, Wuest, Lombardo, & van der Mars, 1987) describes relatively low rates of interaction in the gym, interaction mostly dominated by the teacher. The predominant pattern of interaction is teacher direction, information giving, and predictable student response. This means that teachers give directions telling students to do something, and then students proceed to the task quite automatically. Very seldom do teachers provide content information or allow for student input or questions. This pattern, of course, can negatively affect class climate.

While no research base links interaction patterns directly with student learning in physical education, Dodds (1983) found that teachers who have high rates of interaction provide students with increased rates of appropriate engagement. A note of caution: This correlation should not be interpreted as illustrating a causal relationship between interactions and achievement.

Use of Questions

Effective teachers use clear, concise questions to ascertain students' understanding of directions and content. For example, a teacher who wishes to know what her students gained from an explanation of soccer rules might ask several review questions before continuing the lesson. Inadequate or incorrect responses would indicate that the students did not comprehend her explanations and would signal for further explanation of the rules.

Physical educators, especially at the secondary level, rarely use questions in their teaching. Some curricula at the elementary level are based on teachers' skilled use of questioning to promote student exploration and learning. However, we presently lack research-based descriptions of effective patterns and amounts of teacher questioning in physical education.

Content Development

Content development analysis examines the pattern and sequencing of learning activities to describe how a teacher leads students toward learning outcomes (Rink, 1985; Graham, Holt/Hale, & Parker, 1987). Teacher statements and student learning activities are placed into four categories of increasing complexity:

1. Information
2. Extension
3. Refinement
4. Application

Each category has its own features, which progress on skills and knowledges learned in previous category tasks. Teachers should design class activities that take students from information through application in a mostly linear pattern, based on their observed abilities to perform lead-up tasks. Content development is based upon statements and tasks given to the whole class and is not sensitive to individual student progression. However, even at that level it can provide supervisors with pertinent information about how teachers design sequenced learning progressions for students.

Regular Evaluation of Student Progress

Effective teachers consider the current abilities of students when designing appropriate learning tasks and assessing the amount of achievement relative to stated instructional goals (Waxman & Walberg, 1982). Monitoring formative learning outcomes can be a burdensome, time-consuming activity for physical education teachers. It can lead to a classic dilemma—whether to use class time to make assessments (for increased awareness of student abilities) or to use that time for more learning tasks (at the expense of periodic evaluation).

Teachers who view evaluation as the acquisition of information about how students are doing rather than as formal, structured evaluation can sometimes get that necessary information without expending large amounts of class time. One strategy is to direct students to complete a short task on their own near the end of the period, a task that represents achievement in the class content. By then asking how many students completed the task to varying degrees (e.g., "How many made at least 5 of 10 free throws?" or "How many made at least 7 of 10 free throws?"), a teacher can get a rather good assessment of student progress for that lesson. Regardless of how the information is obtained, it is important for teachers to know how well their students have progressed within instructional units.

Establishment of a Safe Learning Environment

Many activities in the physical education curriculum pose potential risks of injury; most of the risks are minor, but a few can result in serious injury. Although no direct support exists for safety as an effective teaching variable in physical education, it is logical that students must perceive their learning environment as safe before they can strive for maximum achievement (Graham, Holt/Hale, & Parker, 1987). Teachers should inform and periodically remind students of all safety rules in each activity, provide students with safe and functionally protective equipment when warranted, and free the learning area from all potential hazards. One common strategy is to post safety rules on locker room bulletin boards and to review those rules as students prepare for class.

Measurement Criteria and Observation Techniques

Prior to the systematic observation of these physical education teaching/learning processes, the supervisor must decide *which* aspects of teaching and/or learning to monitor. This decision is based upon the relevance of the behaviors: What about each performance process is important for the supervisor to know? Is the performance best understood in terms of time, frequency, rate per minute, or in sequence with other behaviors? Will the focus be on one student at a time, several students, or the entire class? Each of these ways of understanding performance is a *measurement criterion*. The measurement criterion is the most important feature of the teaching/learning process under focus (Sulzer-Azaroff & Reese, 1982). A multiple observation system will contain one measurement criterion for each type of data it produces. Each measurement criterion requires an appropriate observation technique for making data-based recordings of it. A proper match between measurement criterion and observation technique increases the validity of resulting data.

Next, the supervisor decides *how* to monitor those parameters of effective teaching so he or she can gather information for the postteaching conference that can be used to set future performance goals. To do this, the supervisor may use various observation techniques. Insightful and useful supervisory observations originate from using various procedures and techniques for gathering performance information during the teaching episode. Siedentop (1983) divided observation techniques into two general categories—traditional and systematic.

Traditional Observation Techniques

Traditional forms of observation are based on a supervisor's impressions of how well a teacher is doing and result in little more than general statements to the teacher about the episode. Traditional observation has four main techniques for gathering performance information:

- *Intuitive judgment*, having a "feel" for how the teacher is doing, often based on indirect evidence (e.g., conversations with cooperating teachers, promptness in completing related assignments).
- *Eyeballing*, making on-site observations with no permanent recordings of any kind.
- *Anecdotal recording*, making notes on important events that occur in the class, based on the supervisor's designation of critical incidents during teaching.
- *Behavior checklists* and *rating scales*, subjective evaluations on predetermined behavior categories, recorded on a numeric or descriptive continuum reflecting the quality of performance.

Checklists and rating scales comprise the bulk of supervisory techniques in education. They are easy to design and use, are commonly accepted as valid performance evidence, and are familiar to teachers and supervisors. This acceptance is widespread despite the fact that checklists and scales do not provide valid evidence of effective teaching and learning processes.

As a group, traditional observation techniques have several limitations:

- Little or no training is required to use them, which downplays a supervisor's role as skilled observer and subject matter expert. These techniques make supervision largely a passive process, whereby one waits for a critical incident to occur before making note of it or waits until the end of the lesson to check or rate it.

- Teacher and student behaviors as measured by these techniques have little correlation with effective teaching/learning processes; these techniques cannot serve as valid measures of effective teaching/learning indicators.
- These techniques measure a supervisor's perceptions or impressions of teaching, not actual teaching/learning processes.
- Behavior checklists and rating scales in particular are often quite generic and are not sensitive to the observed teaching context. Checked or rated items are designed to be used across many instructional situations, some of which are outside physical education.
- Because these systems are based on impressions, it is not possible to know whether differences over time reflect changes in the supervisor's perceptions or actual changes in teacher performance.
- None of these techniques provide teachers with tangible evidence of current performance levels upon which to establish and monitor future performance goals. They are inadequate for practical attempts to improve teaching skills. It would be ludicrous for a supervisor to say "Today you got a 5 on class management. The next time I observe you, try to make that a 7"!

Traditional observation techniques can have some limited usefulness for supervision. By examining items on checklists or rating scales and identifying some events as critical to good practice, teachers can become aware of more aspects of effective instruction. (This assumes that the items and events are actually manifestations of effective teaching.)

When the teaching context is too complex for systematic observational methods, traditional techniques can be used to round out the monitoring process for effective teaching indicators such as "proper use of questions," "establishing a positive class climate," or "circulating frequently during skill practice segments." Traditional techniques should not be used as actual performance indicators; however, they can be used to alert teachers to additional perspectives of their performance.

Systematic Observation Techniques

Systematic observation techniques are based on objectively measured, direct analyses of teaching/learning processes in physical education. Specific teaching/ learning processes to be monitored are defined prior to a teaching episode. Observers (supervisors) need to be adequately trained to recognize and record instances of occurrence; such training increases the reliability of data gathered for supervision, helping to attain a consistent measurement of behavior across observers.

Systematic observation techniques have several advantages over their traditional counterparts for helping teachers improve instruction.

Advantages

- They are based upon *low inference data recording*, rather than high inference ratings and critical incidences. Teachers can be confident that results (i.e., data) are more representative of actual performance than rating scales and other traditional techniques.
- Systematic techniques are based on predefined categories of teaching and learning processes, allowing supervisors to communicate priorities for instruction through the selection of certain categories for observation. It's a way of saying, "These processes are important to demonstrate in this lesson."
- Effective teaching/learning practices are based on observable behaviors; therefore, the most valid way to measure these practices is through direct monitoring, not impressions or opinions. Effective teaching practices are what teachers and students say and do in class, not what supervisors perceive them as doing.
- Data-based observations can be used to establish baseline teaching/learning patterns, enabling supervisors to more accurately describe teaching skills before attempting to improve them.
- Such obtained baseline measures can be used to set and monitor goals for instructional skill improvement. Comparisons over time become tangible evidence of improvement and the amount of improvement.
- Systematic data can be used to verify the outcomes of supervision itself. Once a supervisor has diagnosed a problematic area and made suggestions for improvement, data-based comparisons can be taken to note the direction and strength of intended changes, verifying their impact. When used in this way, systematic observation can help supervisors be more effective, too.

Systematic supervision techniques have their own limitations. However, these stem mostly from the pragmatics of their use on a regular basis.

Disadvantages

- Some systems take time and expertise to learn. Learning several systems may be prohibitive to some supervisors who cannot devote the necessary time or who lack access to assistance.
- By intentional design, many supervisory systems have tunnel vision. They provide a good picture of only one aspect of the observed lesson, leaving many important teaching/learning processes unnoticed. This limitation

can be greatly reduced with the use of multiple-focus systems (see chapter 5).

A supervision program designed for improving teachers' instructional skills will rely heavily upon several observation systems and will provide all supervisory personnel with the training necessary to record, analyze, and incorporate data-based information to assist teachers. The effectiveness of any supervision program lies in the ability of its personnel to make keen observations and critical decisions; the deployment of systematic observation strategies greatly improves that ability.

Monitoring Teaching Systematically

As explained earlier, once one or more foci have been identified for analysis and the supervisor has decided which measurement criterion (time, frequency, rate, etc.) will be monitored, the next step is to determine how to measure those behaviors during the teaching episode. When choosing to use a systematic observation technique, the supervisor must determine whether to observe teacher behavior, student behavior, or a combination of both for evidence

Table 4.1 Monitoring Effective Process Indicators in Physical Education

	Monitor	
Indicator	Teacher	Students
Time management	X	X
Resource management	X	X
Behavior management and task accountability		X
Task relevance and structure		X
Engagement and success rates		X
Instructional cueing	X	X
Performance feedback	X	X
Class climate	X	X
Planning	X	X
Verbal and nonverbal interaction	X	X
Use of questions	X	X
Content development	X	
Regular evaluation of student progress	X	X
Establishment of a safe learning environment	X	X

of effective practice. Table 4.1 is a useful guide for deciding whom to observe when monitoring teaching/learning processes in physical education.

The supervisor then chooses a specific observation technique. As mentioned earlier, the observation technique is the specific manner in which observational data are recorded for analysis. Selection of the proper observation technique depends upon the supervisor's identification of the measurement criterion. Five observation techniques can be used to systematically monitor teacher and student behavior in physical education.

- Event recording
- Duration recording
- Time sampling
- Planned activity check (PLACHECK) recording
- Multiple-focus recording

Deciding which of the five techniques is best for a given teaching episode depends on the most important dimensions of the behaviors that the supervisor and teacher choose to monitor. Are the defined teaching/learning processes best understood in terms of time (how long they last), frequency (how often they occur), or sequence of events (their order)? Some aspects of performance need to be measured and analyzed in more than one way to provide a complete description for supervisory analysis. Multiple-focus recording allows an observer to combine any two or more of the observation techniques for more descriptive results (e.g., measuring time and frequency to determine rates). Table 4.2 illustrates the most valid ways to measure certain events in the gym, depending on whether the teacher or the students are to be monitored.

Event Recording

Event recording is the tallying of defined events as they occur in class. As the supervisor sees or hears defined behaviors, he or she makes a tally on a coding sheet. That tally represents one occurrence (frequency) of the behavior. Event recording is best used for behaviors that are relatively brief and have clear beginnings and endings. Several kinds of teaching/learning processes in physical education are conducive to measurement with event recording: teacher feedback (verbal and nonverbal), teacher/student interactions, skill attempt trials, trials to criterion, motor appropriate trials, student off-task behavior, teacher's use of questions, and use of students' first names.

Event recording results in a variety of data types for analyzing physical education teaching. The most common is frequency of events, each occurrence represented by one tally on the coding sheet. When all category frequencies are known, the percentage of total events that each category frequency represents can be calculated using Equation 4.1.

$$\frac{\text{Category frequency}}{\text{Total frequency}} \times 100 = \text{Category percentage} \qquad (4.1)$$

Table 4.2 Monitoring Effective Teaching/Learning Processes for Physical Education

Indicator	Event recording Teacher	Event recording Students	Duration recording Teacher	Duration recording Students	Time sampling Teacher	Time sampling Students	PLACHECK recording Teacher*	PLACHECK recording Students
Time management			X	X	X	X		X
Resource management	X	X	X	X	X	X		X
Behavior management and task accountability		X		X		X		X
Task relevance and structure		X		X		X		X
Engagement and success rates		X		X		X		X
Instructional cueing	X	X	X		X	X		

	1	2	3	4	5	6	7
Performance feedback	X	X			X	X	
Class climate	X	X					X
Planning	X	X	X	X	X	X	X
Verbal and nonverbal interaction	X	X	X		X	X	
Use of questions	X	X	X		X	X	
Content development	X						
Evaluation of student progress		X	X	X	X	X	
Establishment of a safe learning environment	X	X			X	X	X

*PLACHECK recording is group sampling and is not appropriate for observing a single teacher.

If the teaching episode duration is known, event frequencies can be converted to a common metric, usually rate per minute (rate/min). A category rate calculation is shown in Equation 4.2.

$$\frac{\text{Category frequency}}{\text{Episode duration}} = \text{Rate per minute} \qquad (4.2)$$

Rates of behavior can be used to equate performance across teaching episodes of varying length; frequency alone is not very useful. If one teacher gave 45 verbal feedbacks in a class and another teacher gave 75, a supervisor would need to know the length of each class to determine which teacher had a higher rate. Event recorded data can be used to analyze the distribution of behavior categories relative to each other. Ratios can be calculated to compare two categories directly with each other. This allows a supervisor to monitor overall rates of events and the desired patterns of events between and within defined categories.

Duration Recording

Duration recording is used to measure the amount of time a defined behavior is observed within a teaching episode. Recordings are made with a timing device (e.g., stop watch or clock with a sweep second hand). Duration recording is most valid for behaviors that last longer and have a clear beginning and end. It can also be used to measure categories comprised of several concurrent events, or those defined by their *function* (rather than topography). For example, *management time* might be defined as the number of minutes students spend in noninstructional activity during class. Regardless of the specific type of behavior observed (e.g., listening to roll call, moving equipment, getting into lines), if it does not involve instructional time, it is considered management time. Each observed occurrence of a defined duration category is called an *episode*. Several important indicators of effective teaching and learning in physical education can be measured with duration recording: management, transition, waiting, motor engagement, motor appropriate engagement, cognitive engagement, and student off-task.

Duration recording produces data on the amount of time teachers and students spend in defined categories. This information is important for supervision. Just like event recorded data, duration data can be analyzed for the distribution of time across categories within the teaching episode (e.g., 25% management, 15% lecture/demonstration, 10% waiting, and 50% practice time). The percentage for each category is determined by following Equation 4.3.

$$\frac{\text{Summed category duration}}{\text{Total duration}} \times 100 = \text{Category percentage} \qquad (4.3)$$

Because each duration episode is noted on the recording sheet, supervisors can also determine the shortest, longest, and average length of episodes for each category.

By recording each episode individually, event recordings are made as well (by tallying how often a duration category occurred). With both duration and event data, teaching/learning processes can be analyzed in two dimensions at once. For example, a teacher might be efficient in cutting down the length of individual management episodes but may have too many such episodes in class, resulting in excessive management time. In that case, the supervisor could suggest ways to reduce the number of management episodes while encouraging the teacher to retain demonstrated efficiency in minimizing their length.

Time Sampling

Time sampling is the systematic monitoring of teacher or student behavior at predetermined intervals during the class (Cooper, Heron, & Heward, 1987). The supervisor records which defined behavior the teacher or student is engaged in at the end of a structured segment of time. The interval length is held constant throughout the observation, typically from 15 seconds to 2 minutes. The actual length of the interval should conform closely to the expected frequency of the observed behavior; the higher the frequency the shorter the interval. This match between frequency and sampling determines how well the sampled data represent actual frequency. Time sampling is useful for supervision because it does not require constant attention to data recording, making it possible for a supervisor to observe other aspects of performance between samplings.

Time sampling results in data on the frequency of observed intervals for each defined category. Supervisors must take some precautions in analyzing and interpreting data from time sampling. Although the data are often considered both event and duration data, they are actually neither. The product is a record of events sampled from actual events. Even though events are sampled at constant intervals of time, they are not duration data. Observing a teacher or student in a certain behavior at the end of the interval does not necessarily mean that behavior occurred throughout the entire interval.

For analyses, supervisors can treat time sampled data like event data, keeping in mind that the data do not represent actual frequencies. The most common analysis is to calculate the percentage of observed intervals each category represents within the entire observation, as shown in Equation 4.4.

$$\frac{\text{Observed intervals (one category)}}{\text{Total intervals}} \times 100 = \text{Category percentage} \qquad (4.4)$$

Time sampling can be used to monitor any defined teaching/learning process from event- or duration-based categories, making it a highly flexible technique for supervision.

PLACHECK Recording

PLACHECK (PLanned Activity CHECK) is group time sampling of student behavior. Instead of observing a single student, the supervisor scans a subgroup or the entire class at predetermined time intervals, observing a predetermined category. Typically, categories for PLACHECKs are dichotomous; that is, students are either in a scanned category or they are not. PLACHECKs are helpful for monitoring several aspects of student process behavior: activity/inactivity, on task/off task, success/failure, and appropriate/inappropriate.

PLACHECK scanning is easy to do. For example, an observer who is scanning for student activity starts from the left side of a group of students and scans toward the right, counting each student who is actively participating at the moment according to the category definition. The observer records the number of active students for the scan. Depending on position and number of students in the class, PLACHECK scans take about 10 seconds and are made six times consecutively for each category (about one minute per set of scans).

PLACHECK data are used to determine how many students at a given time are within a defined behavior category. These data are especially useful for analyzing discrepancies between teacher intent and student process. For example, a teacher might have students in practice time for 90% of the class period, certainly an acceptable percentage in most cases. However, that kind of analysis cannot reveal how many students are actually practicing at any one moment. PLACHECK recording can indicate just how efficiently a teacher designs and implements practice episodes for optimal student engagement. A single calculation is derived for each PLACHECK category by following Equation 4.5. This determines the mean percentage of students observed in that behavior.

$$\frac{\text{Students observed in a defined category}}{\text{Total number of students}} \times 100 = \text{Category percentage} \qquad (4.5)$$

Even though a PLACHECK observation produces a limited number of analyses, it can be a revealing and useful recording technique.

Multiple-Focus Recordings

The four systematic observation techniques discussed previously were developed for various kinds of field-based research and were intended to provide in-depth analyses on rather limited aspects of teaching/learning behavior. Many times, the use of a single technique provides reliable and detailed data on limited teaching/learning processes, at the expense of monitoring other important aspects of effective teaching and learning practice. An event recording system for monitoring teacher feedback tells a supervisor much about rates and types of feedback used by the teacher but reveals nothing else about the teaching episode. Similarly, a duration recording system provides information only about how teachers and students spend their time in class. When used individually, these techniques form *single-focus observational systems*.

Sometimes a single-focus observation technique is adequate for the episode. However, a supervisor most often needs to observe and monitor several teaching/learning processes within one teaching episode, which requires the use of several different observation techniques. This can be done by combining techniques into *multiple-focus observation systems* (Metzler, 1981; Siedentop, 1983). Multiple-focus observation systems provide many different kinds of data from one teaching episode by systematically sampling teacher or student behavior and by incorporating supplemental traditional observation techniques. The overall result is a more complete description of teaching/learning processes. As few as two or as many as six techniques can be combined in one system.

Combining Systems With Measurement Criteria

Table 4.3 illustrates how several measurement criteria presented earlier can be matched with the observation techniques explained here.

Review Table 4.2 for a list of suggested effective teaching/learning processes and the best techniques for monitoring them. In some cases teaching and student behaviors parallel each other, while sometimes different techniques are required for teachers and students. After determining the proper observation technique, the supervisor can employ an observation system to monitor selected

Table 4.3 Matching Measurement Criteria With Observation Techniques

Measurement criterion	Observation technique
Time	Duration recording
Latency (time between events)	Duration recording
Frequency	Event recording
Rate per minute	Duration and event recording
Occurrence/nonoccurrence (1 student or the teacher)	Time sampling
Occurrence/nonoccurrence (Group or whole class)	PLACHECK recording

Select teacher and/or student processes to monitor	→ Determine measurement criterion (most important feature)	→ Determine observation technique (monitoring system)
Time management	Time	Data-based system
Resource management	Frequency	Behavior checklist
Behavior management and task accountability	Rate (frequency/time)	Rating scale
Task relevance and structure	Sequence	Anecdotal notes
Engagement and success rates	Direction	
Instructional cueing	Location	
Performance feedback	Combination of two or more from above	
Class climate		
Planning		
Verbal and nonverbal interaction		
Use of questions		
Content development		
Regular evaluation of student progress		
Establishment of a safe learning environment		
Other preferred processes		

Figure 4.1. Measuring teaching/learning processes for physical education.

teacher or student processes. (Chapter 5 presents examples of single- and multiple-focus observation systems designed exclusively for physical education instructional supervision.)

Figure 4.1 shows the complete schema for considering teaching/learning processes, measurement criteria, and the resulting observation technique. For example, a supervisor might wish to focus on a teacher's use of instructional cues during an observed lesson. Choosing among four likely measurement criteria (event, time, rate, and sequence), the supervisor decides to monitor rate—how many cues the teacher gives per minute. The supervisor then selects an observation system designed to count instructional cues (event) and record elapsed class time (duration). After recording the number of cues stated during a known number of class minutes, the supervisor calculates the teacher's rate of cues during the lesson.

Summary

Fortunately, supervisors today have many options for selecting what to observe during an instructional lesson. They can refer to the growing literature on effective teaching/learning, to teaching skills emphasized in a training program, and to their own list of preferred practices for physical education. They can also ask individual teachers what they wish to focus on during a supervisory visit.

After the supervisor has decided which teaching/learning processes and which aspects of those processes to monitor during an observation, he or she must decide *how* to monitor those processes. These decisions are essential to effective supervisory practice; a supervisor who focuses on relevant teaching/learning processes and monitors those processes in ways that provide valid descriptions of teaching will most likely promote realistic, lasting progress in instructional skill improvement. Chances for success increase when both the teacher and supervisor are confident that the monitored processes will influence student learning and when both have a clear picture of how those processes occur in classes.

Information gained through systematic observation of key teaching skills lends credibility to supervisory decisions, helping teachers and supervisors know whether the supervision made a difference. Focusing on tangential aspects of teaching or basing progress assessment only upon a supervisor's impressions (through traditional methods) contributes little to the improvement of teaching or supervision. Both supervision and teaching work best when they are guided by an overall plan that includes efficient processes for reaching stated goals and sound information for analysis and decision-making.

Chapter 5

Observation Systems for Physical Education Instructional Supervision

The basis of supervisory analysis and decision making lies in the systematic monitoring of teaching/learning processes deemed important by the supervisor and teacher. Through this kind of observation, the supervisor can capture and communicate to the teacher valid descriptions of instructional events. From these descriptions the supervisor verifies effective teaching skills or identifies deficiencies. The supervisor compiles these descriptions of teaching/learning processes using systematic observation instruments, which are really tools that allow the supervisor to focus upon certain instructional events deemed important by the supervisor and the teacher in the preteaching conference. This chapter outlines some general considerations in the design of such instruments and presents several examples of systems designed specifically for physical education supervision.

Designing Systems or Adapting Systems?

The selection of a supervisory monitoring system is based upon two important criteria. First, the instrument must be able to gather valid data on the selected teaching/learning processes; that is, it must be able to focus upon those instructional features identified prior to the lesson. Second, the selected system must be able to apply that focus in a way that is useful to the specific supervisory needs of the moment; it must be sensitive to what the supervisor wishes to analyze within the observed lesson. For example, if a supervisor and a teacher decide to focus on content development in a lesson, they must choose a system that not only can record how many content development tasks are given but also the exact statements made by the teacher and the order in which the teacher presents the tasks to students. Having all that information enables the supervisor and teacher to analyze how well the teacher instructed for content development.

Supervisors who wish to make data-based observations must decide whether to design their own observation systems or to adapt or adopt existing systems for particular applications. The answer to this question should be based on two factors: (1) the availability of time and expertise needed to design and field test a new system and (2) how well existing systems fit the program's supervisory needs. The selected instrument must be useful for each supervisory situation and the decision to design or adapt a system must be made on the basis of the supervisory needs of the moment.

Designing a New System

Designing a supervision system from scratch is a complex task, requiring extensive amounts of time to conceptualize, test, troubleshoot, and finalize for supervisory use. But for supervisors who require custom-made observation systems for many potential applications, the effort is worthwhile.

Supervisors who plan to design their own observation systems must familiarize themselves with the relationships between selected teaching/learning processes for physical education, measurement criteria, and observation techniques outlined in chapter 4. Those relationships are critical for designing a system that will work in its intended supervisory application.

While no standard procedure exists for the design of new observation systems, I have found the following 10-step sequence to be helpful and efficient:

1. Identify teaching/learning processes to monitor.
2. Define those processes in observable and measureable terms.
3. Field test target behavior definitions.
4. Select observation techniques for each process.
5. Design and field test a prototype coding system and coding sheet.
6. Field test the system again.
7. Design and implement observer training program.
8. Develop a decision log for overlapping categories.
9. Practice coding with the system to demonstrate reliability.
10. Make supervisory observations with the system.

Of course, this list lacks details about the entire process and minimizes the amount of trial and error necessary to get the system functioning as needed. Several good references are included in Appendix A for supervisors who wish to design their own observation systems. The complexity of designing a supervisory system from scratch makes the next option—using an existing system for one's specific needs—an attractive route.

Adopting or Adapting
an Existing Observation System

In most cases, someone has likely already designed an observation system that does exactly, or nearly exactly, what you need (Darst, Mancini, & Zakrasjek, 1989). Keen supervisors are always on the lookout for such systems, and they recognize the potential for an existing system to serve a specific purpose.

If a system does just what a supervisor needs for a situation, that system can be *adopted*—used in its current form with no changes. Most often, a system will do almost everything one needs and can be easily *adapted* for a given task. Supervisors who seek to adapt or adopt a system must become very familiar with each system as it relates to their needs for it, ensuring that the system has the potential to do the job at hand. I suggest that a supervisor make two lists during this assessment, one containing functions needed from the observation system in a given instance and the other showing what the existing system can do. If these lists match perfectly, then the supervisor can adopt the system; if the lists differ, the supervisor will need to adapt the existing system. The simplest adaptations usually involve modifying definitions or adding or deleting defined categories. If the lists have great differences, especially in observation technique, the system probably can't be successfully adapted.

Adopting or adapting an existing system involves five steps:

1. Match existing system with observational goals (focus).
2. Obtain and become familiar with observational system materials.
3. Make adaptations for specific supervisory needs (optional).
4. Practice coding to demonstrate reliability with the system.
5. Make supervisory observations with the system.

Using an existing system for physical education supervision requires fewer, less time-consuming steps than necessary for designing a new system, meaning the supervisor can put the system into use much more quickly. This approach is highly practical when many different observation instruments are needed in a total program of instructional supervision.

Supervisory observation systems can be divided into two types—systematic and traditional (Siedentop, 1983). (Chapter 4 provided a complete discussion of the strengths and weaknesses of each type.) This chapter presents examples of several systematic observation instruments plus two more traditional types based on rating scales and behavior checklists.

All of the systematic instruments presented here have been used for various types of physical education instructional supervision, from methods classes to student teaching to in-service teaching analysis. While most of the systems use a single observation technique, the last two are designed as multiple-focus observational systems. The description of each system begins with a brief explanation of its purpose, indicating the specific teaching/learning processes it is designed to monitor. Category definitions follow, along with brief instructions for using the system. Completed recording sheets with sample data are included to provide a picture of what the system looks like in action. Helpful suggestions for collating and analyzing the data resulting from each system (or two similar ones) complete the descriptions.

Monitoring Teacher and Student Time in Class

Time is an important dimension for analyzing instructional events in physical education. Even though time is a common resource (everyone has some of it), it is also an extremely precious one (no one ever has enough of it). As mentioned in chapter 4, effective instruction in physical education is often related to how efficiently time can be used to allow adequate student interaction with lesson content. Students simply cannot learn if they are not provided with sufficient time. The teacher plays a critical role in the way time is spent in the gym, as he or she is responsible for the allocation and expenditure of instructional minutes. Therefore, supervisors will often need to observe and analyze how the teacher and students spend their time in class. Two systems described here focus on teacher time, the other two on student time. They are also classified by two kinds of observation techniques—duration recording and time sampling. In combination, they provide supervisors with contrasting observational foci and observation techniques for monitoring time in physical education classes.

TIME ANALYSIS FOR PHYSICAL EDUCATION— TEACHER FOCUS (TAPE-TEACHER)

Physical education supervisors can use this system to monitor how a teacher spends time in an observed class. The TAPE-Teacher system demonstrates the distribution of a teacher's time across several instructional process categories. This system uses duration recording exclusively.

The observer monitors the teacher throughout the entire episode; this is called *continuous recording*. As an alternative, several samples of teaching behavior can be taken during class, allowing the supervisor to observe other aspects of the lesson when not monitoring for time distribution. If sampling, the observer should distribute observations evenly from the beginning to end of class to get a representative picture of the lesson. The TAPE-Teacher system needs only a few simple materials for its use: a stop watch or watch with a sweep second hand, a clipboard, a pencil, and a TAPE-Teacher coding sheet.

CATEGORIES AND DEFINITIONS FOR TAPE-TEACHER

Management: Teacher activities not directly related to class instructional goals. These include taking roll, setting up equipment, giving directions about class organization, and performing administrative functions.

Behavior Management: Direction of or intervention in student conduct in class. This includes explaining or reminding students of class behavior rules, carrying out disciplinary action, and counseling students.

Lecture/Demonstration: Content information given to students by the teacher. This includes skill demonstrations, explanations of rules and strategies, and audiovisual presentations. (Note: Information about instructional content is coded Lecture/Demonstration; information unrelated to content is coded Management.)

Instruction: Interactive instructional attention given to students. This includes focused (active) observation of skill attempts and delivery of feedback following students' skill attempts.

Monitoring: Passive observation of class activities. This includes watching students as they carry out managerial requests and supervising (but not officiating) games and scrimmages.

Diversion: Focusing of teacher's attention away from class. This includes interruptions from outsiders, responses to emergencies, and the teacher's voluntary choice to be detached from the lesson.

Other/Undefined: A teacher's use of class time not included in any other previously defined category.

USING TAPE-TEACHER

An observer using this system focuses only on the teacher during class. The observer begins timing when he or she observes the teacher in one of the categories. When the teacher moves to another category, the observer stops the clock, records the length of the episode on the TAPE-Teacher sheet, and resets the clock for the new category. Recordings are made only when the teacher changes categories, so the supervisor can monitor other aspects of the class while the teacher stays within one category. Remember, the teacher is always in one of the categories, so the clock should be running constantly except for category changes. The observer can record time episodes in two ways: by recording the exact length of each episode (e.g., 3 minutes) or by recording an episode's start/stop times (e.g., 9:15-9:18). The latter method allows for the making of a time line denoting the sequence of teacher process episodes during the class. A completed sample recording made using the TAPE-Teacher system is shown on page 88.

Time Analysis for Physical Education — Teacher Focus (TAPE-Teacher)

Date __4-7-89__   Teacher __PAUL PRUSAK__

Grade __2__   School __Chico HS__

Observer __S. VARLEY__   Content __BASKETbALL-FREE Throws__

Time Begin __9:00__   Time End __9:45__

Elapsed Time __45 min.__

	Episode 1	Episode 2	Episode 3	Episode 4	Episode 5
Management	9:00-9:04	9:10-9:12	9:25-9:27	9:44-9:45	
Behavior Management	9:09-9:10				
Lecture/ Demonstration	9:04-9:09		9:42-9:44		
Instruction	9:19-9:25	9:28-9:35	9:37-9:42		
Monitoring	9:12-9:19	9:27-9:28	9:35-9:37		
Diversion					
Other/ Undefined					

Physical Education Engagement

Lecture/ Demonstration __7__ min = __15.5__ %

Instruction __18__ min = __40__ %

Monitoring __10__ min = __22.2__ %

Total __35__ min = __77.7__ %

Non-Physical Education Engagement

Management __9__ min = __20__ %

Behavior Management __1__ min = __2.2__ %

Diversion ____ min = ____ %

Other/Undefined ____ min = ____ %

Total __10__ min = __22.2__ %

TIME ANALYSIS FOR PHYSICAL EDUCATION— STUDENT FOCUS (TAPE-STUDENT)

The TAPE-Student system monitors how students spend time during class. The supervisor can focus on an individual student, one or more groups of students, or the whole class. The TAPE-Student system uses duration recording for all but two categories. Because measuring the duration of some kinds of practice trials (e.g., batting) is not feasible and in many cases not valid, students' attempts at skill tasks are monitored with event recording techniques. TAPE-Student requires a stop watch or watch with a sweep second hand, a clipboard, a pencil, and a TAPE-Student recording sheet.

CATEGORIES AND DEFINITIONS FOR TAPE-STUDENT

Management: Student activities not directly related to instructional goals. These include waiting for class to begin, listening to roll being called, listening to teacher managerial directions, setting up equipment, and spending time in transition between instructional activities.

Knowledge: Listening to, reading, or watching explanations of instructional content material. This includes listening to lectures, watching demonstrations, receiving cues and feedback, watching media presentations, and taking written tests. Knowledge includes reading task cards if the cards contain content related to the learning task. (Reading cards and receiving other information on class management is coded under Management).

Warm Up/Fitness: Preparatory or repetitive exercises for warm up or fitness enhancement. These include stretching, jogging, aerobic exercise, and weight lifting.

Skill Practice: Student time engaged in the active pursuit of skill acquisition, limited to motor skill practice only. Getting ready to make an attempt and watching the results of a motor skill trial are considered practice (e.g., alignment routines, focused concentration prior to an attempt, and watching the results of a golf shot). Active participation in scrimmages and games is recorded in this category. Normal time needed to retrieve balls, arrows, and shuttlecocks for the next trial is recorded as Skill Practice. (Excessive time spent doing this should be recorded as Management.)

Tasks: Single motor task trials (or set of trials combined into one attempt) not reaching a stated or implied level of proficiency. This category is recorded with event coding as frequencies within Skill Practice episodes.

Tasks to Criterion: Any single motor task or set of tasks reaching a stated or implied level of proficiency. The criterion can be stated by the teacher directly (''Try to hit the blue ring on the target'') or implied by the task itself (e.g., making foul shots while practicing them). If the teacher assigns tasks as groups of attempts, record each set as one trial (e.g., ''See if you can make five in a row" or "Try to get 8 of 10 shots onto the green"). This category is recorded with event coding as frequencies within Skill Practice episodes.

Off-Task: Inappropriate disengagement from the lesson. Disengagement can result from misbehavior (not paying attention, causing distractions, fighting, cheating on a test) or inappropriate task engagement (practicing a different task than requested or expected). If a student should be participating but takes an unauthorized break, it is recorded as Off-Task (not as Resting/Break).

Waiting: Student time spent waiting for the next skill attempt. It typically occurs as students are standing in line or waiting to share equipment or space. Preclass waiting and time between activity segments are recorded as Management.

Resting/Break: Disengagment from class authorized by the teacher. This includes teacher-approved water breaks and rests between exercises. If the break is not authorized by the teacher, this is coded Off-Task.

Other/Undefined: Student in-class activities not included under a previously defined category. This includes answering emergencies and responding to external interruptions.

USING TAPE-STUDENT

The TAPE-Student system uses duration recording for all categories except Tasks (T) and Tasks to Criterion (C), which are monitored with event recording. Each time a motor skill attempt is made, the observer should record T if not performed to criterion, C if performed to criterion.

The supervisor makes duration recordings by observing one student at a time in 5-minute blocks. The observer randomly selects four or five students before class and focuses on each one separately during the lesson. The student in focus at the moment is the "target." Time is recorded when the target is observed in one of the defined or other categories. Time can be entered by the *exact length* of the episode (e.g., 3 minutes), or by the episode's start/stop times (e.g., 11:30-11:33). When the target student is in a Skill Practice episode, Tasks or Tasks to Criterion are event recorded in the appropriate row and column.

Student time in class can also be recorded by whole class observation, using the "Rule of 51%." Under this rule, the category that represents over one-half of the class's engagement is monitored. When one category alone does not account for 51% of the students, the predominant category is monitored.

Differing pictures of student engagement will likely result from single and whole-class observations. Single-student focus will represent how individuals spend their time within general class activities. This is usually a more sensitive measure of how efficiently teachers arrange the learning environment in physical education than is a whole-class focus. When using TAPE-Student for whole-class analysis, supervisors should delete the event recording of Tasks and Tasks to Criterion.

A sample completed TAPE-Student observation sheet is shown on page 91.

Time Analysis for Physical Education — Student Focus (TAPE-Student)

Date __1-14-89__   Teacher __SUE MAGLIARO__

Grade __3RD (LESH)__   School __MENDHAM ELEM.__

Observer __G. WEBSTER__   Content __Throwing TO TARGETS__

Time Begin __1:30__   Time End __1:50__

Elapsed Time __20 min.__

	S-1 RED HAIR	S-2 TALL GIRL	S-3 BLUE SHOES	S-4 RED SHORTS
Management		1:35-1:36		
Knowledge		1:36-1:38		
Warm Up/Fitness	1:32-1:35			
Skill Practice		1:38-1:40	1:40-1:45	1:45-1:48
Tasks (T) Tasks to Criterion (C)	T T T CCCCC (SIT-UPS)	TTT TT T T TT	T T T T T T T TT T TT CCCCCCC CCCCCC	T T T CCCCCCC
Off Task				
Waiting	1:30-1:32			
Resting/Break				1:49-1:50
Other/Undefined				

Physical Education Engagement

Knowledge __3__ min = __15__ %

Warm Up/Fitness __3__ min = __15__ %

Skill Practice __10__ min = __50__ %

Total __16__ min = __80__ %

Non-Physical Education Engagement

Waiting __2__ min = __10__ %

Management __1__ min = __5__ %

Off Task ____ min = ____ %

Resting/Break __1__ min = __5__ %

Other/Undefined ____ min = ____ %

Total __4__ min = __20__ %

Tasks to Criterion __25__ ÷ Tasks Attempted (T+C) __52__ x 100 = __48__ % Success

DATA ANALYSIS FOR TAPE-TEACHER AND TAPE-STUDENT

Both TAPE systems use duration recording for individually defined categories of teacher or student behavior. Therefore, resulting data can be calculated similarly for both systems, as each one depends on the same procedures for translating raw data into coherent units for supervisory analyses.

When using both TAPE systems, supervisors should record the starting and stopping times for the observation to determine *elapsed time* for the teaching episode. Once the observation has been completed, the *category summed times* are calculated by adding up all recorded durations for each category. The number of recordings for each category determines its *frequency* for that lesson. All pertinent data analyses can be accomplished by knowing elapsed time, category summed times, and frequency.

The most important information for supervision is how the teacher or students distributed time during the episode. This can be computed for each category by dividing a category's summed time by elapsed time, shown in Equation 5.1.

$$\frac{\text{Category summed time}}{\text{Elapsed time}} \times 100 = \text{Category percentage} \qquad (5.1)$$

In some cases, the summed time alone for a category is useful and sufficient for illustrating examples of extreme expenditures of time in class. Dividing a category summed time by its corresponding frequency results in the *mean episode length* for that category, another measure often used by supervisors. And, just like raw summed time, raw category frequencies can be analyzed to isolate wasteful and repetitious patterns of class time usage. The success rate for students' observed motor tasks trials can be computed with the formula on the bottom of the TAPE-Student coding sheet.

TIME SAMPLING—TAPE-TEACHER (TS-TEACHER) AND TIME SAMPLING—TAPE-STUDENT (TS-STUDENT)

Recall that time sampling involves the recording of behavior codes at constant, predetermined intervals. The focus of time sampling is the same as the focus of duration recording—to determine how teacher and students distribute their activity during an episode. Duration recording does that directly by measuring time; time sampling does that somewhat less directly by systematically asking "What is the teacher or student doing now?" many times within an observation. Because the focal points of duration and time sampling recording are similar, it is possible to use identical categories under both techniques. The Time Sampling (TS) systems do just that, using the same categories and definitions as the duration-recorded TAPE-Teacher and TAPE-Student systems just described.

Both Time Sampling (TS) systems monitor how the teacher or students are engaged during observed lessons; the TS-Teacher focuses on the teacher while the TS-Student focuses on one student at time, rotating across several students throughout the class. The two systems are based upon 20-second time samples. That is, every 20 seconds the observer records onto the data sheet the category best describing the teacher or student behavior at that moment. The time between samples can be used to monitor other class activities by the supervisor. Using the TS systems requires a watch or 20-second timer, a clipboard, a pencil, and the appropriate recording sheet.

CATEGORIES AND DEFINITIONS
FOR TS-TEACHER AND TS-STUDENT

Categories and their definitions for both time-sampling systems are identical to their respective TAPE systems, except for the deletion of Skill Practice in the TS-Student system; this category is not necessary since all skill trials are coded under Tasks or Tasks to Criterion. Shifting from duration recording to time sampling conveniently allows a supervisor to keep previous definitions, altering just the observation technique in the transition. If necessary, refer to the TAPE categories and definitions of the following terms.

TS-Teacher Management
Behavior Management
Lecture/Demonstration
Instruction
Monitoring
Diversion
Other/Undefined

TS-Student Management
Knowledge
Warm Up/Fitness
Tasks
Tasks to Criterion
Off-Task
Waiting
Resting/Break
Other/Undefined

USING THE TIME SAMPLING SYSTEMS

Most supervisors wish to know more than just what the teacher or target student is doing at an observed moment. They want to know the predominant class activity of the moment as well, as one indicator of the context of the recorded category. Both TS systems enable the observer to record broad descriptions of that context. The entire teaching episode is divided into 3-minute segments, with codes to denote Management (M), Instruction (I), Practice (P), Lecture/Demonstration (L/D) and Other (O). The supervisor describes the overall activity during each 3-minute segment, writing this above each column for the TS-Student and circling it for TS-Teacher.

When using the TS-Teacher, the supervisor focuses on the teacher throughout the class. Every 20 seconds the supervisor asks, "What is the teacher doing now?" and records a tally (or a check) under the corresponding behavior column in the proper time segment row. Nine tallies should be entered for each 3-minute segment of class time. At the end of each segment the supervisor circles the code that best describes the predominant class activity in that 3 minutes. The supervisor can circle multiple codes if no single category is representative of the segment.

The TS-Student system uses the same target student sampling strategy described in the duration TAPE-Student system. A supervisor can monitor a single student throughout the entire class; however, an overall picture of student activity is usually more advantageous for supervisory applications, necessitating sampling several students in the class. Four to eight students should be sampled in a class, each one observed in rotation for 3-minute segments. Selected students should comprise a reasonably representative group from the class (in terms of gender, skill level, etc.). If the supervisor wishes to denote that specific tallies represent certain students, each student can be assigned a number and tallies made with that number while the student is being observed.

Regardless of the sampling procedures, the observation strategy is identical to the TS-Teacher system. At the end of each 20-second interval, the supervisor asks "What is the target student doing now?" and makes the tally in the appropriate category/segment intersection.

Samples of completed TS-Teacher and TS-Student observations are shown on pages 95 to 97.

DATA ANALYSIS FOR TS-TEACHER AND TS-STUDENT

Because both systems share common lists of definitions and the time sampling feature, similar data analyses can be used for them. Both systems provide a total number of tallies for the entire observation, and each category will have its own sum for the observation. These two pieces of information form the basis of all data analyses. Time sampling does not measure duration or actual frequency of behavior, so those two measurement units are not appropriate for interpreting data from these systems. Dividing each separate sum by the total tallies and multiplying by 100 calculates the percentage each category was observed within the class, as shown in Equation 5.2.

$$\frac{\text{Category sum}}{\text{Total tallies}} \times 100 = \text{Category percentage} \qquad (5.2)$$

Although not the same as actual duration or frequency percentages, the time sampled calculations can provide supervisors with a reasonably valid picture of how the teacher or students distributed their time in class. Further analyses can be based on the comparisons between observed categories and the

Time Sampling Time Analysis for Physical Education — Teacher Focus (TS-Teacher)
(tallies made every 20 seconds)

Date **2-18-89** Teacher **RANDY O'NEILL**

Grade **7TH** School **TERRAPIN JR. HS**

Observer **J. BURTON** Content **TUMBLING**

Time Begin **11:15** Time End **11:45**

Elapsed Time **30 min.** # Tallies **90**

Segment	Min	Management	Behavior Management	Lecture/ Demonstration	Instruction	Monitoring	Diversion	Other/ Undefined
1 (M) I P L/D O	0-3 min	✓✓✓✓ ✓✓					✓✓✓	
2 (M) I P L/D O	3-6 min	CLASS RULES →	✓✓✓✓✓ ✓✓✓✓					
3 M I P (L/D) O	6-9 min		✓✓	✓✓✓✓ ✓✓				
4 M I (P) (L/D) O	9-12 min	✓✓		✓✓✓✓		✓✓✓		
5 M I (P) L/D O	12-15 min				✓✓✓✓✓ ✓✓	✓✓		

(Cont.)

TS-Teacher (Continued)

Segment	Min	Management	Behavior Management	Lecture/ Demonstration	Instruction	Monitoring	Diversion	Other/ Undefined
6 M I (P) L/D O	15-18 min		✓✓	✓✓	✓✓✓	✓✓		
7 M I (P) L/D O	18-21 min				✓✓✓✓✓	✓✓✓✓		
8 M I (P) L/D O	21-24 min				✓✓✓✓ ✓✓	✓✓		
9 M I P (L/D) O	24-27 min	✓✓✓		✓✓✓✓✓				
10 M I P (L/D) O	27-30 min	✓	✓	✓✓✓✓ ✓✓				

Physical Education Content

Lecture/Demonstration   _26_ tallies = _28.9_ %

Instruction   _22_ tallies = _24.4_ %

Monitoring   _13_ tallies = _14.4_ %

Total _61_ tallies = _67.8_ %

Non-Physical Education Content

Management   _12_ tallies = _13.3_ %

Behavior Management   _14_ tallies = _15.5_ %

Diversion   _3_ tallies = _3.3_ %

Other/Undefined   ____ tallies = ____ %

Total _29_ tallies = _32.2_ %

Time Sampling Time Analysis for Physical Education — Student Focus
(TS-Student)
(tallies made every 20 seconds)

Date _2-22-89_   Teacher _BRENT MYDLAND_

Grade _9TH_   School _SAN RAFAEL HS_

Observer _S. WHEELER_   Content _TENNIS_

Time Begin _1:45_   Time End _2:15_

Elapsed Time _30 min._   # Tallies _90_

M/I/P/LD/O	min 0 — O	min 3 — M	min 6 — P	min 9 — P	min 12 — P	min 15 — P	min 18 — P	min 21 — I	min 24 — I	min 27 — P
Management	✓✓✓ ✓✓✓	✓✓✓ ✓✓								
Knowledge				✓✓✓ ✓✓				✓✓✓ ✓✓	✓✓✓	
Warm Up/Fitness		✓✓	✓✓✓ ✓✓✓ ✓✓✓							
Tasks					✓✓✓ ✓✓✓ ✓✓	✓✓✓ ✓✓✓	✓✓✓ ✓			✓✓✓
Tasks to Criterion					✓	✓✓	✓✓	✓✓✓	✓✓✓ ✓✓	✓✓✓ ✓
Off Task						✓	✓✓✓ ✓✓✓			✓✓
Waiting	✓✓									
Resting/Break									✓	
Other/Undefined										

Physical Education Content

Knowledge _15_ tallies = _16.7_%

Warm Up/ Fitness _11_ tallies = _12.2_%

Tasks _21_ tallies = _23.3_%

Tasks to Criterion _17_ tallies = _18.9_%

Success Rate _17/38_ = _44.7_%

Non-Physical Education Content

Management _14_ tallies = _15.5_%

Off Task _9_ tallies = _10_ %

Waiting _2_ tallies = _2.2_ %

Resting/Break _1_ tallies = _1.1_ %

Other/ Undefined ___ tallies = ___ %

predominant activity (context) within each segment (e.g., noting excessive waiting by students during class practice times).

By segmenting the lesson into 3-minute blocks, a supervisor can derive a useful time line of activities within the class period. The codes representing the predominant activity in each segment provide a description of class level involvement, thus providing a concurrent student level description of activity.

Monitoring Instructional Information

Physical education teachers typically provide students with much verbal and nonverbal information related to class management, discipline, organization, nonclass events, and the learning of intended lesson content. While all of this information is important at various times, instructional information consistently holds a priority. Many times, that information is the key to the total effectiveness of a lesson. The specific information provided to students in an attempt to help them learn relevant motor skills is of particular value to effective teaching/learning in physical education. For that reason, supervisors often choose to monitor and analyze a teacher's patterns in providing students with skill-related information. The observation system described next is designed exclusively for that purpose.

PHYSICAL EDUCATION INSTRUCTIONAL INFORMATION SYSTEM (PEIIS)

The Physical Education Instructional Information System (PEIIS) monitors frequency and types of instructional information; the system can be used to record what information teachers provide, or it can be used to record what information students receive, depending upon the supervisor's choice for analysis. The PEIIS employs event recording techniques, in which each instance of defined information is considered one occurrence. An observer needs only a pencil, a clipboard, and a PEIIS recording sheet.

Effective teachers communicate information to students prior to, during, and after skill attempts; the PEIIS separates instructional information on that temporal basis alone. Information that precedes a skill attempt and is intended to provide strategies, models for performance, or tips for completing a skill is called a *cue*. Information provided simultaneously with a skill attempt is called *guidance*. Information following a skill attempt, related to some aspect of that or previous trials, is called *feedback*. Thus, the timing of the information in relationship to a skill trial determines the main differences between cues, guidance, and feedback. All three types of information serve the same purpose—to increase students' opportunities to complete a motor skill task.

All three kinds are important for student learning, and all three can be measured quite easily with event recording techniques.

CATEGORIES AND DEFINITIONS FOR PEIIS

Cues: Information given by the teacher or through a communication medium that contains a strategy, prerequisite knowledge, or skill analysis intended to prepare students for an upcoming skill attempt. A cue can impart information on the whole skill, or a partial feature of the skill. Five kinds of instructional cues are monitored with the PEIIS:

- *Verbal*: Cues passed from teacher to students through oral communication.
- *Model Before*: A demonstration of the desired learning task by the teacher.
- *Manipulative*: A demonstration of the skill with teacher-student contact; a hands-on cue.
- *Mediated*: Cues provided by audiovisual media.
- *Other*: Cues provided to students by persons other than the teacher (e.g., another student, teacher's aide).

Sometimes information can contain multiple delivery mechanisms (e.g., verbal and nonverbal simultaneously). When this happens the observer should code all observed types in their appropriate places. The observer should also monitor the focus of instructional cues and guidance, whether partial (p) or whole (w), to denote whether information is directed to a subcomponent of the skill or to the entire skill. For example, "A good golf swing is smooth and even" (w), or "It is important to keep your head down on the backswing" (p).

Guidance: Information communicated from teacher to student while the student is actively making a skill trial. The trial can be any portion of the skill attempted at any speed. The guidance category definitions are the same as those of cues, differing only in their timing: Verbal, Model Along, Manipulative, Mediated, and Other.

Feedback: Information communicated by the teacher to students on the result or adequacy of a completed motor skill trial or other class activity. The PEIIS monitors both verbal and nonverbal feedback, by coding with V or N to denote which type the teacher provided. For the PEIIS, feedbacks are divided into two main groups:

- *Skill Attempt:* Feedback referring to an attempted motor task trial or one of its component parts
- *Non-Skill Attempt:* Feedback referring to behavior management or class activities other than skill attempt trials (e.g., making comments on student behavior, denoting appreciation for assisting the teacher, acknowledging student sportsmanship efforts).

The PEIIS categorizes feedback by two features, the direction (positive or negative) and the content (general or specific). The combination of these two features yields four types of feedback for monitoring in physical education teaching:

- *Positive General*: Information denoting approval/correctness and containing no specific reference about the origin of that approval (e.g., "Nice try," "Way to go," "I really like that," "Good shot").
- *Negative General*: Information denoting disapproval/incorrectness and containing no specific reference about the origin of that disapproval (e.g., "You missed the shot," "That's not how you do push-ups, is it?" "You are not behaving well today").
- *Positive Specific*: Information denoting approval/correctness and providing specific reference about the origins of that approval (e.g., "That was a great follow-through on your jump shot, Bobby," "I really like the way everyone got quiet when I asked you," "You kept your head down nicely on the backswing that time, Brent").
- *Negative Specific*: Information denoting disapproval/incorrectness and providing specific reference about the origin of that disapproval (e.g., "Your shot had no backspin on it that time, so it rolled off the rim," "Don't take your eye off the ball next time, Jerry").

USING PEIIS

The supervisor need only be within comfortable listening distance of the teacher to use the PEIIS. When instructional information is provided through an audio or visual medium, the supervisor must get in a position to see or hear it. Each time the supervisor hears or sees a cue, guidance, or feedback, he or she records it in the proper section of the coding sheet.

The supervisor can focus on the teacher and the students when monitoring instructional information. Using *subscript codes*, the supervisor can monitor how much information the teacher gives to students and identify which students received it. Subscript codes are labeled codes (rather than simple tally marks) used for entering data onto recording sheets. The code denotes an instance of a behavior, and distinguishes it from other instances of the same behavior (e.g., directed to another student). Assigned numbers or students' initials are commonly used for this purpose. For instance, whenever the teacher directs some piece of defined information to Bill Graham, it could be coded as *BG* or *1*.

Two final features add greatly to the use of PEIIS for supervision. Both features can be applied to cues, guidance, and feedback. The first denotes target—whether the information is directed to a single student (coded with an "I" or with that student's initials), a group of students (coded with a "G"), or the entire class (coded with a "C"). The second feature is sequence—recording consecutive instances of information being given to the same student. This is denoted by placing a 1, then a 2, then a 3, and so on after the student's initials or code. This enables the supervisor to monitor *cue/guidance/feedback chains*—instances when the teacher provides one student with several consecutive and related pieces of information. Examples of PEIIS target and sequence codes look like this: VI1 (verbal, to an individual student, first in sequence); NI2 (nonverbal, to an individual student, second in sequence); and VC (verbal, to the whole class).

An example of a subscripted coding session appears on page 102. The supervisor can make simple tallies instead of subscripted codes if he or she does not wish to designate target or sequence. The selected recording procedure is continued until the end of the teaching episode.

DATA ANALYSIS FOR PEIIS

The PEIIS yields an interesting array of data for supervisors to use in helping physical education teachers. The most prominent data will be frequencies for each category and classification under cues, guidance, and feedback. If the observation elapsed time has been recorded, rates can be computed for each PEIIS category, as shown in Equation 5.3.

$$\frac{\text{Category frequency}}{\text{Elapsed time}} = \text{Category rate per min} \qquad (5.3)$$

Computing a grand rate for all the various kinds of information combined is not particularly helpful, as each type of instructional information means something different for analyzing effective teaching.

Supervisors might also monitor patterns of instructional information: for example, the ratio of whole cues to partial cues and guidance; the percentage for each category within cues, guidance, and feedback; a teacher's tendencies when delivering information (i.e., needless repetitions, exclusion of some types of information, dependence on one type of information); reliance on student- , group-, or class-target information; and other patterns that might affect student learning in physical education. Analysis of patterns should be left to individual supervisors, because interpretation of those items must reflect the unique context of the teaching environment and lesson content.

In addition to rate and information type, a supervisor might choose to monitor cue/guidance/feedback chains, which are series of information given to the same students consecutively in one communication episode. A chain can be comprised of any number and combination of instructional information directed to a single student or group of students.

Using the PEIIS can be as simple or as complex as the nature of instructional information needed by a supervisor. Parts of the PEIIS can be used in micro and peer teaching to monitor preservice students as they acquire skills in presenting information. Supervisors can easily develop systems with additional categories or subscripting, expanding the capabilities of PEIIS for specialized uses.

Physical Education Instructional Information System (PEIIS)

Date __3-29-89__   Teacher __TERRY WILDMAN__

Grade __5TH (HART)__   School __PROMISED LAND ELEM.__

Observer __J. GARRISON__   Content __TRACK-SPRINT STARTS__

Time Begin __10:15__   Time End __10:50__

Elapsed Time __35 mins.__   # Students __N/A—TEACHER FOCUS__
__(21 min. PRACTICE)__

	Cues			Guidance	
Type	Whole	Partial	Type	Whole	Partial
Verbal	IIIIIII CCCCIII	CII CCIII	Verbal	CCCC II	
Model Before	IIII CCCC	IIII CCCC	Model Along	IIIII IIICC	IIIII CC
Manipulative	___	___	Manipulative II		IIIII
Mediated	___	___	Mediated	___	___
Other	___	___	Other	___	___
Totals	22	16	Totals	18	12

Feedback [Code Verbal (V) or Nonverbal (N)]

	Skill Attempt	Non-Skill Attempt	Totals
+ General	VI1, VI2, VI3, VI4, VI1 VI1, VI1, UI1, UI1, UI1	UI1, VC1, VC2	13
- General	NI1, NI1, NI1, UI1, UI1, UI1, VI2	VI1	8
+ Specific	VC1, VC2, NI1, NI2 VI1, VI2, VI3, VI4		8
- Specific	VC3, VC4, VI1, VI2, VI1, NI1	VI1, VI2	8

Total Feedback __37__ / __35__ Elapsed Time = Feedback Rate __1.1__ / min

Skill Feedback __31__ / __21__ Practice Time = Skill Rate __1.5__ / min

Use of Student First Name ~~HHH HHH HHH HHH HHH HHH HHH~~ = __45__ Times

Monitoring Academic Learning Time—Physical Education (ALT-PE)

Research on physical education teaching has recently identified an effective teaching variable for use in supervisory analyses. Academic Learning Time—Physical Education (ALT-PE) is the amount of time a student spends in motor skill tasks that are considered relevant and appropriate learning tasks (Metzler, 1983). Descriptive studies indicate that students get very little of this kind of time in physical education classes (Dodds, Rife, & Metzler, 1982). Some correlational evidence exists on the positive relationship between ALT-PE accrual and student learning (Metzler, 1989). Several other research studies have shown that students' ALT-PE accrual can be increased through simple changes in class planning and structure (Metzler, 1989). ALT-PE is a powerful concept for effective teaching because it indicates a teacher's ability to keep students in relevant and appropriate motor skill learning tasks—two necessary conditions for learning.

When monitoring ALT-PE for research purposes, the observer must pay strict attention to a few students in a class and constantly be ready to make several decisions within a short period of time. That total focus for research poses some drawbacks for monitoring this important process indicator for instructional supervision; measuring it the same way requires an undue amount of attention on one aspect of teaching while ignoring nearly all else in the teaching episode. As this is not practical, supervisors must devise alternative ways to monitor student ALT-PE. Two of those ways will be explained here after the three component parts of ALT-PE—which must be observed simultaneously—are defined.

Task Relevancy: The logical and observed relationship between the current learning tasks and the instructional goals of the lesson; the ability of the tasks to lead to intended learning outcomes. Practicing skills unrelated to the lesson goals (e.g., shooting jump shots during free throw shooting drills) does not contribute to ALT-PE.

Motor Engagement: The actual practicing of a skill or the direct preparation for an impending skill attempt. This feature is easily discerned in drills. In games or scrimmages the student must be in the action or clearly showing preparedness for play. For example, a goalie in a soccer match who is obviously paying attention and responding as the ball moves in the distance is accruing ALT-PE. However, a goalie who is leaning on a post or is otherwise unprepared is not considered in ALT-PE.

Task Appropriateness: Learning tasks that reflect a student's current skill abilities and past experiences; tasks that the student can accomplish about 80% of the time (Siedentop, 1983). Appropriateness does not require success on all observed trials but requires only that the task is appropriate for the student's abilities and experience at the time.

Directly measuring student time accrual during an observed lesson is not a simple task, especially when time, like ALT-PE, has three determining characteristics. Because the construct of ALT-PE is so important for effective teaching/learning, alternative ways must be devised to monitor it in supervisory situations. The following two systems offer differing, but valid, solutions to this logistical problem, basing student ALT-PE on event recording and PLACHECK analyses. Supervisors must take care not to interpret the resulting data in units of time but rather as proxy indicators of a teacher's ability to provide students with learning tasks that contain all three features of ALT-PE accrual.

ALT-PE Event Recording System (ALT-PEERS)

Even though ALT-PE is a time-based aspect of instruction, it can be monitored with nonduration techniques for supervisory purposes. Student ALT-PE accrual can be monitored with event recording, to determine if an observed motor task trial fulfills the three-part criterion for ALT-PE. The ALT-PE Event Recording System (ALT-PEERS) allows a supervisor to monitor student task trials for ALT-PE characteristics.

Siedentop, Tousignant, and Parker (1982) renamed the ALT-PE term as *motor appropriate* trials, thus eliminating the confusion stemming from the reference to time in the original label. Motor appropriateness can be measured by how much time students accrue or in this case by how many of such trials they complete in class. The ALT-PEERS monitors student motor appropriate task engagement by focusing on discrete student responses (trials). Because a supervisor cannot observe all students in a class simultaneously, he or she selects 4 to 8 students in a class and observes them individually on a rotating basis. The system requires only a clipboard, a pencil, and an ALT-PEERS recording sheet.

CATEGORIES AND DEFINITIONS FOR ALT-PEERS

The ALT-PEERS uses only three categories, labeled and defined according to the three components previously described. All three must occur simultaneously for a trial to be classified as motor appropriate (ALT-PE).

USING ALT-PEERS

The ALT-PEERS employs a simple strategy to record the number of observed tasks, relevant motor engagement, and motor task appropriateness. The observer watches one student at a time for 4-minute segments of the class. When the supervisor observes a motor task, he or she places a tally under Task. If the task is relevant to the learning activity and has a motor emphasis, the supervisor places another tally under Relevant Motor Engagement. Note that this column combines both task relevancy and motor engagement. Finally, if the task reflects an appropriate level of difficulty for that student, the supervisor makes a third tally under Motor Task Appropriateness.

The supervisor makes decisions about relevancy and appropriateness based on information the teacher provides students about task criteria and by assessing whether a task reflects the current student abilities. If the teacher requests students to "get five in a row," then each set of five attempts counts as one task. When the motor skill task involves an extremely high rate of responding (e.g., dribbling a basketball), the supervisor can count each response silently and then record the numbers for relevant and appropriate trials once the student stops that task. At the end of each 4-minute segment, the supervisor selects another student and repeats the recording process.

Supervisors can use periods of nonmotor engagement to observe other aspects of the teacher's performance in class; this free time is a great advantage of the ALT-PEERS. A sample of a completed ALT-PEERS observation appears on page 106.

DATA ANALYSIS FOR ALT-PEERS

Because ALT-PEERS is an event recording system, data analyses are based on category frequencies. Those frequencies must be interpreted on three different dimensions: frequency of motor skill attempts, frequency of relevant trials, and the percentage of motor appropriate trials within all trials. Determining the first two involves simple tabulations of all observed trials in the class. The percentage of motor appropriate trials is calculated by the formula in Equation 5.4.

$$\frac{\text{Motor appropriate trials}}{\text{Total observed trials}} \times 100 = \text{\% Motor appropriate} \qquad (5.4)$$

Consider three different scenarios and what each might mean for a supervisor going into the postteaching conference. *First*: During a 45-minute teaching episode only 20 motor skill trials are observed, fewer than one every 2 minutes. If 15 of those trials were relevant and appropriate, students had a 75% motor appropriate (success) rate on their observed skill attempts. *Second*: In another 45-minute class, 200 motor skill trials were recorded, over four per minute. All 200 were of relevant content but only 20 were observed as appropriate, a percentage of only 10% motor appropriate trials. *Third*: In the same amount of time, another class was observed in 100 motor trials, with 100 being both relevant and appropriate (100% motor appropriate trials).

The first scenario characterizes a teacher who can design appropriate learning tasks but has difficulty involving students in enough such tasks. The second scenario illustrates a teacher who can involve students in many practice attempts but pays little attention to the match between students' skill level and learning tasks. The third teacher shows the ability to involve students in a relatively

Academic Learning Time—Physical Education Event Recording System
(ALT-PEERS)

Date __10-15-88__   Teacher __S. BLUE__

Grade __11TH__   School __FENWAY HS__

Observer __J. GARCIA__   Content __Softball – Bunting__

Time Begin __2:00__   Time End __2:44__

Elapsed Time __44 mins.__

Student/Segment		Task	Relevant Motor Engagement	Motor Task Appropriateness
S __1__	0 - 4	卌	卌	111
S __2__	4 - 8	卌 卌 卌 卌	卌 卌 卌 卌	卌 卌 1111
S __3__	8 - 12	NONE – OFF TASK		
S __4__	12 - 16	卌 卌 卌 卌 卌 卌 卌	卌 卌 卌 卌 卌 卌 111	卌 卌 卌 卌
S __1__	16 - 20	卌 卌 卌 卌	1111 (WAS HITTING AWAY)	1111
S __2__	20 - 24	卌 卌 卌 1	卌 卌 卌 1	卌 卌 卌 1
S __3__	24 - 28	NONE – TEACHER DEMO		
S __4__	28 - 32	卌 卌 卌 卌 1	卌 卌 卌 卌 1	卌 111
S __1__	32 - 36	111	111	
S __2__	36 - 40	卌 卌	卌 卌	卌 1111
S __3__	40 - 44	Q + A REVIEW		

Total Relevant Motor Trials = __112__ / __44__ Elapsed Time = __2.5__ / min

Total Appropriate Tasks = __74__ / __130__ Trials = __56.9__% Motor Appropriate moderate amount of practice but is careful to design those tasks to promote student success on every trial. The ALT-PEERS is sensitive to the amount of motor appropriate responses made in class, which can be viewed as an indicator of a teacher's skill in task orientation—knowing the proper match between learning tasks and each student's current abilities relative to that task.

ALT-PE PLACHECK RECORDING SYSTEM (ALT-PEP)

Recall that the PLACHECK observation technique involves regularly scanning students in a class to determine how many of them are engaged in a predefined category of behavior. Because the scans are made at constant intervals, this is essentially a group time sampling procedure. PLACHECK techniques can be employed to monitor motor appropriate engagement for entire classes of students in physical education (Siedentop, Tousignant, & Parker, 1982); the ALT-PE PLACHECK (ALT-PEP) recording system does just that, as explained next.

The ALT-PEP involves systematically observing all students in a class and counting how many meet the three criteria for ALT-PE engagement during each scanning moment. An observer needs only a clipboard, a pencil, and an ALT-PEP recording sheet.

CATEGORIES AND DEFINITIONS FOR ALT-PEP

Categories and definitions in this system are based directly upon the three-part definition of ALT-PE. Readers should refer back to those definitions, keeping in mind that all three conditions must be met for student ALT-PE engagement.

USING ALT-PEP

A supervisor can use ALT-PEP to monitor ALT-PE patterns for groups of students or for the entire class using PLACHECKs, analyzing how many students at one moment in time are in motor appropriate engagement. PLACHECKs are regularly scheduled scans of the gymnasium to monitor how many students are engaged in a certain manner; for the ALT-PEP system that means how many students are engaged in relevant and appropriate motor skill tasks.

Supervisors should make ALT-PEP scans only when students have an opportunity to be actively engaged, not at unlikely times such as during management, lectures, and transitions. The ALT-PEP system yields its best information when used during drills, games, scrimmages, and other designated practice times. Supervisors can focus on other aspects of the lesson when students are not in skill practice segments of class. This is a helpful feature of this particular system.

Making PLACHECK scans is a simple procedure. The observer should be located so that all students are visible within a half radius turn of the head. Typically this means being stationed in a corner of the room. Starting from the left, the observer counts how many students are engaged in relevant motor activity and how many are at an appropriate task difficulty. Each scan should last about 10 seconds, with six scans to a set. The number of students who are Relevant Motor Engaged is recorded under that column in the proper scan row. Among those recorded under Relevant Motor Engaged, the number of students engaged at an appropriate difficulty level is recorded in the same row under Appropriate. This procedure is repeated six times during each scanning period (approximately 1 minute).

A sample ALT-PEP observation appears on page 109. Note that each scanning sequence has a place to record the number of students being scanned. That number can represent either the whole class or a subgroup of the class. If all students are in the same learning activity, the supervisor can scan the whole class; if the students are engaged in several different learning tasks (e.g., at stations) the supervisor should select one group for each 1-minute scanning sequence.

DATA ANALYSIS FOR ALT-PEP

After all the ALT-PEP scans are completed, the supervisor must compute the data to prepare for the postteaching conference. The ALT-PEP data are computed the same way for all scans combined and for individual scanning sequences. Two operations are needed for ALT-PEP analyses, shown in Equations 5.5 and 5.6. First the total number of students is determined by summing the # Scanned column in each sequence. Then the Relevant Motor Engaged and Appropriate columns are summed. Dividing the Relevant Motor Engaged figure by the total and multiplying by 100 gives the mean percentage of students in that category on any single scan. The same procedure is repeated for Appropriate to yield that mean percentage of students.

$$\frac{\text{Sum relevant motor engaged}}{\text{Sum \# scanned}} \times 100 = \% \text{ Relevant motor engaged} \quad (5.5)$$

$$\frac{\text{Sum appropriate}}{\text{Sum \# scanned}} \times 100 = \% \text{ Appropriate} \quad (5.6)$$

If all scans involve the same number of students, an overall mean percentage can be calculated for the whole class period. If scan series are based on different numbers, then only individual scanning sequence percentages should be computed.

The ALT-PEP system monitors class-level motor appropriate engagement—the teacher's ability to keep many students at one time in relevant and appropriate motor tasks. Thus, the calculated percentage of Relevant Motor Engaged students should approach or exceed 70% in most lessons, allowing

Academic Learning Time—Physical Education PLACHECK Recording System (ALT-PEP)

Date __5-7-89__   Teacher __DONNA MILLER__

Grade __7TH__   School __WALSH JR. HS__

Observer __B. HANNA__   Content __Volleyball- Bump__

Time Begin __11:15__   Time End __11:50__

Elapsed Time __35 mins__ # Students __24__

Task __BUMP TO PARTNER__   Time __11:23__

Scan:	# Scanned	Relevant Motor Engaged	Appropriate
1	24	16	16
2	24	17	13
3	24	16	10
4	24	18	18
5	24	0	0
6	24	12	10
Totals	144	79 = 55 %	67 = 47 %

Task __TRIANGLE BUMP__   Time __11:31__

Scan:	# Scanned	Relevant Motor Engaged	Appropriate
1	24	24	15
2	24	24	15
3	24	21	18
4	24	18	9
5	24	18	9
6	24	12	9
Totals	144	117 = 81 %	75 = 52 %

Task __TRIANGLE BUMP__   Time __11:39__

Scan:	# Scanned	Relevant Motor Engaged	Appropriate
1	24	12	12
2	24	12	12
3	24	9	9
4	24	9	9
5	24	15	15
6	24	12	12
Totals	144	69 = 48 %	69 = 48 %

Task _____   Time _____

Scan:	# Scanned	Relevant Motor Engaged	Appropriate
1			
2			
3			
4			
5			
6			
Totals	_____	_____ = _____ %	_____ = _____ %

for situational and necessary detachment from activity. Regardless of the actual percentage within Relevant Motor Engaged tasks, the percentage for Appropriate should match it closely to reflect that all or nearly all students can perform the task as expected. Naturally, the percent of Appropriate can never exceed the percent of Relevant Motor Engaged, but effective teachers plan learning tasks so that those two percentages match closely.

Monitoring Content Development

Promoting student skill development in physical education depends greatly upon the design of sequenced, logical, and progressive learning tasks. Effective teachers are keenly aware of students' skill development to date and have an eye for leading students from simple to complex learning progressions. Teachers accomplish this best through monitoring individual students' progressions. However, supervisors who cannot know each student's skill level will find general monitoring extremely helpful for postteaching conferences. This monitoring of a teacher's sequencing of learning tasks is called *content development* (Graham, Holt/Hale, & Parker, 1987; Rink, 1985) and is based on four levels of task progression and instructional information: Information, Extension, Refinement, and Application.

Information: The process whereby the teacher imparts the initial, most basic information about a task to students (Rink, 1985). This includes verbal and nonverbal demonstrations, lectures, and any audiovisual devices that provide students with basic task information.

Extension: A teacher's attempts to reduce the complexity and difficulty of a task by ordering its parts logically to form a sequence (Rink, 1985). This involves slowly building on the initial information given to students and breaking the task into component parts for learners to perform. Students can also be given tips or strategies for completing the task within extensions. Noncriterion tasks are usually given to students; that is, learning tasks are pursued without measuring performance or outcomes on them.

Refinement: Focuses on what it means to perform the task well (Rink, 1985). Students are given some tangible performance criteria to strive for in practice and are able to work toward those goals. Refinement includes more tips and strategies, but that information centers on how to accomplish specific rather than general tasks (e.g., how to bunt a curve ball to third base, rather then bunting in general).

Application: Developing the learning tasks for the work setting (i.e., games, drills, performances, recitals, and personal experiences outside of class). Application is learning for utilitarian purposes with sport and movement skills (Rink, 1985). Application tasks are characterized by a narrow focus (situation-specific skills) and often are competitive in nature (competition against an opponent, some expected standard, or some expected outcome).

   An example from golf will help illustrate content development in physical education. A teacher who is trying to help students with putting skills tells students about the equipment, intent, timing, rules and basic principles of the putting stroke during Information. During Extension she introduces students to the proper grip, stance, and alignment for putting, either verbally or through demonstration. Students then engage in a general type of practice to get acquainted with the new skill. For Refinement, the teacher designs a series of tasks that specify certain putting situations (various distances, degree of break) and specifies performance criteria to be met before going from one task to the next. When most students complete the final refinement task for putting, the class is then ready for Application. Application tasks for putting might involve putting competition at a miniature golf course or the monitoring of putting accuracy during a complete round of golf.

CONTENT DEVELOPMENT FOR PHYSICAL EDUCATION (CDPE) SYSTEM

As content development involves placing teacher-stated learning tasks into one of the four described categories, supervisors can easily use event-recording techniques to monitor content development in physical education classes. Each observed or heard instance in which a teacher provides the class with Information, Extension, Refinement, or Application is properly identified and counted as a single event. The CDPE system monitors whole-class learning task progressions provided by teachers for their classes. Such group-directed statements are easy to hear and their relative infrequency usually allows supervisors ample time to record and classify each one. An observer needs only a clipboard, a pencil, and a CDPE coding sheet.

CATEGORIES AND DEFINITIONS FOR CDPE

The CPDE system uses the four definitions of content development explained earlier: Information, Extension, Refinement, and Application. Readers should refer to those definitions and the examples provided. For a more complete description of physical education content development, see Rink (1985).

USING CDPE

Content development is monitored on a whole-class basis by analyzing learning tasks and teacher statements about those tasks. Teachers most frequently make statements to the whole class at once about the lesson's content and learning tasks. Matching those statements with the descriptions given for each kind of content development determines the content of the moment. The observer records each content development statement made by the teacher and the nature of the class' learning tasks on the CDPE sheet. This procedure is maintained throughout the teaching episode. Because the observer needs only to record each content development statement, the time between statements can be used to focus on other aspects of the lesson.

Following the class, the supervisor places each statement and task into one of the four content development categories. Each occurrence of content development is plotted in order of occurrence on the content development series at the bottom of the page. A sample CDPE observation appears on page 113.

DATA ANALYSIS FOR CONTENT DEVELOPMENT

Two types of data can be derived from content development analysis. The first is a simple frequency of each content development category (e.g., two occurrences of Information, six of Extension, etc.). Using these data, the supervisor can calculate the percentage each category represents within the whole lesson, shown in Equation 5.7.

$$\frac{\text{Category frequency}}{\text{Total frequency}} \times 100 = \text{Category percentage} \qquad (5.7)$$

The second kind of analysis should be even more useful for supervisors during the postteaching conference. The completed content development series actually represents a sort of content map of the observed lesson, showing how many (and what kind of) content statements were made, the order in which they were made, and how many were repeated. Ideally, the graph will show progressions from Information to Extension to Refinement to Application for each skill. At times several skills need to be refined individually before being applied simultaneously (e.g., pitching, catching, batting, and fielding before softball game application). Whatever the specific situational need, content development is a useful tool for supervisors to monitor how teachers sequence learning tasks in physical education classes.

Multiple-Focus Observation Systems

All of the data-based systems presented so far represent single- or limited-focus observation techniques. As discussed previously, single-focus observation systems give the supervisor a superb picture of limited aspects of effective teaching/learning processes in physical education. These systems are especially useful when the supervisor wishes to help a teacher improve one or a few instructional skills. Frequently, however, a supervisor needs a larger picture and must be able to monitor many and varied teaching/learning processes in a single observation. This is usually the case with student teachers, as opportunities to observe them are limited and rather infrequent with university-based supervision.

Two or more observation techniques can be combined into multiple-focus systems for monitoring several key teaching skills in the same episode. Two

Content Development for Physical Education System (CDPE)

Date __5-15-89__   Teacher __WENDY MUSTAIN__

Grade __3__   School __GLEN VIEW ELEM.__

Observer __R. CREGGER__   Content __KICKING__

Time Begin __2:30__   Time End __3:05__

Elapsed Time __35 MINS.__   # Students __26__

Write down the statements the teacher makes to the entire class when students are stopped—not to individual students. Classify each one related to the motor skill content of the lesson as either Information, Extension, Refinement, or Application. Graph the statements at the bottom in the order they occur.

1. KICK TO YOUR PARTNER, STOP BALL WITH FEET (E)
2. INSTEP KICK WITH CONTROL (R)
3. KICK TO YOUR PARTNER, 5 TIMES IN A ROW (A)
4. KICK THE BALL TO YOUR PARTNER'S RIGHT SIDE (E)
5. WATCH HOW DAVID KICKS WITH HIS INSTEP (R)
6. KICK FOR DISTANCE, TO YOUR PARTNER (E)
7. KICK THE BALL BETWEEN THE CONES (E)
8. SEE HOW MANY TIMES YOU AND YOUR PARTNER CAN
9. KICK TO EACH OTHER BETWEEN THE CONES (A)
10.

(Continue on back if needed)

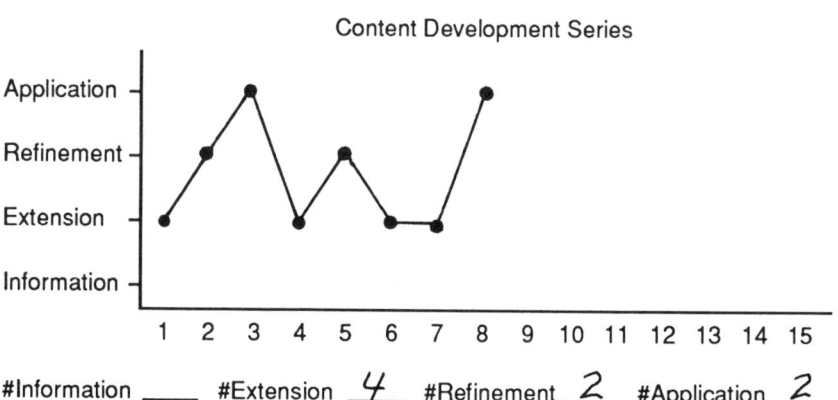

Content Development Series

#Information ____   #Extension __4__   #Refinement __2__   #Application __2__

considerations make multiple-focus systems easy to use for physical education instructional supervision. First, two or more observation techniques can be combined into one component system, rather than using several single-focus systems simultaneously. Second, teacher and student behaviors can be sampled within the teaching episode, as monitoring all desired processes continuously throughout every episode is not feasible. Even though multiple-focus systems must use sampling, they offer the potential to monitor many and different parts of the teaching performance and provide a supervisor with comprehensive information on which to base a postteaching conference.

TIME ANALYSIS—INSTRUCTIONAL INFORMATION SYSTEM (TA-IIS)

This simple multiple-observation system combines the TAPE-Student system and the PEIIS. TAPE-Student monitors student time allocations while PEIIS monitors a teacher's use of cues, guidance, and feedback. Even though using TA-IIS places more demands upon a supervisor for recording, the resulting increase in analytic information is well worth the added attention. However, supervisors can informally observe other aspects of a lesson and make marginal notes, as the TA-IIS does allow some free time for the supervisor.

CATEGORIES AND DEFINITIONS FOR TA-IIS

The TA-IIS takes its target categories and definitions directly from the TAPE-Student system and the PEIIS. Refer back to the previous descriptions of those systems to review the category definitions of these terms.

TAPE-Student   Management
Knowledge
Warm Up/Fitness
Skill Practice
Off Task
Waiting
Resting/Break
Other/Undefined

Instructional Information System:

Feedback	Cues	Guidance
General skill attempt (+ or −)	Whole	Partial
General nonskill attempt (+ or −)	Partial	Partial
Specific skill attempt (+ or −)		
Specific nonskill attempt (+ or −)		

The key to the merger of these two systems is in the design of the recording sheet, based on a time line approach. A completed TA-IIS recording sheet appears on pages 116 and 117. The TA-IIS categories and their respective recording symbols are listed on the second page of the coding sheet to remind supervisors of them.

USING TA-IIS

When using the TA-IIS, the observer codes the activity that best describes what the majority of students are doing at a given time. When the supervisor observes a majority of students in one of the defined modes of time allocation, he or she places the corresponding letter code on the time line. When the time mode changes, the supervisor places a bar on the time line corresponding to that moment of class, and enters the next category code. This is repeated throughout the episode. The supervisor should set a stop watch to zero and start it when coding begins.

To monitor instructional information, the supervisor looks or listens for a defined cue, guidance, or feedback. Hearing or seeing one, the supervisor records the proper symbols on the time line in the corresponding place. If several identical cues, guidances, or feedbacks occur quickly, one symbol can be recorded with a number before it to denote the repetitions (e.g., 4CW, 3SS+, 4GN). Another alternative is to circle all cue/guidance/feedback chains that occur during the lesson. As each one is coded near others in the chain, this procedure is both simple and informative. The recording procedures for time analysis and instructional information are continued throughout the observed lesson.

One advantage of the TA-IIS is that the supervisor doesn't make any recordings until the students change engagement category or the teacher provides some instructional information. Moments between those events allow supervisors to monitor other aspects of the lesson and to take anecdotal notes.

DATA ANALYSES FOR TA-IIS

Data from the TA-IIS are computed, analyzed and interpreted just as those from the respective TAPE-Student and PEIIS systems. The percent of class taken for each time category can be calculated with the formula in Equation 5.8.

$$\frac{\text{Category summed time}}{\text{Total class time}} \times 100 = \text{Category percentage} \qquad (5.8)$$

Rates of occurrence for each information category can be calculated by the formula in Equation 5.9.

$$\frac{\text{Category frequency}}{\text{Total class time}} \times 100 = \text{Category rate per min} \qquad (5.9)$$

Time Analysis—Instructional Information System for Physical Education
(TA-IIS)

Date __1-20-89__   Teacher __Pamela Schmitt__

Grade __5__   School __Delta Elem.__

Observer __M. Scott__   Content __Catching__

Time Begin __9:00__   Time End __9:25__

Elapsed Time __25 mins.__   # Students __25__

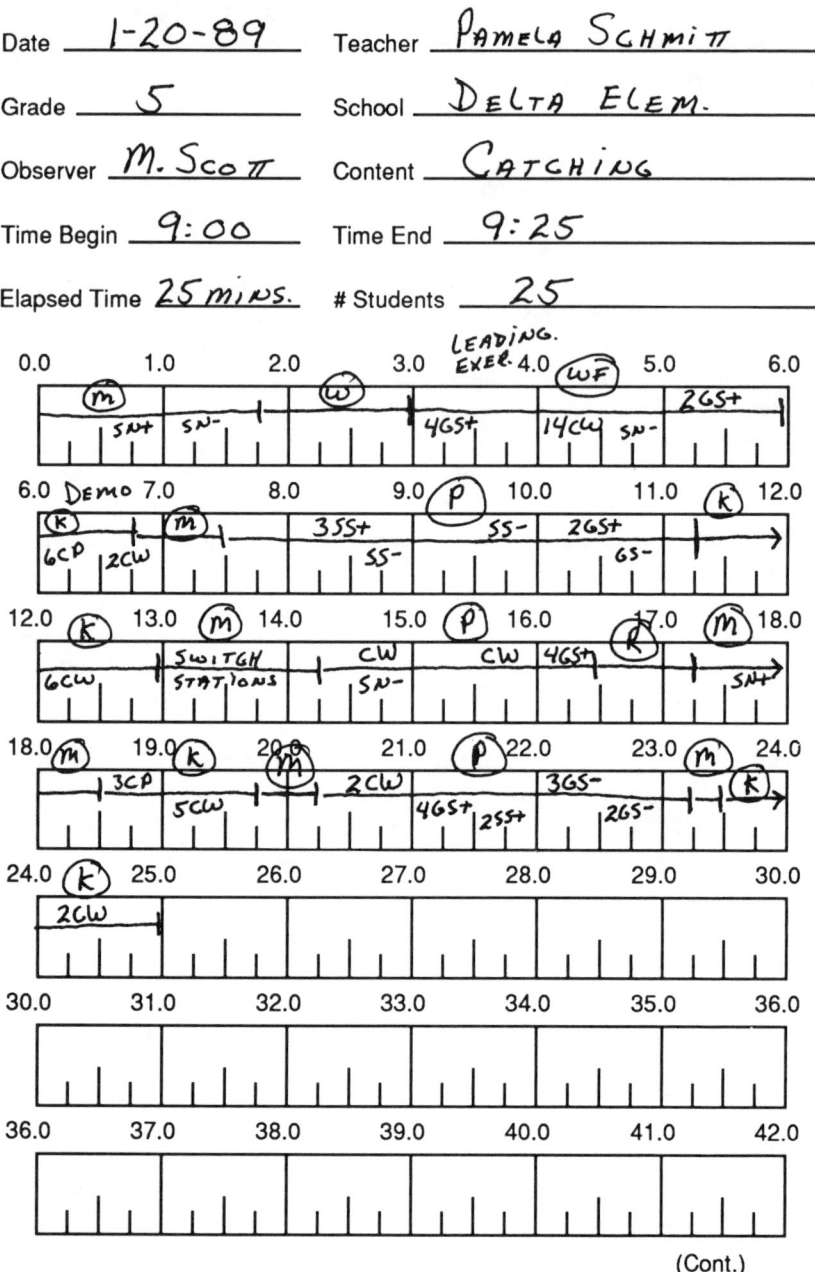

(Cont.)

TA-IIS (Continued)

Time Category (Code)	Feedback Category (Code)
Management (M)	General Skill (GS + or -)
Knowledge (K)	General Non-Skill (GN + or -)
Warm Up/Fitness (WF)	Specific Skill (SS + or -)
Skill Practice (P)	Specific Non-Skill (SN + or -)
Off Task (OT)	
Waiting (W)	Cues and Guidance [(Code)]
Resting/Break (R)	Cue [Whole (CW) or Partial (CP)]
Other/Undefined (O)	Guidance [Whole (GW) or Partial (GP)]

Category Calculations

Time Analysis	Min	%	Instructional Information	
Management (M)	5:45	= 23	+ General Skill (GS +) = 16	Total
Knowledge (K)	5:15	= 21	+ General Non-Skill (GN +) = ∅	Feedback
Warm Up/Fitness (WF)	3:00	= 12	+ Specific Skill (SS +) = 5	34
Skill Practice (P)	9:00	= 36	+ Specific Non-Skill (SN +) = 2	
Off Task (OT)		=	- General Skill (GS -) = 6	Rate/min
Waiting (W)	1:15	= 05	- General Non-Skill (GN -) = ∅	1.4
Resting/Break (R)	:45	= 03	- Specific Skill (SS -) = 2	
Other/Undefined (O)		=	- Specific Non-Skill (SN -) = 3	

Cue—Whole (CW)	= 31	
Cue—Partial (CP)	= 9	Total
Guidance—Whole (GW)	= ∅	40
Guidance—Partial (GP)	= ∅	

Notes and Comments

- STATION TRANSITIONS WERE TOO LONG

- TOO MUCH INFO IN LECT/DEMOS, CUT BACK ON THIS

The time line feature also allows a supervisor to visually scan the data sheet for patterns that occur during class. Patterns of student time could include unnecessary flip-flopping of engagement categories, excessive time spent listening to the teacher, and inefficient transitions between class learning tasks. Teacher information patterns could be analyzed for the use of chains, repetitive use of one type of feedback, or certain periods within the class that the teacher provides no information to students.

MULTIPLE OBSERVATION OF STUDENT TEACHERS IN PHYSICAL EDUCATION (MOST-PE)

This multiple-focus system has been in use for several years and is now the sole systematic observation tool for Virginia Tech physical education student teachers. It is called Multiple Observation of Student Teachers in Physical Education (MOST-PE) (Metzler, 1981). Even though it was designed for use with student teachers, a supervisor can use it for comprehensive analysis of many teaching/learning processes in any observation. MOST-PE has undergone several revisions, each one reflecting new developments in teaching effectiveness research, an evolving set of preferred teaching skills at Virginia Tech, and trained supervisors' abilities to record more and complex data within observed teaching episodes.

MOST-PE incorporates several measurement criteria and observation techniques: duration recording for student time analysis, event recording for instructional information and first name use, PLACHECK recording for monitoring motor engagement and task appropriateness, and content development analysis. The system also depends upon anecdotal note taking and to a much lesser extent a rating scale. The system does not use a behavior checklist because the data-based analyses provide sufficient evidence of a teacher's demonstration of observed skills and competencies.

The MOST-PE recording procedures are broken into six operations for the supervisor, represented by the five recording sheet sections and another, note taking, which can be done anywhere on the front or back of the sheet. Supervisors can make notes alongside data entries for easier recall and more explicit comments in the postteaching conference. The current version of the MOST-PE recording sheet from a completed teaching episode is shown on pages 119 and 120.

STUDENT TIME ANALYSIS

The MOST-PE uses three categories of student time during class: Management, Lecture/Demonstration, and Skill Practice. All class time must be placed into one of these categories—whichever category best describes what the majority of students are doing at the moment.

Multiple Observation of Student Teachers in Physical Education (MOST-PE)

Date __2-7-89__   Teacher __JERRY NiLES__

Grade __4__   School __OLDE MiLL ELEM.__

Observer __J. BURTON__   Content __ROPE JUMPING__

Time Begin __8:30__   Time End __9:00__

Elapsed Time __30 mins.__   # Students __25__

Management	Lecture/Demonstration	Skill Practice WARM UP
1 8:30 - 8:31 = 1	1 8:31 - 8:33 = 2	1 8:33 - 8:37 = 4
2 8:47 - 8:48 = 1	2 8:37 - 8:40 = 3 REVIEW	2 8:40 - 8:47 = 7
3 8:59 - 9:00 = 1	3 8:57 - 8:59 = 2	3 8:48 - 8:57 = 9
4 ___ - ___ = ___	4 ___ - ___ = ___	4 ___ - ___ = ___
5 ___ - ___ = ___	5 ___ - ___ = ___	5 ___ - ___ = ___
__3__ min = 10 %	__7__ min = 23 %	__20__ min = 67 %

Was management appropriate? (Yes) No   Explain _____

SEE NOTE ON BACK

	Feedback			Cues	Guidance
	General	Specific			
+ Skill	‖‖‖ ‖‖ ‖‖ ‖‖‖ ‖‖ ‖‖ ‖‖ ‖‖ ‖‖ ‖‖ ‖‖ ‖‖‖ ////	‖‖‖ ///	Verbal	wppPww	
- Skill		‖‖‖ ‖‖ //	Modeling	wwwww	
+ Non-Skill		///	Manipulative		pppw pp
- Non-Skill			Mediated		
+ Management	"Thanks" ///		Other		
- Management			Whole (W) or Partial (P)		

OK, DiDN'T NEED MANY

65 Feedback = 2.2 /min   # 17 Cues + Guidance = 0.6 /min

First Names ‖‖‖ ‖‖ ‖‖ ‖‖‖ ‖‖‖ ‖‖‖ /// (33) GREAT!

(Cont.)

MOST-PE (Continued)

PLACHECK 1 _INDIVID. PRACTICE_
25 Students scanned

1	2	3	4	5	6
E/A	E/A	E/A	E/A	E/A	E/A
13/13	14/10	17/15	10/10	20/18	19/15

PLACHECK 2 _W/ PARTNER_
25 Students scanned

1	2	3	4	5	6
E/A	E/A	E/A	E/A	E/A	E/A
22/22	14/14	18/18	18/18	16/16	16/16

PLACHECK 3 _W/ PARTNER_
25 Students scanned

1	2	3	4	5	6
E/A	E/A	E/A	E/A	E/A	E/A
10/10	10/10	16/16	20/20	18/18	18/18

PLACHECK 4 _____

1	2	3	4	5	6
E/A	E/A	E/A	E/A	E/A	E/A

% Motor Engaged = _64_   % Motor Appropriate = _62_

Content Development Graph

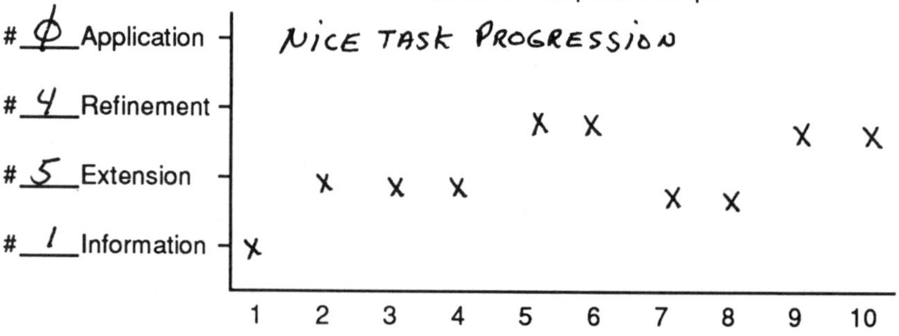

_∅_ Application

_4_ Refinement

_5_ Extension

_1_ Information

NICE TASK PROGRESSION

Scatter plot with axis labeled 1 through 10.

Clarity of Information	1	2	3	4	5	6	7	⑧	9	10	NA
Task Orientation	1	2	3	4	⑤	6	7	8	9	10	NA
Enthusiasm	1	2	3	4	5	6	7	8	⑨	10	NA
Planning and Preparation	1	2	3	4	5	6	⑦	8	9	10	NA
Pos. Atmosphere	1	2	3	4	5	6	7	8	⑨	10	NA

Notes and Comments

- FEEDBACK _RATE_ WAS GOOD, BUT TOO MANY GENERAL COMMENTS (42 GENERAL — 23 SPECIFIC)

- TASKS WERE TOO EASY FOR THEM

- POSSIBLY USED MORE REFINEMENTS

Management: Student class time spent in noninstructional activities. This includes waiting for class to begin (past designated starting time), setting up equipment, transition to and between learning tasks, and outside interruptions.

Lecture/Demonstration: Student class time spent listening to or watching instructional content. This includes watching skill demonstrations, listening to rules/strategy/history for content, and reading task content material. (Directions that explain what, where, and when to perform skills are classified as Management; directions that explain techniques and other content information are classified as Lecture/Demonstration.)

Skill Practice: Student class time focused on the development of motor skills or applications of skills in game-like settings. This includes learning drills, fitness activities, scrimmages, games, and also practice during concurrent lectures/demonstrations.

Time categories are determined on the basis of the teacher's intended focus of the class. The chosen category is that activity in which most of the students are expected to be engaged at the moment. The category is not determined by individual student engagement patterns.

INSTRUCTIONAL INFORMATION

The categories for MOST-PE duplicate those from the PEIIS. Readers can refer back to that system for definitions of the respective feedback, cues, and guidance categories.

Cues	Guidance	Feedback
Verbal	Verbal	+ Skill Attempt
Model Before	Model Along	− Skill Attempt
Manipulative	Manipulative	+ Non-Skill Attempt
Mediated	Audiovisual	− Non-Skill Attempt

Feedback is further categorized as general and specific, depending on content. General feedback has no reference to particular aspects of the performance (e.g., "Nice shot" or "I liked that one"); specific feedback points out exactly what parts of the performance warranted comment (e.g., "Your follow through was great on that shot" or "I liked that one because you kept your head down on the backswing"). Teacher's use of students' first names is also noted and tallied in this section.

PLACHECK FOR MOTOR ENGAGEMENT
AND MOTOR APPROPRIATENESS

When the class is in Skill Practice time, the supervisor can monitor students' motor engagement and appropriate motor task difficulty through periodic PLACHECKs, using category definitions and recording procedures taken directly from the ALT-PEP system. The supervisor scans the class from left to right, counting how many students are motor engaged and how many of them are engaged in tasks appropriate for their skill level. The number in motor engagement is recorded to the left of each slash (under the E); the number in appropriate level of difficulty is recorded to the right of each slash (under the A). The number of students in the group scanned by PLACHECK is recorded on top of each series of six scans. For purposes of later recall, supervisors should note the learning activity during each scan.

CONTENT DEVELOPMENT

Content development is monitored with an abbreviated version of the CDPE system. The four content development categories remain the same: Information, Extension, Refinement, and Application. Rather than write an entire statement, however, the observer instantly classifies each statement and then records it on the MOST-PE content development time line. The result is a content development graph identical to that of CDPE but made without writing out every statement made during class. A compromise can be made by writing abbreviated content development statements when possible, for later recall.

RATING SCALES

The supervisor uses rating scales to record impressions of performance aspects not measured systematically on other parts of the instrument. To allow for greater discrimination on rated items, a scale of 1 to 10 is used, with an NA (Not Applicable) code for items not relevant to that teaching episode. Four permanent scales are now on the MOST-PE, along with one open category for any additional aspect of the episode gaining the supervisor's attention. If the supervisor wishes to rate something not currently listed, he or she can add that new category on the last line and assign a performance rating.

Clarity of Information: The manner in which the teacher provided managerial and task information to students. Did the teacher give information at a level students could understand? Did the teacher provide enough information? Did the information result in efficient and immediate action by students?

Task Orientation: The degree to which the teacher addressed student skill levels when determining learning tasks. Did the teacher allow for individualized responding when skill level was variable? Were the tasks sufficiently challenging—not too boring and not too difficult?

Enthusiasm: The degree to which the teacher portrayed interest in and excitement about the lesson material and the students.

Planning and Preparation: The manner in which the teacher delineated an intent and plan of action for the class. Planning refers to actions and decisions made prior to the lesson; preparation refers to interactive decisions that reflect a teacher's readiness or anticipation of unplanned events.

ANECDOTAL NOTES

An overriding design consideration in the MOST-PE is easy recording of data, which frees the supervisor to make anecdotal notes throughout the episode. Except for the PLACHECK section, recordings are made only when the teacher exhibits one of the defined behaviors; the rest of the time is available to make general observations and notes on important class events. I suggest that when a data entry needs to be annotated, the notes be made on the front of the coding sheet close to the data. Other more lengthy notes can be made on the back of the sheet in the designated area.

USING MOST-PE

A supervisor needs only a MOST-PE recording sheet, clipboard, pencil, and stop watch. Because MOST-PE is a multiple-focus system, the supervisor will probably need to move around the instructional area to hear the teacher's verbal behaviors and to make PLACHECK scans. The supervisor should get only as close to the teacher and the students as is necessary to make recordings.

The supervisor's watch should always run from the beginning of the episode. The supervisor can monitor actual start/stop time for each time category (e.g., 9:44-9:53) as it happens or record the elapsed time at the end of each episode (e.g., 9:00 min). The latter method is usually the simpler approach. The watch is stopped, recordings are made, and the watch is reset only when changes occur in time allocation categories.

Concurrent with keeping time records, the supervisor watches and listens for the three kinds of instructional information: Cues, Guidance, and Feedback. As the supervisor sees or hears this information, he or she quickly makes a tally (or other code) in the proper box on the second section of the MOST-PE sheet. The supervisor also makes an event recording tally when the teacher uses a student's first name (except during roll).

Four series of PLACHECK scans are provided in the system on the third level (second page) of the sheet. The supervisor can record more series at the bottom if necessary. The supervisor should make PLACHECK scans for motor engagement and motor appropriateness only during practice segments, as the scans are intended exclusively for that time in class. Before making the first series of scans, the supervisor records the number of students to be scanned along with a note identifying the observed activity (e.g., a bump drill, half-court scrimmage, rebounding drill). Six scans are made of that activity, each taking about 10 seconds. PLACHECK scanning sometimes causes the supervisor to take attention away from instructional information monitoring, but the period is brief. I suggest supervisors try to hear the information during the scan and record it afterwards. As explained above, the supervisor enters the number for motor engagement to the left of the slash mark and the number for motor appropriate to the right.

The content development recording simply involves the immediate classifying of each class-level task statement by the supervisor followed by an entry onto the content development graph. To help recall each statement later, the supervisor can write abbreviated versions of each statement near the graph.

DATA ANALYSIS AND INTERPRETATION FOR MOST-PE

The MOST-PE produces a large array of data for the supervisor to take into the postteaching conference. The data computations can be made quickly and easily, usually as the teacher is completing end-of-class duties. The summed duration for each time category is divided by the elapsed time and multiplied by 100, indicating the percentage of class time each one accounted for. The supervisor determines if the amount of management time was appropriate and makes comments if needed.

The summed feedback is divided by the elapsed time to compute overall feedback rate per minute. A sometimes useful computation is the *instructional feedback rate*, derived by counting only skill feedbacks and dividing that by the number of practice time minutes. Cue and guidance rates can be derived similarly, depending on the specific rate desired.

The Content Development Graph on the second page is visually analyzed for patterns of student task progressions. A space is provided next to each content development descriptor for the supervisor to enter the frequency of that category during the observation. As the supervisor plots each statement immediately during the class, there is no need to transform the data in any way.

Supervisors often find it useful to analyze content development along with the PLACHECK data. The percentage of students observed in motor appropriate tasks should be a factor in the teacher's decision to proceed from Extension to Refinement to Application. That is, progression from one content task to a more difficult one should occur only when most or all students can complete the current task (reflected in the PLACHECK percentages).

Unless the number of students in every PLACHECK series is constant, each of the four series must be analyzed by itself. The procedure typically requires a calculator and takes two steps, shown in Equation 5.10a and 5.10b. First, sum up the motor engaged and motor appropriate numbers respectively and divide by 6 (the number of scans in a series). Then, for each category, divide the quotient by the number scanned and multiply by 100. This results in the mean percentage of students engaged and at appropriate levels (ALT-PE) in each series, respectively.

$$\frac{\text{Sum of motor engaged or motor appropriate scans}}{6} = \text{Series mean} \qquad (5.10a)$$

$$\frac{\text{Series mean}}{\text{Number of students scanned}} \times 100 = \text{Category mean percentage} \qquad (5.10b)$$

Each of the four rating scales is completed at the end of the lesson. A fifth one is left blank for the supervisor to use at his or her discretion to point out an aspect of the lesson not monitored elsewhere in the system. The complete data analysis takes less than 5 minutes, easily allowing enough time to prepare for the postteaching conference. All sections are interpreted as they would be for single-focus systems and are intended to be used in similar ways to provide the teacher with feedback on that lesson and goals for future lessons.

Traditional Techniques for Physical Education Supervision

Sometimes systematic data-based observation techniques are neither convenient nor usable for all aspects of physical education instructional supervision. In these cases supervisors must employ more informal ways to monitor teaching performance. Chapter 4 suggested that supervisors use traditional methods sparingly. If these methods are to be used, they should retain a focus on effective teaching/learning processes.

Rating Scales

Most supervisory observation and evaluation practices in physical education are based on rating scales. These scales, when used as the only supervisory instrumentation, have four serious deficiencies:

- Items on rating scales are notoriously invalid measures of teaching behavior; what most rating scales monitor has little relationship to effective teaching/learning processes.
- Rating scale evaluations are not reliable; recordings across time and supervisors tend to show little agreement.
- Rating scales do not actually measure teaching/learning processes. They measure a supervisor's impressions of those processes, something possibly quite different from objective performance measures.
- Due to the first three weaknesses, rating scales are ineffective for setting and monitoring teachers' performance goals and progress. Rating scales simply cannot reflect actual improvement in skills, only a supervisor's notion that the teacher improved.

Supervisors should use rating scales only for monitoring processes and factors not amenable to direct observation with a data-based system and should consider rating scales only as supplemental methods.

Rating scales used to monitor teaching should at least overcome the first limitation cited previously, thus observing for and rating only performance

Rating Scale for Physical Education Teaching Supervision

Date __3-17-89__   Teacher __Jon Poole__

Grade __9__   School __Auburn HS__

Observer __J. Straw__   Content __Archery__

For each listed area of teaching, assign your evaluation rating. Rate each item from 1 (poor) to 10 (excellent), based upon your observation of the class period.

Planning:

1. Clarity of lesson plans.   Rating __6__ NA

2. Clarity of lesson objectives.   Rating __5__ NA

3. Organization of instructional materials.   Rating __5__ NA

Class Management: Your Strongest Area

1. Use of preventive management strategy.   Rating __8__ NA

2. Maintenance of adequate control during class.   Rating __8__ NA

3. Awareness of student behavior in class.   Rating __9__ NA

4. Effectiveness of interactive management.   Rating __8__ NA

Instructional Management:

1. Consideration of individual student abilities.   Rating __7__ NA

2. Provision of learning opportunities.   Rating __6__ NA

3. Circulation during practice time.   Rating ____ (NA)

4. Amount and content of feedback.   Rating __3__ NA

5. Use of cues for student comprehension.   Rating __3__ NA

Communication Skills:

1. Presentation of lecture/demonstrations.   Rating __4__ NA

2. Use of language.   Rating __6__ NA

3. Clarity of verbal information.   Rating __7__ NA

4. Communication at student level.   Rating __10__ NA

(Cont.)

Rating Scale for Physical Education Teaching Supervision (Continued)

Others:

1. Enthusiasm for teaching.	Rating __8__ NA
2. Rapport with students.	Rating __8__ NA
3. Professional deportment.	Rating __7__ NA
Overall Rating of This Lesson	Rating _6-7_ NA

Comments:

- NEED TO EXPLAIN CONTENT BETTER, STUDENTS SEEMED CONFUSED.

- YOU USED THE RIGHT AMOUNT OF PREVENTION AND CONTROL — IT WAS A SAFE CLASS.

- THE AMOUNT OF INSTRUCTIONAL INFORMATION SEEMED LOW. BUT, YOU DID TRY TO EXPLAIN IT AT THE STUDENTS' LEVEL.

- ENTHUSIASM AND RAPPORT WERE GREAT.

- WORK ON PREPARING LECT/DEMOS BETTER.

parameters that reflect effective teaching and learning processes. A completed sample rating scale for physical education supervision appears on page pages 126 and 127.

Because of the relatively sparse information communicated by rating scales, supervisors should take detailed notes when using scales. A number on a scale, or even an evaluative term (e.g., good, poor), tells the teacher very little about how that determination was made. Detailed notes help the supervisor recall why a certain rating was assigned and provide the teacher with better information in the postteaching conference.

Behavior Checklists

Behavior checklists are an acceptable alternative to rating scales. Rather than placing performance on a continuum, behavior checklists merely indicate whether or not a predefined process/feature/competency was observed in the episode. Thus, the problem of estimating degrees of performance (and observer reliability) is reduced because only two choices are available for each item. School districts in many states now use behavior checklists to monitor new teachers and to observe teachers for retention, promotion, and career ladders.

The basis for behavior checklists lies within the definitions of monitored performance items. Those items should be written in objective and clear language, focusing on observable behaviors that represent effective teaching/learning processes. Well-written checklist items should also specify the outcome or function of the desired process so that different teachers can demonstrate the ability to bring about those effects in their own way (rather than simply mimicking a process without purposeful results). For example, "Teacher uses an attention signal to cue students to cease activity" or "Teacher posts first activity to reduce preclass waiting time" are well-written checklist items.

A completed sample of a physical education teacher behavior checklist is shown on pages 129 to 131. The sample checklist is divided into several broad groupings of effective decisions and actions. Some of the items focus on student processes, supporting the notion that some aspects of effective teaching involve student behavior as well.

Note that the supervisor has only three choices: Demonstrated, Not Demonstrated, and Not Applicable. The last choice reflects the expectation that some items on the checklist will not be demonstrated in every lesson. This checklist has space under each item for the supervisor to write notes on just how the teacher did or did not demonstrate that process.

Supervisors can use behavior checklists in one limited way to help teachers improve. While checklists can't monitor the amount of improvement, they can inform the teacher whether certain desirable performance aspects were present in the lesson. If the teacher did not demonstrate those aspects, the supervisor can recommend that the teacher show those competencies in the next observed lesson. Shifting from Not Demonstrated to Demonstrated represents at least a gross estimate of improvement on effective teaching/learning performance items.

Summary

This chapter presents many examples of observation systems for physical education instructional supervision. Of course, many others are available, and readers should become familiar with a wide variety of systems and their usefulness for supervisory programs. A supervisor's most important challenge is finding one or more systems that will provide the kind of analytical information needed in a given situation—the "right tool for the job." If no system has been yet designed for your needs, then you might wish to design your own.

The systems presented here focus mainly on skill-related instruction for physical education, rather than on processes for effective teaching/learning

Behavior Checklist for Supervising Physical Education Teachers

Date __4-25-89__   Teacher __JOSELLE EDWARDS__

Grade __1__   School __HARDING AVENUE ELEM.__

Observer __K. EDDLEMAN__   Content __CATCH IN PERSONAL SPACE__

Students __32__

	Demonstrated	Not Demonstrated	Not Applicable
Preparation for Class			
States clear intentions and objectives prior to start of class.	✓		
Evidenced by: STATED LESSON CONTENT Slowly, CLEARLY			
Prepares and arranges equipment and facilities before class.		✓	
Evidenced by: DID NOT SET bALLS OUT bEFORE CLASS			
States learning goals and activities to meet objectives.	✓		
Evidenced by: LESSON INTRO- JUST RIGHT			
Plans for potential problems.	✓		
Evidenced by: ANTICIPATED THEY WOULD ARRIVE LATE			
Efficient Use of Class Time			
Plans preclass activity.			✓
Evidenced by:			
Maintains academic focus.	✓		
Evidenced by: KEPT "STRAGGLERS" ON-TASK			
Arranges for smooth transitions into and between activities.	✓		
Evidenced by: STUDENTS WENT TO "PS" RIGHT AWAY			
Uses efficient roll-taking plan.			✓
Evidenced by:			
Reduces wait time in class.	✓		
Evidenced by: STARTED RIGHT AWAY			

(Cont.)

Behavior Checklist for Supervising Physical Education Teachers (Continued)

J. EDWARDS 4/25

	Demonstrated	Not Demonstrated	Not Applicable
Efficient Use of Class Time			
Monitors for student engagement during activity.	✓		
Evidenced by: CIRCULATED A LOT			
Designs learning tasks for maximum opportunity to learn.	✓		
Evidenced by: USED ALL AVAILABLE EQUIPMENT			
Task Orientation for Activities			
States criteria for tasks.		✓	
Evidenced by: THEY WERE CONFUSED TO BEGIN WITH			
Manages tasks.	✓		
Evidenced by: GOT TO "PS" AND STAYED THERE			
Plans for varying student skill levels.		✓	
Evidenced by: EVERYONE DID THE SAME TASK			
Clearly states task structure and accountability.	✓		
Evidenced by: REVIEWED "PS" RULES			
Interactive Instruction			
Provides sufficient performance information.	✓		
Evidenced by: LOTS OF FEEDBACK			
Provides task cues to students.	✓		
Evidenced by: COMMENTS WHILE CIRCULATING			
Provides performance feedback.	✓		
Evidenced by: SEE ABOVE			
Relates performance outcomes to form and effort.		✓	
Evidenced by:			
Circulates during learning tasks.	✓		
Evidenced by:			

(Cont.)

Behavior Checklist for Supervising Physical Education Teachers (Continued)

J. EDWARDS 4/25

	Demonstrated	Not Demonstrated	Not Applicable
Preventive Management			
Anticipates potential sources of misbehavior. Evidenced by:			✓
Posts or states conduct rules. Evidenced by:	✓		
Reminds students of rules. Evidenced by:	✓		
Interactive Behavior Management			
Monitors student behavior while attending to other tasks. Evidenced by:			✓
Maintains class flow during behavior management episodes and outside interruptions. Evidenced by:			✓
Class Climate			
Establishes positive atmosphere. Evidenced by: LOOKED LIKE A "NEAT" CLASS TO bE iN!	✓		
Supports and encourages student suggestions. Evidenced by: ASKED ThEm FOR ThEiR IDEAS	✓		
Evaluation of Student Progress			
Provides formal or informal monitoring of student progress. Evidenced by:		✓	
Maintains updated records on student achievement. Evidenced by:			✓
Reflection on Teaching			
Documents outcomes of completed lessons and activities. Evidenced by: KEEPS A "DiaRY" OF +'s/-'s EACH DAY	✓		

in the cognitive and affective domains. There are two reasons for this emphasis. First, relating in-class processes to potential outcomes is extremely difficult in those domains; that is, deciding what to observe as indicators of effective instruction in these areas is not easily resolved, at least not within the limited observation time typically given for supervision. Second, this lack of observable and measureable processes for cognitive and affective outcomes leads to a dependence on subjective, high-inference (i.e., traditional) monitoring systems. This book does not promote such a reliance, which hinders the acquisition of instructional skills in physical education. If we can isolate certain teaching/ learning processes that foster student learning in these domains and devise valid and reliable ways to measure those processes, we can create systems of valuable assistance to all supervisors in physical education.

The use of systematic observation techniques is probably not widespread at this time; most supervisors still rely upon one of the traditional techniques, most likely rating scales. Chapters 4 and 5 attempt to show the theory and the practice of making direct observations of teaching/learning processes in physical education supervision. Certainly, supervisors will notice that using systematic techniques is much more complex and time consuming for them. However, the advantages of using these systems, and the contribution they can make to supervisory decision making and instructional skill development, are apparent. The more valid and useful information supervisors have, the better they can do their job of teaching teachers.

Chapter 6

Systematic Supervision: Observing, Decision Making, and Goal Setting

Effective supervision goes well beyond familiarity with appropriate observation systems. The supervisor must have confidence in the records made from an observation and must be able to use that information to help a teacher maintain or improve instructional skills. This chapter outlines several important considerations necessary for the conduct of systematic supervision in physical education: training for reliable observations, data-based decision making, and instructional goal setting. These three parts of the overall supervision process are highly interrelated, and all stem from the commitment to base a supervision program on logical and systematic foundations.

Training for Reliable Observations

The key for supervisory use of the systems described in chapter 5 lies in the demonstration of reliable data coding in live settings or from tapes. Reliability is the degree of agreement between two observations made of the same subject at the same time while using the same coding system (Baer, 1977). It is a measure of how well target behaviors have been defined and how well they are understood, observed, and recorded by persons using a coding system. Observer reliability is acquired and maintained through a program of observer training; it involves more than merely reading the description of a system and then using it for supervisory observations. Thus, reliability and observer training go hand in hand; the former is the direct result of the latter.

A typical observer training sequence includes up to seven steps and should be specific for each data-based system in use:

1. Familiarization with the purpose of the system
2. Familiarization with written target definitions

3. Recognition of examples of target behaviors—knowing when a defined behavior has occurred and when it has not occurred
4. Familiarization with the system's recording sheet and procedures
5. Practice coding with the system in a limited setting (live or videotaped samples with little complexity)
6. Practice for progressively more complex examples during entire lessons and in actual settings of supervisory observations
7. Demonstration of acceptable, consistent reliability with the complete system in the anticipated environment (live or videotaped)

Observer training is much more efficient and more likely to improve reliability if the training is facilitated by someone who is familiar with the system. That person can serve as the reference observer in practice coding exercises and can answer questions that might arise. If such a person is not available, a single user must learn a system well enough to code a videotape or audiotape twice in a row demonstrating at least 80% agreement across all categories. The next section discusses more about calculating agreement.

The length of time needed to learn an observation system depends on the complexity of the system and the number of categories it contains. More complexity and more categories usually require a longer training period (i.e., not necessarily more steps, but more time spent on each step). The supervisory systems described in chapter 5 can be learned in 2 to 10 hours. Learning the MOST-PE system first might be helpful, because many of its components are taken from other single-focus systems. If an observer can use each of those components reliably in MOST-PE, he or she can learn the single-focus applications more easily.

The National Association of Sport and Physical Education (no date) has produced a useful videotape for observer training called Videotape Observation Systems for Physical Education Programs (VOSPEP). The tape contains three samples of physical education teaching, one each for elementary, junior high, and high school. Two production features can help observers in training learn a selected system more quickly and easily: a split screen always showing the teacher on one side and individual students on the other and a digital clock projected on the bottom of the screen. Thus, an observer can use VOSPEP to practice coding for any of the systems described above, regardless of whether the system focuses on teacher, students, or both; plus the observer can replay scenes from exact points in time with the assistance of the on-screen clock.

Reliability

As mentioned, reliability is the degree of agreement between two observations made of the same subject at the same time while using the same coding system (Baer, 1977). In essence, it is corroboration of two observation records. Two kinds of observer reliability are typically used for the systems described in chapter 5—intraobserver and interobserver. *Intraobserver reliability* is demonstrated by a single observer recording the same videotape of a lesson twice and then comparing the resulting two records. *Interobserver reliability* is measured when two independent observers watch the same lesson, focusing on the same persons throughout, then comparing their records. In this application, being independent means that the observers are not able to see each other's coding sheet. This kind of reliability checking is most commonly used in research when one person (e.g., a system designer) must train several observers at once. Because many supervisors work alone and will probably learn the various systems in isolation, intraobserver reliability is more practical and is quite acceptable.

Calculating Reliability

Regardless of which reliability procedure is used, the purpose remains the same—to illustrate an observer's ability to translate defined behaviors into recorded data as they occur. The first consideration in determining reliability is a separate examination of each category. If a system has eight defined behavior categories, then the observers must make eight separate reliability calculations. Observers should not calculate an overall agreement for all categories, because that statistic will be confusing and may camouflage specific sources of observer disagreement that could indicate serious problems or misunderstandings by one or both observers. The example in Table 6.1 illustrates why single category calculations are necessary. Two observers have recorded three types of instructional information in a lesson: cues, guidance, and feedback. The reported frequency for each observer is shown. Even though the observers recorded 53 and 59 occurrences of instructional information, they obviously did not see the same ones!

The second consideration for calculating reliability is the selection of an appropriate equation, based on the kind of data collected for each category: event, duration, time sampling, or PLACHECK. Single-focus systems require only one kind of reliability equation, while multiple-focus systems require one equation for each kind of data produced. The following descriptions imply

Table 6.1 Differences Between Overall and Category Agreement Calculations

Category	Observer A	Observer B	Agreement (%)
Cues	10	20	50
Guidance	8	24	33
Feedback	35	15	43
Total events	53	59	90

that two observers are used to check reliability—Observer A and Observer B. If you use intraobserver reliability, simply compare the data from Observation 1 and Observation 2 instead.

Event Recording Reliability

Event recording results in frequency counts for each defined category of behavior. Those category frequencies are the basis for calculating reliability using Equation 6.1.

$$\frac{\text{Lowest observed frequency}}{\text{Highest observed frequency}} \times 100 = \% \text{ Agreement} \qquad (6.1)$$

The two observers described in Table 6.2 used the PEIIS, and each recorded cues as indicated, calculating each category separately. When only one observer records in a category (e.g., Manipulative), the equation yields an impossible result. Because 0% agreement cannot exist, the term None is used. When neither observer records in a category (e.g., Other/Undefined), no calculation is made.

Table 6.2 Calculating Event Recording Reliability

Cues	Observer A	Observer B	Equation	Agreement (%)
Verbal	23	26	23/26 × 100	88.5
Model before	8	6	6/8 × 100	75.0
Manipulative	2	0		None
Mediated	7	7	7/7 × 100	100
Other/undefined	0	0		—

Duration Recording Reliability

Duration recording systems result in the number of minutes and seconds a supervisor observes each category during a lesson; category durations then become the basis for calculating reliability in those systems. The equation for determining duration category agreement is similar to that used for event category agreement, and is shown in Equation 6.2.

$$\frac{\text{Lowest duration}}{\text{Highest duration}} \times 100 = \% \text{ Agreement} \qquad (6.2)$$

The TAPE-Student is used in Table 6.3 to illustrate duration category reliability. The TAPE-Student focuses on several students, one at a time; there-

Table 6.3 Calculating Duration Recording Reliability

Category	Observer A	Observer B	Equation	Agreement (%)
Waiting	0.6	0.6	.6/.6 × 100	100
Management	1.3	1.5	1.3/1.5 × 100	86.7
Off task	0.5	0.0		None
Warm up/fitness	1.8	2.0	1.8/2.0 × 100	90.0
Knowledge	0.0	0.0		—
Skill practice	0.8	0.9	.8/.9 × 100	88.9

fore, category reliabilities must be determined for individual students; individual categories must be determined as well. The Tasks and Tasks to Criterion categories are not included here because they are event recorded and use the calculation for event category reliability.

Time Sampling Reliability

Because time sampled data are recorded as frequencies—the number of times an event is observed within each category at the end of an interval—they can be treated the same as event data for calculating reliability. For each observer, the frequency of observed intervals is the basis for the reliability calculation in Equation 6.3.

$$\frac{\text{Lowest recorded frequency}}{\text{Highest recorded frequency}} \times 100 = \% \text{ Agreement} \tag{6.3}$$

Table 6.4 describes how two observers recorded several category frequencies from the TS-Teacher system.

Table 6.4 Calculating Time Sampling Reliability

Category	Observer A	Observer B	Equation	Agreement (%)
Management	14	23	14/23 × 100	60.9
Lecture/demonstration	5	5	5/5 × 100	100
Instruction	18	15	15/18 × 100	83.3
Monitoring	12	12	12/12 × 100	100
Behavior management	2	0		None
Diversion	0	0		—

PLACHECK Recording Reliability

PLACHECK recording involves the periodic scanning of the students, with scans typically made in sets of six. Each observer's entry for an individual scan becomes the basis for calculating agreement percentages. Therefore, each set of six scans requires six separate reliability calculations with Equation 6.4.

$$\frac{\text{Lowest number}}{\text{Highest number}} \times 100 = \% \text{ Agreement} \qquad (6.4)$$

Table 6.5 shows two observers using the ALT-PE PLACHECK recording system in the same lesson, making their scans for relevant motor engagement at precisely the same times. One set of scans produces these data and the resulting agreement percentages.

Table 6.5 Calculating PLACHECK Reliability

Scan #	Observer A	Observer B	Equation	Agreement (%)
1	24	24	24/24 $\times$ 100	100
2	18	10	10/18 $\times$ 100	55.6
3	21	18	18/21 $\times$ 100	85.7
4	16	16	16/16 $\times$ 100	100
5	0	0		—
6	15	14	14/15 $\times$ 100	93.3

Prior to using any data-based system for monitoring lessons, an observer should demonstrate a proficient level of reliability. Consistent category reliability at or above 80% is typically considered acceptable. Because PLACHECK scanning is sometimes done in large classes and students will be in or out of defined behaviors quickly, observers will at times exhibit low agreement on some scans. Unless low agreement percentages are quite regular, these periodic low agreement percentages are acceptable.

As mentioned before, reliability and observer training go hand in hand. Well-planned and conscientious training helps establish reliability before using a system for supervision. In fact, demonstration of acceptable reliability should be the evidence that an observer is sufficiently trained and ready for field observations.

Data-Based Supervisory Decisions

Systematic observations in physical education provide a rich compilation of data to be analyzed and shared with teachers. The data are highly valid indicators of the effective teaching/learning processes monitored for supervision. The data can indicate many things about observed teaching/learning but only after the supervisor interprets them according to instructional context and the teacher's developmental stage.

However, data alone cannot capture effective teaching. In one sense data are merely descriptors of what happened during the class. The supervisor's familiarity with the instructional context, the intended teaching/learning processes, and the results of the data analyses all are relevant in interpreting what occurred in the observed lesson. The data are best viewed as judgmental aids that can be used by knowledgeable supervisors to make informed decisions about what was observed and what it means for a teacher's instructional skill development. Observational data are useful to teachers only to the extent supervisors can interpret them, communicate them, and make diagnostic/prescriptive decisions from them.

Effective teaching is context specific, and supervisory data analyses must reflect this reality. Two identical sets of data can actually indicate different degrees of effective teaching when the context of each situation is considered. For example, one teacher might have insufficient space and equipment for a class of 50 students, while another teacher, teaching the same activity, might have plenty of space and equipment for a class of 20 students. If both teachers were observed with the TAPE-Student instrument and the resulting data were nearly similar, the observer would conclude that the second teacher did not use the more beneficial circumstances for increased effectiveness over the first teacher.

Physical education supervisors should resist setting rigid data-based standards for parameters of effectiveness when contextual factors vary widely across teachers, schools, grade levels, and lesson content. However, performance standards should be devised for common teaching situations (e.g., peer teaching in a methods lab) and for individual teachers whose context will not change significantly over a series of observations. With time and experience, supervisors can learn to recognize acceptable data-based performance indicators by experimenting with ranges of those indicators in familiar situations and contexts. Because teaching contexts can vary so greatly, clear-cut parameters cannot be established for effective teaching in all situations. The consideration of expected and reasonable performance indicators in each observed lesson requires expert, informed, and professional decisions of the physical education supervisor.

Goal Setting

The several single- and multiple-observation systems described in chapter 5 result in large amounts of data on various teaching and learning processes. Having those data in hand is only the beginning of intentional and systematic supervision for the improvement of physical education instructional skills.

The next step, using those data to help teachers, is also vital; in fact, initiating decisions and actions is the most important part of teaching teachers.

A goal-setting program can become the basis of an instructional improvement effort lead by the supervisor. Such a program should be based on six steps:

1. Determining baseline performance on effective teaching skills
2. Determining priorities for instructional skill improvement
3. Considering the context of the instructional situation
4. Setting specific goals on targeted teaching skills and strategies for their achievement
5. Systematically monitoring performance on skills and goals
6. Providing strategies for self-maintenance

Determining Baseline Levels of Teaching/Learning Processes

Baseline levels of teaching performance describe abilities before any systematic attempt to improve teaching skills. Baseline skills are instructional skills relative to effective teaching practices that a teacher brings to the first monitored instructional episode; the baseline level is the starting point. Regardless of his or her developmental stage, a teacher already has some level of skill in effective teaching practices.

For the beginning preservice teacher, this existing skill level might be the ability to mimic the way former physical education teachers instructed. The powerful influence derived from many years as a student prior to formal teacher training should not be underestimated; only recently has this influential source of teaching practice been addressed in preservice programs (Lawson, 1983, 1986).

Baseline skills analyses in the later stages of preservice teaching should reflect those aspects of effective teaching sought in the training program. To some extent, every teacher training program attempts to help students acquire a set of signature instructional skills prior to and during student teaching. Baseline measures of those skills should be taken before each major pedagogical component in the program: methods courses, lead-up field experiences, and student teaching placements. Systematic monitoring of preferred teaching skills at several key times is a useful way to evaluate the ongoing effectiveness of teacher training programs.

For the induction stage, baseline levels of teaching skills reflect the degree to which teachers carry over preservice effective practices into daily teaching in schools. A considerable amount of evidence suggests that teachers learn much more about how to teach while on the job than they do in university training programs (Feiman-Nemser, 1983; Locke, 1979). Baseline skills evolve constantly, especially over the first two or three years of service as a teacher adjusts to a new school, new students, new colleagues, and new expectations and as he or she encounters various constraints on teaching performance. Determining baseline measures during induction takes into account that performance is quite likely to change gradually as a result of the teacher's new environment and new working conditions. To get accurate baseline measures the supervisor must make more observations in a shorter period of time, another reason for considering school-based mentoring and clinical programs for induction stage supervision.

At the veteran stage, baseline measures represent teaching patterns fully evolved and deeply engrained. Veteran teachers are likely to show little variation in their instructional practices, so relatively fewer baseline observations are needed for more experienced teachers.

To develop baseline measures at any stage, the supervisor makes some initial observations with one or more data-based systems until a pattern emerges. If time does not allow for an adequate pattern to emerge, the supervisor can proceed as if such a pattern were evident, but must take caution to avoid overgeneralizing from those few performance measures. True baselines can be established only on measureable aspects of effective teaching and learning; supervisors should not develop baselines for performance aspects monitored with rating scales or behavior checklists.

Determining Priorities for Improvement

If baseline measures are determined for several aspects of effective teaching behavior, then the supervisor (and the teacher, when appropriate) may select just one or a few skills to focus on for improvement. This is applicable for preservice teachers who do not have well-developed teaching skill repertoires and who probably cannot concentrate on multiple areas for improvement; these teachers must become proficient in one skill at a time.

When several skills have been monitored in baseline measurement and improvement is necessary on many or all of them, the supervisor and teacher must set priorities that determine which skills will get immediate attention. Three criteria are suggested for making those decisions. *First*, focus on that aspect of the teaching/learning process most likely to make the greatest impact on student achievement. Helping students to develop motor skills, attitudes, and knowledge should be the primary objective for any physical education program. Thus, instructional supervision should assist teachers with those processes above all others. *Second*, focus on preventive strategies for teachers. Sometimes a teacher will try so hard to do things correctly that he or she will divert attention from practices that can prevent problems in the first place. For example, some teachers use organizational patterns that foster student inactivity and eventually lead to student misbehavior that the teacher cannot control adequately amidst all other teaching functions. The problem must be correctly identified as an organizational one, rather than an inability to exert sufficient disciplinary action in class. *Third*, identify and focus on teaching skills that have the greatest chance for immediate improvement and attend to more difficult problems later. For example, annoying idiosyncratic verbal patterns (excessive use of "OK") can often be reduced by just making the teacher aware of them. Teachers, like other learners, enjoy seeing results and steady progress toward goals. Attempting to correct long-term, complex problems right away leaves other problems unresolved, resulting in a seeming lack of progress that can discourage a teacher.

Considering the Teaching Context

Good teaching is situation specific, and so is effective instructional supervision. Supervisors should consider context on two levels for goal achievement. *First*, what is the nature of the teaching experience being monitored? Is it a peer-teaching laboratory on campus, a lead-up to student teaching, student teaching itself, or a teacher's first year or two on the job? Each of these situations requires a supervisor to plan for, implement, and evaluate supervisory processes quite differently. *Second*, what are the specific features of the program in which the teacher practices? How large are classes? How much equipment is available? What is the curriculum like? Is physical education important in that school? How often do students have physical education scheduled in that school? All of these factors plus many others influence the kind of teaching observed by a supervisor and cannot be ignored or taken lightly.

A supervisor needs to be keenly aware of the nature of the teaching experience and the realistic potential for effective teaching in each situation. Many factors must come together at once to allow teachers a chance to exhibit skills for effective teaching. All physical education teachers are not given the same opportunities to be good at their jobs; it is easier to be an effective teacher in some situations than others. Supervisors must come to recognize those differences and take them into consideration when outlining instructional improvement plans with teachers.

Setting standardized performance expectations for all teachers at all stages of development in all programs would be very easy but very unfair. The wise supervisor spends as much time initially studying the context of the teaching as observing teaching/learning processes themselves. The supervisor should ask, "How good can this teacher be at this stage and in this context?" Any baseline assessment and subsequent performance expectations should include an evaluation of the potential for effective teaching by a particular teacher in a particular setting.

Setting Performance Goals and Providing Strategies for Attainment

A supervisor who has baseline data available and who understands the teacher's developmental stage and specific teaching context can set performance goals for future observations. Sometimes those goals can be set for all teachers in a common teaching experience (e.g., a peer-teaching laboratory), but most often the goals must be highly individualized.

Standardized goals and expectations can be set for micro teaching, peer teaching, and other lead-up teaching experiences as each one has similar contextual features for all teachers in a group. Also, these experiences are designed to allow preservice teachers opportunities to exhibit and practice certain preferred instructional skills; a firmly established set of goals is highly desirable in preservice programs.

However, supervisors should not always hand down performance goals and expectations to teachers. As teachers develop, they should be given more responsibility for selecting which aspects of performance need improvement and determining how adept they should be on those skills. Analyses of present skills, goal identification, and determination of desired levels of proficiency are important processes for personal professional growth; good supervision should facilitate that growth, not rigidly direct it. Chapter 7 presents several instructional improvement schemes and offers suggestions for their use.

The most important part of setting goals is prescribing ways to attain those goals. Merely having goals is not enough, especially for preservice, student, and induction teachers; teachers need viable avenues for accomplishing those goals in their own teaching contexts. Most supervisors draw upon their own experiences and bag of tricks, passing along what has worked for them. Too often these well-intended suggestions become quick remedies defined for quite narrow applications. They might work once or twice, but they cannot serve the teacher over the entire spectrum of teaching contexts and future experiences.

One promising strategy for helping teachers identify and resolve instructional problems has been outlined by Hawkins, Wiegand, and Landin (1985). It involves calling upon the collective wisdom of teacher educators and teaching research for instructional problem solving. Rather than advocating specific and narrow plans of action, these researchers suggest that supervision can be based on a process of mapping out several reasonable courses of action for the teacher. The teacher then selects and experiments with one or more of these new plans that he or she thinks might work best. The analytic and prescriptive model by Hawkins, Wiegand, and Landin (1985) is based on a taxonomy of common pedagogical problems, each one with resolutions stemming from general practice and research-based documentation. A sampling of this collective wisdom taxonomy is shown in Table 6.6.

When given opportunities to identify and set their own performance goals, teachers are more likely to strive to meet those goals. Veteran teachers especially are aware of what can and should be done to improve their own teaching, once they know baseline levels of performance. As teachers proceed through the developmental stages of their careers, supervision should become less direct and more dependent upon teacher expertise and input for instructional improvement.

Table 6.6 Taxonomy for Supervisory Prescriptions

Student process indication	Supervisory feedback or prescription
1. Low motor appropriate—high waiting:	A. Use additional equipment or improve utilization of current equipment.
	B. Reduce group size.
	C. Incorporate activities not requiring much additional space or equipment (e.g., fitness).
	D. Design and implement competitive drills.
2. Low motor appropriate—high interim:	A. Develop settings in which equipment is less likely to ''get away'' (e.g., use hitting cage in golf lessons).
	B. Design and implement an extrinsic motivation system when students display high interim levels as a means to avoid the prescribed activity (e.g., allow students to participate in an activity of their choice after they complete a set number of objectives).
3. Low motor appropriate—high off task:	A. Planning error: Use additional equipment or reduce group size to reduce waiting time, which often provides opportunities for off-task behavior.
	B. Planning error: Use activities that may not need more equipment in order to reduce waiting, thus decreasing opportunities for off-task behavior.
	C. Revise supervision and instruction pattern. Target students who need help and/or attention prompts and then provide the necessary instruction and feedback.
	D. Employ an extrinsic motivation system.
	E. Revise instructional sequence by including more rigorous and challenging tasks.

4. Low motor appropriate—high on task:	A. Communication error: Teach the system early and thoroughly so students have a clear understanding of what to do, where, and when *before* the class moves into activity.
	B. Employ an extrinsic motivation system.
5. Low motor appropriate—high cognitive:	A. Not always undesirable. Certain activities require detailed demonstrations or instructions. If the teacher's instructional episodes were few but occupied much class time, it suggests students had little time to engage in the activity. Teacher trainee needs to establish activities in which the students can begin working and then offer as many short, individual episodes as necessary.
	B. Use other visually or task oriented cognitive activities such as stations in which students read materials, watch film loops, make paper-pencil responses, etc. Such a station is designed to enhance the student's cognitive understanding of the activity while involving him/her more actively in the subject matter.
6. Low motor appropriate—high motor supporting:	A. Motor supporting activities are often essential in the teaching/learning process of motor skills. Generally not detrimental. Can be beneficial when the motor supporting student can offer pertinent feedback to the performer. Also, many motor skills need to be practiced in a controlled setting to allow the performer to concentrate on the proper mechanics.
	B. Revise the management plans to avoid the need for motor supporting (e.g., practice soccer kicking techniques using a wall for rebounding and "feeding").
7. Low motor appropriate—high motor inappropriate	A. Planning error: Revise the objectives or their sequence in light of student abilities. The objectives should challenge all students, yet allow them to succeed.
	B. Task may seem inappropriate due to the students' not understanding how to perform it. Teacher should offer supplementary and more intense instruction.
	C. Design and employ an extrinsic motivation system when planning and instruction errors are not the cause of high levels of motor inappropriate activity.

Note. From "Cataloguing the Collective Wisdom of Teacher Educators" by A. Hawkins, R.L. Wiegand, and D.K. Landin, 1985, *Journal of Teaching in Physical Education,* **4**, pp. 246-247. Copyright 1985 by Human Kinetics Publishers, Inc. Adapted by permission.

Monitoring Goal Attainment

Once teaching/learning processes have been selected and performance goals for them have been set, the supervisor's next step is to monitor for their attainment. This involves two processes. *First*, the supervisor makes follow-up observations with the data-based systems used to establish baseline performance targeted for improvement. The supervisor goes back into the same or similar teaching context to monitor the teacher's performance once again. The supervisor must take care not to let expectations influence these follow-up observations (i.e., sometimes a supervisor will perceive an event in a way that favors goal attainment because the teacher is supposed to show improvement after suggestions are made!). *Second*, supervisors should not anticipate that teachers will meet goals just because the goals are being targeted for improvement; teachers often need additional suggestions, strategies, and several opportunities to practice those teaching skills before goals can be reached. A helpful strategy is to establish interim goals, which lead to long-range goals

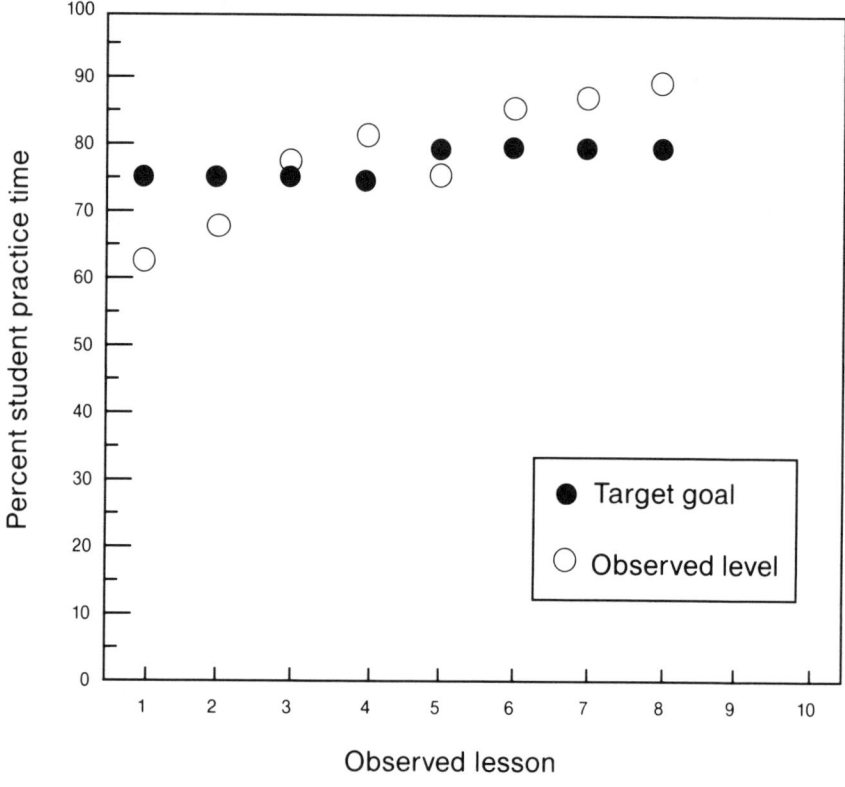

Figure 6.1. A sample graph charting a student teacher's progression in one area throughout a term.

in small increments. For example, in a series of micro lessons on campus, the supervisor and teacher might set goals to reduce class management gradually from 25%, to 20%, to 15%, and then to 10% as the final indicator of proficiency. A teacher is more likely to show improvement in gradual and steady steps rather than by struggling over a long period of time to meet a single terminal goal. Remember that teachers acquire their skills in much the same way other learners achieve—through progressive and sequential attainment of relevant goals and tasks.

Supervisors at Virginia Tech use a simple combination of data graphing and tables to monitor a student teacher's progression throughout the term. Each time a supervisor visits and observes, he or she places the resulting data for each monitored teaching skill on a graph, like the one shown in Figure 6.1. A composite table is then kept for each student teacher on all aspects of teaching/ learning considered important for student teachers to demonstrate across the term (see the chart below). The graph for each teaching skill allows a supervisor to quickly see trends across the term for a particular aspect of instruction; the composite table allows the supervisor to see if a student

Student Teaching Goals Summary Chart

Name _Gail Webster_ School _Ironto HS_

Supervisor _L. Treanor_ Co-op _J. Hunt_

	Baseline	Goal 1	Goal 2	Goal 3	Goal 4
Feedback (rate/min)	(Tennis) 1-7 8/27	(2.0) 8/30	(2.5) 9/17	(2.5) 10/15	
Student Practice Time (%)	(Tennis) 57 8/19	(63) 8/29	(70) 9/5	75 Did Not Reach	
Management Time (%)	(Tennis) 26 8/19	(20) 8/29	(15) 9/22	(10) 9/24	
Lecture and Demonstration Time (%)	(Volleyball) 10 9/30	(10) 10/3	(10) 10/10		
Motor Appropriate (%)	(Volleyball) 45 9/30	(60) 10/3	(70) 10/10	(75) 10/15	80 Did Not Reach

teacher has reached goals on the listed parameters of performance. Together, these allow a supervisor to keep abreast of a teacher's development and, more importantly, to see if suggested supervisory prescriptions have resulted in desired improvements.

Providing Self-Monitoring Strategies

Supervisors are rarely present when teachers work on targeted instructional skills; this is one overriding contextual limitation of supervision as practiced today (except for clinical supervision, discussed in chapter 7). Teachers, then, can benefit by learning ways to monitor their own progress and goal attainment when no other supervisor is present. While it is not practical for the same person to teach and collect extensive data simultaneously, teachers can keep "pocket records" on some parts of their performance, especially time analyses. Using a handwritten recording form and a small pencil, a teacher can make notes on how long the class spends in certain activities. When the class changes activity, the teacher pulls the page out of a pocket and jots down the time. This kind of note taking should not disrupt a lesson in any way. Later in the day, the teacher can sum up each category and calculate duration data for the lesson.

Other strategies for self-monitoring involve innovative use of student, collegial, and audiovisual resources. A teacher might explain to a gym aide what feedback means and ask the student to record each time feedback is used. Or, one teacher might ask another teacher to count the number of students actively engaged at specified points in a lesson. More advanced monitoring could be provided by training several teachers in one school to observe each other using one or more of the data-based systems described in chapter 5. This type of monitoring could lead to a positive and supportive team effort and could improve the entire staff's performance. Most schools now have sophisticated audiovisual recording equipment, and many high schools have student television clubs. Teachers can make their own video recordings or request students or other teachers do this for them. Later, the teachers can use data-based observation systems for self-analysis. At Virginia Tech we often use miniature audiotape recorders to make voice records during classes. The teachers then use a system similar to PEIIS to make self-evaluations from the tapes and then report their results to methods lab and student teaching supervisors.

If adequate personnel and media resources are available, a program can easily be set up for a teacher to self-monitor progression through a series of performance goals. Technological advances in electronic recording equipment make this self-supervision possible for more teachers. Limited financial and time resources for campus-based supervision of student teachers make self-supervision an attractive avenue to explore for three reasons. First, self-supervision shifts some dependency for the supervisory process back to the teacher, the person who ultimately will have to find ways to help himself or herself become a better instructor. This reflects a more realistic view of the physical educator's world in schools today. Second, it provides a greater potential for teachers to receive more regular supervision than is possible when others must deliver supervisory processes. Third, self-help is likely to promote more autonomous professional decision making by teachers. The teachers decide what to focus on for improvement, how much improvement is needed and possible in their context, and how to proceed toward solving instructional problems in their own classes. Supervision can do no more for a teacher than provide effective strategies for self-help.

Summary

The systematic gathering of even the most insightful data using observation techniques presented in chapter 5 does not complete the process of supervision; in many ways it represents only an interim step to using that information in the postteaching conference for the benefit of supervisor and teacher alike. Systematic data are best viewed as judgmental aids upon which to base supervisory decisions rather than as hard facts. Such data facilitate the supervisory process best by providing the supervisor and teacher with evidence linking what was attempted in a lesson to what occurred in the lesson. Once that information is gathered, it must be incorporated into the interactive processes of the postteaching conference, including analysis, the identification of prescriptive strategies, and the establishment of future performance goals.

The supervisor and the teacher are still the key agents in the process of improving instructional skills. The decisions and actions necessary for effective supervision cannot be taken from an infallible set of rules; good supervision must rely upon the individual supervisor's ability to keenly observe and correctly analyze teaching and to properly prescribe the best possible avenues for improvement. Those key skills work best within a scheme of systematic observation, contextually guided interpretations, and directed goal setting for improved teaching/learning processes in physical education.

Chapter 7

Improving Instructional Skills in Physical Education

The PEIS Model, described in chapter 3, separates the processes of supervision into two levels—program and implementation. The program level is comprised of many decisions and factors that determine the overall supervisory system. The supervisor, or the supervisory team, examines the potential to implement each of the several supervisory guidelines and functions and plans which supervisory personnel are to be trained and available for performing supervisory processes. The implementation level outlines a series of information-gathering, observation, and conferencing activities, which are intended to provide effective supervision for improving physical education teachers' instructional skills. This chapter takes the PEIS Model one step further by describing ways to actually arrange and implement instructional improvement efforts for better supervisory results.

Besides those considerations reflected in the PEIS Model, two other considerations must be made to complete the total picture of instructional supervision in physical education. The first is determining the overall structure or plan given to the supervising context, that is, how to provide supervision with the best chances of being effective in a given situation. The second consideration is determining what specific strategies to use to help teachers improve their instructional skills. The former set of plans works on a macro level to establish the environment in which supervision will be carried out; the latter plans operate on a micro level, suggesting specific ways to improve teaching/learning process skills. Figure 7.1 shows the components of this 2-tiered approach.

Supervision Structuring Plans

The overall structure refers to the manner in which the supervision program works to arrange and facilitate the environment to promote better supervisory

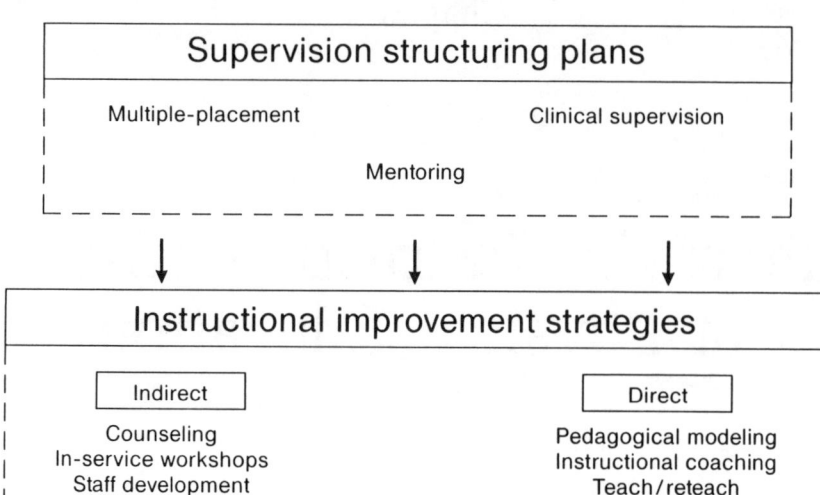

Figure 7.1. It takes both an overall supervisory plan plus specific instructional improvement strategies to create an effective instructional supervision program.

practice. The three ways suggested here are multiple placement, clinical supervision, and mentoring. The traditional arrangement of a university-based supervisor working with a single student teacher is not included due to its familiarity and demonstrated inability to foster effective assistance to teachers.

Multiple-Placement Plan

This plan, designed for preservice field teaching experiences and the student teaching stage, provides an alternative to the more traditional intern/cooperating teacher model currently used by most teacher training programs. The plan places several interns in the same school simultaneously for these field experiences. Verabioff (1983) proposed that as many as five student teachers could be under the tutelage of a single physical education teacher. Our experiences with multiple placements at Virginia Tech suggest that placing two or three student teachers in the same school allows for the maximum benefit intended under this plan.

The multiple-placement plan is intended to enhance the effectiveness of supervision for field experience and student teaching interns who comprise a cluster at one site.

Advantages

• All of the interns are likely to be in the same developmental stage, have similar needs, and exhibit similar teaching skills. This stage sharing can reduce the isolation and anxieties sometimes associated with these field placements. The clustered interns have a feeling of "strength in numbers."

- The interns share the same teaching context by virtue of being in the same school. Therefore, they can work as a team to identify problems and to suggest solutions that will work for all of them in that school. This single context can enhance the group's instructional and professional interactions, as they all share similar problems and experiences; the resolution of a problem for one intern will likely work for the others.

- The multiple-placement plan is viewed as an effective way for interns to bridge the two worlds of university and schools. A team of interns can plan for and implement instruction in ways familiar from their training program on campus; they can become a bit less resistant to practices that might conflict with effective teaching skills learned previously. This can contribute to their confidence when implementing familiar teaching processes in new settings.

- The group of interns becomes a miniclass with which the cooperating teacher and the supervisor can interact. This reduces much repetition in the delivery of supervisory processes as information and feedback can be passed along to the whole group at once. This also allows both supervisor and cooperating teacher to make group assignments and to design group experiences at a time when other student teachers are left to accomplish tasks alone.

- With planning and help, the interns can learn to provide one another with peer supervision on many aspects of instructional improvement. One intern can systematically observe another intern teaching lessons, for the benefit of both; the teacher is provided with necessary supervisory functions and the observer becomes more aware of teaching practices through data analyses and subsequent interactions with the teaching intern.

- By designing observation and interaction experiences (e.g., reflective teaching) for the interns, the cooperating teacher or supervisor can encourage collegial communication patterns that become the basis of positive attitudes toward professional dialogue throughout the interns' careers.

Placing several interns or student teachers in the same school can also have disadvantages, and certain precautions need to be taken to eliminate or reduce potentially negative effects.

Disadvantages

- Such an arrangement can result in reduced opportunity for an intern to plan for and teach entire classes, especially in small departments. We have observed a natural tendency to share all responsibilities, sometimes reducing each intern's opportunity to assume the full range of instructional and professional responsibilities inherent to field placements.

- The team concept might conceal the inabilities of some members who could not function adequately on their own. A teacher who cannot carry out the entire spectrum of instructional skills necessary for individual responsibility can potentially hide, thus failing to develop those skills.

- Finally, this arrangement increases demand on the cooperating teachers as they provide supervision to more than one intern. Not only must the cooperating teachers plan for instructional improvement, they must be aware of and responsive to the dynamics of the intern group as the experience progresses.

Even though the multiple-placement plan has potential drawbacks, commitment and regular planning can increase viability of the group intern model. By carefully selecting and properly training cooperating teachers to work with several interns at once, supervisors can create multiple-placement plans that provide instructional, professional, and career-related social enhancement for every member of the intern cluster.

Clinical Supervision

Nearly 20 years ago, Robert Goldhammer (1969) proposed a major theoretical shift in the supervision of student teachers. His clinical supervision model proposed a change in the process, context, and personnel of instructional supervision, including the student teaching experience. Recognizing the power of the teaching context to influence the acquisition of practical and effective teaching skills, he argued that the best place to learn how to teach was in the school itself. He argued further that due to this shift in the context of learning how to teach, the best supervisory personnel were likely to be those teachers who worked in the placement school and who daily saw student teachers attempt to acquire teaching skills. According to this model, the foundation of clinical supervision lies in the shifting of instructional supervisory responsibilities from the university staff to the cooperating teacher, who is given a new title—clinical supervisor.

At the time Goldhammer presented his ideas, they received only mild support. The theory of clinical supervision offered a viable solution to the problems of university-based supervision; however, this movement lacked the development and implementation of effective clinical supervision models. Few—if any—ongoing and effective clinical supervision programs could exemplify Goldhammer's theory. Possibly due to a combination of that theory and some recent calls for better interaction between university teacher training programs and school-based placement sites, clinical supervision is once again gaining attention (Acheson & Gall, 1987), and it offers some important advantages over university-based supervision.

Advantages

- University-based supervision is costly and time consuming. Clinical supervision reduces most of those costs by placing the clinical supervisor directly with the intern teacher in the school.

- As university supervisors often spend as much time traveling to placement sites as actually providing supervisory functions, clinical supervision is much more efficient. This goes beyond fiscal concerns; the clinical supervisor has far greater opportunity to observe, interact, and communicate with teachers just by being present when many important supervisory processes should be implemented.

- Logic supports Goldhammer's original position that the best place to learn teaching skills and receive supervisory input is the professional work setting (i.e., the school). Medical interns, for example, are supervised by physicians who work in hospitals, not by ones who can only drop in periodically.

Potential drawbacks to the clinical supervision model are few; most of them are simply logistic hurdles to be overcome in the establishment of such a plan.

Disadvantages

- Time and other resources are needed to recruit, identify, and train in-service physical education teachers for this role. This involves more than simply placing a student teacher with a veteran teacher.

- Clinical supervision requires new arrangements in the clinical supervisor's schedule to allow for these expanded duties.

- Clinical supervisors who work with student teachers must acknowledge the expectations of the university training program. Even though clinical supervisors are not full members of the university staff, they certainly are an integral part of the teacher training program and must work toward that program's goals.

- Communication between the university program, school administrators, and clinical personnel is critical yet is often not easily maintained. An effective program must provide good communication between these three parties.

A clinical supervision plan offers the best chance for implementing the PEIS Model outlined in chapter 3, especially as the model pertains to student teaching. Providing the right person to perform timely supervisory processes in the instructional setting greatly increases the effectiveness of instructional supervision during the student teaching stage.

One clinical supervision model for physical education has been developed and implemented at the University of South Carolina under the direction of Dr. Melissa Parker. Most of the following descriptions of clinical supervision for physical education were provided by Dr. Parker in published papers, personal communications, and presentations at professional meetings (Parker 1986a, 1986b). The program was established as an experimental arm of that university's physical education teacher training program.

In addition to Goldhammer's original assumptions, other factors contribute to the effectiveness of clinical supervision for physical education.

• Good teachers can be found in many schools to serve as instructional role models and effective supervisory personnel. Teacher training programs must establish criteria for clinical supervisors, find teachers who meet their criteria, and recruit them as integral contributors to the teacher training effort.

• The context of school physical education programs can be varied and, at times, quite constraining (Griffin & Locke, 1986; Lambdin, 1986). Student teachers must receive their primary supervision from someone who is familiar with the placement context and who is able to provide inside information that contributes to a successful student teacher term.

• In-service teachers can be oriented and trained to effectively implement all of the supervisory processes now assumed by the university staff member. Once provided with sufficient information about the teacher training program goals and expectations, clinical supervisors make and carry out decisions about the student teachers' instructional skill development. Also after training, clinical supervisors can be entrusted as the primary supervisory personnel during student teaching and can be held accountable for the decisions they make in the development of student teachers' instructional skills. The resulting combination of their experience, familiarity with the context, and supervisory training greatly enhances the effectiveness of instructional supervision at this stage.

• The clinical supervisor will likely benefit from the program as well. The clinical supervisor can improve his or her own instructional practices through the training exercises and regular supervision of the student teacher and may experience renewed professional enthusiasm when given a direct and key role in the development of the next generation of physical educators.

• Clinical supervision calls for a change in the role of the university faculty person as well. If the total supervisory responsibility shifts to the clinical supervisor, the faculty supervisor may not need to continue a sporadic and often ineffective profile in the "noble triad" (Locke, 1979). The university supervisor may need to assume the role of clinical supervisor trainer or supervision program director, who would direct the entire program for instructional skill development from the design of early field experiences, to the management of teaching methods courses, and finally to recruitment, selection, training, and evaluation of clinical supervisors.

An effective clinical teaching program requires a reallocation of existing resources and likely the acquisition of new resources. Current temporal and fiscal resources must be reallocated to allow sufficient training and compensation for the cadre of clinical supervisors working in the program. At the start, the training will most likely come from the university faculty and must be extensive enough to allow the clinical supervisors to assume nearly all of the current supervisory staff's field responsibilities with student teachers.

In recognition of the clinical supervisors' increased responsibilities and central role in the teacher training program, these supervisors must receive adequate considerations and remuneration. Some considerations can come in the form of status and new on-campus privileges, such as appointment as adjunct faculty to the university, recognition as master teachers by the local school agency, release time during the school day, reduced or waived graduate course tuition, campus bookstore discounts, campus parking privileges, and a substantial stipend for each student teacher supervised.

The university department must also reconsider its supervisory staff resources. Some of the current fiscal and temporal resources must be shifted from faculty to clinical supervisors. As the university faculty will have no direct supervisory duties, those former supervisors can be reassigned to other responsibilities in or out of the teacher training program. Finally, one or a few faculty members must be designated director or directors of the clinical supervision program, with new job responsibilities outlined to reflect this changed role in the teacher training program.

The preceeding assumptions and new perspectives illustrate that a move to clinical supervision requires radical changes in and outside the physical education teacher training program. Adopting the theory and logic of clinical supervision without a concurrent commitment to changing the entire supervisory program will probably result in supervision even less effective than that now provided by most university-based programs. Acknowledging that the design and implementation of any clinical supervision program must take into account many departmental, university, and school contextual factors, the following list outlines steps for establishing an effective clinical supervision program for physical education student teaching. Items on the list do not appear in any necessary temporal order; some must be completed ahead of others, but many can be completed before or during the implementation of the clinical supervision program.

1. Discussion of the role responsibilities and skills needed for clinical staff (a job description)
2. Recruitment and selection of the clinical supervision staff
3. Orientation to the training program (goals, students, curriculum, certification, etc.)

4. Training in supervisory skills, including systematic observation for physical education
5. Establishing communication channels between training program and clinical personnel
6. A gradual but steady shifting of supervisory responsibilities to the clinical staff
7. Securing appropriate considerations and remuneration for the clinical staff
8. Conducting frequent review and evaluation of clinical teaching staff and the entire program

Clinical supervision can provide solutions to many of the problems that have plagued university-based student teaching supervision for years. Preliminary studies within the physical education clinical supervision program at the University of South Carolina indicate that student teachers in fact receive much more instructional supervision time, feedback, and overall assistance from the clinical supervisors (Parker, 1986a, 1986b). Clinical supervision requires fundamental changes in how student teaching supervision is viewed, funded, staffed, and implemented, but its potential for helping young teachers acquire field-based instructional skills far outdistances the effort required to make those changes.

Mentoring

In recent years awareness has increased concerning the importance of the induction period for teachers. Induction is usually thought to begin during the student teaching experience and extend into the first 2 or 3 years of in-service teaching. Because student teachers have a cooperating teacher who assumes primary responsibility for their development, similar *mentoring* efforts are now being made for beginning in-service teachers. Educators now regard the induction period as the most important time in a teacher's career. During that time, a teacher learns not only how to teach but also about teaching as a way of life. These two kinds of learning involve many aspects, such as attitudes toward students, administrators, colleagues, and education as a whole; life as a teacher, both in and way from school; dispositions toward future professional growth avenues; personal preferences toward curricular offerings in physical education; student discipline; and effective instructional practices. Most physical educators also must learn to prioritize time and energies between coaching and teaching responsibilities (Lawson, 1983).

What happens during the induction years undoubtedly establishes attitudes and instructional patterns that become indelible marks, both positive and negative, that characterize a teacher throughout his or her entire career. When the negative begins to outweigh the positive, or if some critical needs are left unattended, professional unhappiness and possibly an early exit from the teaching force can result. For many years, administrators and the public assumed that new teachers possessed fully developed teaching skills, were already capable by virtue of their training, and were professionally acclimated, needing only a little experience on the job. This hands-off approach results in nearly one half of all new teachers in the United States leaving the teaching force in their first seven years of service; most of those who leave do so in the first three years (Templin, 1987). While many leave for reasons unrelated to induction problems, most cite dissatisfaction with schools and the difficulty of learning how to be a good teacher as the major reasons for leaving. Educators now acknowledge that induction teachers need highly focused guidance, support, and supervision efforts to help them become effective teachers with positive professional dispositions that lead to long and productive teaching careers.

To address induction teachers' needs, many states and school districts have initiated formal mentoring and other early career support programs. The basis of all mentoring programs is the assigning of a new teacher as the direct charge of a veteran teacher from the same school building. Early mentoring efforts focused mostly on assisting the new teacher with operational and socialization needs—learning the many ins and outs of life as a teacher, both in general and as applied to a school or district. The mentor was viewed primarily as a support person and was expected to be available when the new teacher needed advice, consolation, praise, or a companion during the sometimes lonely first years on the job. Lately the mentor's role is viewed more broadly and includes direct assistance in the development of the new teacher's instructional skills. Part of this expanded role stems from a realization that much of the anxiety and concern voiced by new teachers originates from their desire to be effective teachers, while other forces simultaneously inhibit the attainment of that goal. Eventually this frustration can lead to pronounced job dissatisfaction and early exit from the teaching force. The mentor as support person can address only some of the new teacher's needs; in order to help in a more complete way, the mentor must also serve as an instructional supervisor. In this expanded role, a mentor becomes much like the clinical supervisor described earlier.

As mentors have their own classes to teach, they cannot be expected to provide supervisory functions as frequently as a true clinical supervisor. However, the two roles are almost identical during those times intended for instructional assistance. Following are criteria for the selection of a mentor teacher:

1. The mentor and new teacher should teach the same subject area.
2. The mentor should be located near the new teacher for on-the-spot help in emergencies.

3. The mentor should be a veteran teacher, recognized both as an effective teacher and a positive professional role model.
4. The mentor should be adequately trained in all aspects of this new role: systematic observation, instructional effectiveness, interpersonal relationships, and teacher counseling.

Like clinical supervision, effective mentoring programs require some reconceptualization of the mentor's role in the school; adjustments must be made in a mentor's teaching day to allow adequate time to perform mentoring functions. Like the clinical supervision model for student teachers, mentor teaching has the potential to provide positive outcomes for all teachers involved in the process. The new teacher gets a wide range of supervisory and support functions, while the mentor takes on new challenges in the direct development of another teacher's career.

Instructional Improvement Strategies

A supervisor must at some point address the question, "What can I do to help this teacher acquire the instructional skills we have identified as needing improvement?" This question surfaces in every teacher training situation, regardless of the teacher's developmental stage or the supervisory plan in operation. Supervisors can benefit greatly by having a repertoire of instructional improvement strategies. The following section suggests several potentially effective ways to help teachers improve their skills. As illustrated in later chapters, each of the strategies can be implemented for the improvement of various teaching skills along all stages of the teacher development continuum. Some of the strategies will work best in just one stage or for just one purpose, while other strategies can be used within any of the developmental stages.

Instructional supervision is any attempt to improve a person's teaching skills. Such attempts can be made through two kinds of approaches—indirect or direct. *Indirect strategies* do not involve the supervisor actually observing (systematically or otherwise) the teacher in an instructional episode. Examples include counseling, in-service workshops, staff development, and awareness activities. *Direct strategies* do involve a supervisor's personal observation of the instruction, leading to a series of interactions with a teacher to assist him or her in the improvement of pedagogical skills. The direct strategies described here include pedagogical modeling, instructional coaching, teach/reteach strategy, and reflective teaching.

Indirect Strategies

Indirect strategies for supervision all share one common feature— they do not rely upon the supervisor making actual observations of the teacher. The presumed problem is identified through communication from the teacher to the supervisor. In some instances, the supervisor simply assumes that a problem or situation exists and proceeds on that basis without consulting the teacher. Because of this lack of observation, indirect strategies hold limited potential for the kind of effective supervision needed in physical education.

Counseling

Sometimes a teacher will approach a supervisor with verbal accounts of instructional problems. The supervisor gathers as much information as possible by listening and asking questions, in order to isolate and identify the source of the teacher's problem and to then offer suggestions for alleviating it. This counseling can occur in any location and is characterized by the supervisor's unfamiliarity with the teaching context and day-to-day events that contribute to the problem.

A concerned and well-meaning supervisor will try to learn about the teacher's stated problem, offer one or more suggestions, and then leave the teacher alone to carry through with the solution. For example, new teachers often consult supervisors about difficulties with class management and discipline in physical education. The descriptions are always of past events and usually involve specific problematic situations or students. The informed supervisor may be able to offer one or more general suggestions, but this third-party advice has limited potential in the absence of direct observation of the problem. Counseling is useful only if the supervisor can capture the true nature of the instructional problem through verbal reports and make rather general suggestions that are effective.

In-Service Workshops

The in-service workshop is one common strategy for helping teachers to improve instructional skills. Such a workshop is held on a common theme for a group of teachers away from the actual teaching context yet in a manner that simulates a classroom lecture period. The workshop can last from just a few hours to several days (e.g., during the summer). All teachers attending receive the same information and advice, based on the assumption that all of them have similar knowledge and experience related to the current topic. The topic, in many cases, is an existing problem for many teachers (e.g., how to work with mainstreamed students) or the learning of new curriculum and instructional approaches. Some or many of the teachers may already be acquainted with the workshop topic, as it usually has been chosen for them!

The most limiting feature of the in-service workshop is that the person giving the workshop, an acknowledged expert, is usually far removed from the day-to-day activities of teaching and is surely unfamiliar with the specific context in which each member of the audience must teach. In many cases the in-service approach has neither the design nor the potential for helping teachers improve instructional skills.

The in-service workshop strategy does have three positive features: It allows teachers to discuss common instructional problems, share each one's unique perspective, and offer each other workable suggestions for resolving these problems. The in-service workshop strategy does promote this kind of useful professional interaction and support, even if at times these are not the primary reasons for holding the workshop.

Staff Development

The staff development strategy is similar to the in-service workshop strategy but has one important advantage. In staff development, all of the teachers share the same context; typically, they teach in the same department, school, or school district. In addition, staff development usually involves a small group of teachers and activities are spread over a series of meetings or workshops. The coordinator of the staff development series comes to know the teachers and their concerns, problems, and context quite well through the many small group discussions they hold. Even though some topics might be quite generic, they are always pursued from the perspective of a common context and can lead to highly focused efforts to improve instruction in that unique context. As with the other indirect strategies, however, staff development does not involve observing the teachers in classes, and leaves many of the suggestions for improvement for the teachers themselves to interpret, implement, and evaluate.

Awareness Activities

Possibly the least effective of all instructional improvement approaches, awareness activities are based on the assumption that to know better is to teach better. While all of the indirect strategies above can help teachers become aware of problems and potential solutions, this particular approach goes no further. Typical strategies involve reading articles or books on teaching, watching videotaped examples of good teaching practices, or discussing with supervisors or other teachers certain aspects of curriculum and teaching.

Siedentop (1983) makes the distinction between learning about teaching and learning how to teach. Merely imparting supervisory information to teachers falls squarely into the former category and must be viewed as less effective than the latter for the improvement of teaching skills.

Awareness activities are also characterized by the offering of many prescriptive suggestions; the source (a person, article, or book) typically says, "Effective teachers should/shouldn't do . . ." and leaves teachers with the pressing practical problem of how to implement the suggestion in their classes! In addition, these awareness sources rarely offer teachers advice about how to evaluate the effectiveness of the newly-suggested practice. For example, even if a teacher becomes alert to the importance of content development by reading a textbook, that awareness alone will not enable him or her to select and implement new task patterns to apply those concepts correctly; much more must be done to assist the teacher with appropriate content development skills.

Awareness activities often leave teachers asking, "What will my teaching look like or produce when I can successfully implement this new action?" For these and many other reasons, approaches that go no further than merely alerting teachers to effective instructional practices hold little hope for helping teachers become better.

Direct Strategies

Many strategies for instructional improvement involve ongoing observation, analysis, and interaction. These strategies are characterized by the supervisor actually observing a teacher in action, usually with systematic instrumentation. That teaching action can occur in many forms and places, including micro teaching, peer teaching, student teaching, and in any other clinical setting regardless of the teacher's stage of development. Direct strategies are based on the notion that the supervisor must have a firm understanding of the teacher's instructional skills and needs prior to any attempt to interact with and help that teacher. Direct strategies also assume that there are many effective ways to help teachers teach better and the supervisor must select the one most likely to result in demonstrable improvement of instructional skills within a particular context.

Pedagogical Modeling

In many supervisory arrangements, the teacher instructs while the supervisor observes and later makes diagnoses and prescriptions for the teacher. Using the pedagogical modeling strategy of supervision, these roles are reversed so the teacher can actually see how the supervisor would like certain teaching/learning processes carried out. This strategy is particularly effective when the supervisor wants the teacher to practice an instructional skill or procedure for the very first time.

Pedagogical modeling has three component parts: (a) a briefing on what is about to be seen, including a detailed explanation of all contextual factors influencing the upcoming teaching demonstration; (b) the actual demonstration of the model lesson, either in part or in its entirety; and (c) postlesson discussion between supervisor and teacher to review and clarify the points made in the exercise.

Briefing. Teachers can most likely imitate even the most difficult instructional skills shown them; however, those skills must be applied correctly—at the proper time and for the right reason—if they are to have maximum effectiveness in classes. The supervisor must spend adequate time prior to the model lesson providing rationale and information the teacher needs to consider when using the demonstrated skill elsewhere (e.g., "Notice that when I want to increase students' attention for this free throw demonstration, I make sure they are not holding the basketballs in their hands. If you don't remember to do this, they will typically toss the balls around and disrupt you"). Inadequate briefing may result in the teacher using the demonstrated skills inappropriately at a later time.

The Model Lesson. The best model lesson is taught to an intact class in the teacher's own gym using only available equipment and facilities. This arrangement, however, can have too much ecological validity and can increase potential for the context to interfere with a proper demonstration. For example, the supervisor would have difficulty carrying out a model lesson not knowing students' names or their skill abilities and being unfamiliar with many other contextual features. Because the purpose of the model lesson is to show teachers why, when, and how to perform certain instructional practices, predetermined arrangements sometimes must be made for setting, equipment, and content, and by scripting the roles of students in the class. Of course, too much contriving can make the model lesson unrealistic (the opposite of the previous problem); a balance must be sought between both extremes.

Often, modeling only a portion of a teaching lesson, focusing on just one or a few instructional skills, is useful. Demonstration topics could include how to gain students' attention at the start of class, how to communicate managerial information to very young students, and how to end classes in an orderly manner. Limiting the focus this way helps the novice teacher avoid intimidation by expectations to do so many things well so early. For the veteran teacher, the isolation of just a few skills acknowledges that he or she probably does not need help on every teaching skill. Most likely a veteran teacher will wish to see how one small procedure is carried out by the supervisor.

One very effective part of this strategy is talking through or explaining ongoing procedures to the audience (one or more teachers). When the supervisor is about to carry out a highlighted teaching action (e.g., stopping a gymnastics class for safety reminders), he or she can alert the audience in order to explain the reasons, procedures, and anticipated outcomes for it.

> "I am going to stop the class because I see a few students not spotting properly. It's not a major problem right now, but I want to prevent it from escalating. The soft reminder is in line with the minor inattentiveness I observe. If a problem is not severe, don't make a big issue out of it. Just remind them of their tasks, and get them back to work."

This also points out that most effective teaching skills are implemented intentionally and with premeditation. If no opportunity arises to make explanations prior to certain performance aspects, then the supervisor should review his or her thinking and decisions with the audience at the soonest available pause in the lesson. Because this is a demonstration lesson, the supervisor can stop when necessary to prepare for, highlight, and review key points with the audience. Remember, the purpose is to help the audience understand and observe key teaching skills, which justifies unnatural breaks in the lesson that would disrupt normal continuity.

Postlesson Discussion. A discussion following the model lesson allows the supervisor to explain parts of the lesson that were not demonstrated as intended. This lets the audience know that even model lessons can be less than perfect, and it avoids confusion about whether those aspects were or were not examples of effective teaching. After the supervisor makes this disclaimer, the audience and the supervisor should interact freely about the lesson. The audience should be encouraged to ask questions about anything just observed and the supervisor should provide detailed responses.

Recording the model lesson on video is extremely helpful, allowing review and analysis by the supervisor and audience together. The supervisor can stop the tape at certain points in the lesson to pose two kinds of questions to the audience: "If this were your lesson, what would you have done here?" and "After seeing my decision and its outcome, would you have tried something different? If so, what?" This interaction helps teachers to recognize decision points in their own lessons and to shape intentional, rational, and effective courses of action at these points. The selected teaching/learning processes might not always be 100% correct or effective, but at least the teacher will apply them for a reason.

Finally, the supervisor can use the videotape of the model lesson to generate systematic observations by the audience. Within the context of that lesson, the audience can quantify teaching/learning processes that typify effective instruction, providing the audience with a match between those processes and resulting data analyses.

For many reasons, pedagogical modeling is an innovative and effective strategy for improving teachers' instructional awareness, decision making, and skills. More than imitating good teaching, modeling can illustrate and promote good teaching practice by alerting the audience to the many reasons effective instructional procedures are implemented.

Instructional Coaching

Although teachers can learn much by observing model lessons, nothing can substitute for actual teaching experience. However, a teacher sometimes should not practice those skills alone, especially during the early stages of learning to teach. Just as a teacher might use some type of guidance technique to help a student perform a task correctly for a first time, so too can supervisors guide or coach teachers through the initial acquisition of some instructional procedures. This instructional coaching strategy effectively promotes the acquisition of instructional skills and monitors a teacher's interactive decision processes as they occur.

The instructional coaching strategy can be used in any kind of teaching episode, from micro teaching to teaching intact classes. First the supervisor must provide the teacher with a full description of the teaching context and some explanation of the instructional skills on which the lesson will focus. The supervisor can also alert the teacher to any potential situations that might arise during the lesson and offer preclass advice for handling them. Once both teacher and supervisor understand the game plan, the teacher implements the lesson under the watchful eye of the supervisor. The supervisor stays close to the teacher throughout the lesson, being careful not to hinder the teacher's mobility or unnecessarily break the continuity of the lesson. The supervisor should take plentiful notes and monitor ongoing performance aspects systematically so that some data-based decisions and comments can be communicated to the teacher immediately.

The key feature of the instructional coaching strategy calls for the supervisor to interact with the teacher as the lesson is being taught. Several kinds of interactions are possible. They include alerting the teacher to ongoing or upcoming events ("Are you aware of how many students are standing around right now?" or "Don't forget to tell the class about tomorrow's tournament"); posing questions about why certain actions were taken ("Why did you cut that part of the lesson short?" or "Why did you decide not to punish Bruce for misbehaving?"); providing feedback on performance aspects just completed ("Your demo went well because you proceeded slowly and spoke clearly"); and giving tips about performing certain instructional procedures successfully ("When you call the class together in a minute, have them go to the middle of the gym to cut down on straggling").

The supervisor should also encourage the teacher to ask questions during the class ("What do you think will happen if I skip this next refinement task?") and to think aloud as the lesson progresses ("Let me see, I guess it's time to advance into long iron strokes; they have had enough time to work on their stance"). Certain parts of the lesson can be repeated, allowing the teacher to try alternative ways to implement some instructional procedures.

The teacher should understand that this strategy allows for the class to be stopped periodically. However, the supervisor must avoid making too many interruptions or stopping the class completely. The supervisor should adequately brief the teacher and students prior to the lesson so everyone understands the purpose of the exercise; this will reduce the potential for interactions to be viewed as scoldings or to take on other negative connotations. In the terms used by team coaches, this is viewed as a *controlled scrimmage*, in which the primary purpose is to provide the teacher with interactive help for improving instructional skills. This strategy is intended to be highly dynamic, having the potential for innovation, cooperation, and mutual experimentation between teacher and supervisor. For the teacher, instructional coaching means having someone at his or her side to hear suggestions, pose pedagogical questions, and provide feedback on the spot. For the supervisor, it means having an opportunity to make and evaluate ongoing suggestions for the improvement of a teacher's decision-making and instructional skills.

Teach/Reteach Strategy

One characteristic of most supervisory situations is that prescriptions made to teachers in the postteaching conference are not implemented immediately; some lag usually exists between the conference and the next opportunity to follow through on supervisory suggestions with the supervisor present. This is especially true for university-based student teaching supervision. The teach/reteach strategy eliminates this delay by arranging consecutive opportunities for a teacher to implement the same or a similar lesson. This arrangement should be made prior to the supervisory visit to ensure that at least two consecutive, contextually similar teaching episodes can be observed. An exception can be made for the time requirement if the first teaching episode is videotaped; in this case the teacher and supervisor could review the tape and confer immediately before the next lesson, as though the first one had just taken place.

The first teaching episode in the pair is observed and analyzed like any other lesson; the teacher implements the lesson while the supervisor makes systematic observations of designated parts of the teacher's performance. (Anecdotal notes are also useful with this strategy.) The postteaching conference focuses on those performance aspects identified before the lesson and on any others that become apparent while the lesson is in progress.

The basis of the teach/reteach strategy is the collective wisdom approach described by Hawkins, Wiegand, and Landin (1985). This approach specifically identifies instructional performance deficiencies through systematic diagnoses, with the resulting prescriptions derived from research on effective teaching and accepted pedagogical practices (see chapter 6). The research evidence and the general acceptance of the prescriptions lend a great deal of validity to those prescriptions as viable suggestions for improving teaching skills.

The effectiveness of the teach/reteach strategy comes from providing the teacher with some suggestions and alternatives for the first lesson that he or she can incorporate into the next lesson with the supervisor present. The supervisor can use the same systematic observation instruments for the second lesson as for the first, offering the teacher direct evidence for how those changes affected the second lesson. Comparing the data from the two lessons helps the teacher understand the relationship between teaching decisions, teaching processes, and student learning processes. If the systematic observation is properly sensitive to the teaching and learning processes being monitored, the supervisor can provide the teacher with tangible evidence of the differences between two courses of decisions and actions. For example, the teacher uses one plan for moving students between instructional tasks that results in 33% management time. From suggestions made by the supervisor for the next (and similar) lesson, an alternative plan results in just 15% management time, clearly showing the impact of the supervisor's prescription in that situation.

Data from consecutive teach/reteach lessons can also illustrate how two divergent approaches might result in similarly effective process outcomes, thus legitimizing both approaches for the teacher. If a teacher experiments with two different arrangements for student engagement in a volleyball drill, and both approaches result in more than 90% motor engagement rates in consecutive lessons, that teacher has validated two satisfactory ways to structure that drill and knows that both can accomplish similar process goals. Thus, the teach/reteach strategy can illustrate how one set of actions might be superior to another, or the strategy can help teachers develop different teaching actions to bring about similar results. Both uses are powerful learning exercises for improving teachers' instructional skills.

Reflective Teaching

Educators have given increased attention in recent years to teachers' decision-making and thinking processes as sources for improving instructional skills (Clark & Peterson, 1986). This attention is based upon the assumption that the more teachers are aware of ongoing and upcoming events in the gymnasium, the better able they are to choose among many possible courses of action, leading to more effective teaching patterns. A second assumption is that teachers can improve their awareness and decision-making patterns by having regular opportunities to reflect upon and discuss their own teaching with others. Supervisors surely can play a key role in the development of these reflective/analytic skills for teachers. Reflective teaching is based on arranging opportunities for anticipation of upcoming lessons or reflection on recent lessons and on considering suggestions for modifying decisions or processes in both cases (Cruickshank & Applegate, 1981).

Many strategies can comprise supervisory use of reflective teaching. One such strategy is the *leading question*, a purposeful inquiry from a supervisor to a teacher about an upcoming or completed teaching decision, action, or situation (Gitlin, Ogawa, & Rose, 1984). This inquiry can lead teachers in one of two ways. First, it helps them understand events that the supervisor already understands; second, the leading questions allows teachers to verbalize to other persons (a supervisor or other teachers) their reasons for making certain decisions and taking certain actions in class. Preservice and student teachers need to have opportunities to preview lessons for a supervisor. Because induction and veteran physical education teachers typically work in isolation, they rarely have opportunities for interactive, reflective thought with peers, colleagues, or administrators. The supervisor can help all teachers understand and reflect upon their own instructional decisions and actions.

Marland (cited in Clark & Peterson, 1986) describes the following four categories of teacher thought as reflected in verbal reports.

- *Perceptions*: Sensory experiences (i.e., something that has been seen or heard)
- *Interpretations*: Subjective meanings attached to a stated perception
- *Anticipations*: Speculative thoughts or predictions made during class about what could happen later in that class
- *Reflections*: Thoughts about past aspects or events in the lesson, especially what decisions resulted in and how different decisions could cause different outcomes

In combination with these four levels of thinking, supervision for reflective teaching can focus on making decisions and observing events from three time perspectives: preparation (before class), interaction (during class), and review (after class). Teacher thought patterns and these time perspectives come together in a schema for posing leading questions to physical education teachers, shown in the chart on page 170.

Reflective teaching based on thoughtful, meaningful questions can be a useful strategy for helping teachers understand and act upon their own instructional decisions. A supervisor must first be aware of the many and complex decisions made by a teacher in a lesson in order to skillfully pose appropriate leading questions and provide effective explanations to help that teacher become a better decision maker in the gym.

Summary

The plans for structuring supervisory environments and the improvement strategies presented in this chapter represent some of the best ongoing approaches to instructional supervision in physical education. Most educators feel that direct strategies for working with teachers toward better pedagogical skills are inherently more effective than indirect ones. No physical education teacher expects students to improve motor skills merely by watching, reading, or listening; the same applies to acquiring complex instructional skills.

By setting the stage for supervision with overall plans, supervisors can employ the specific strategies needed to improve teachers' instructional skills. Alert supervisors will recognize which strategies work best with the teachers they supervise; the strategies are actually a repertoire from which a supervisor can select a given approach most likely to be effective in certain situations. Undoubtedly, individual supervisors will need to experiment with each of these plans and strategies, exploring possible variations that work best in familiar situations. The direct strategies actually evolved through such exploration and variation; innovative and unique applications are encouraged. At some point in time a supervisor is faced with the question, "What can I do to assist this teacher?" Implementing one or more of these strategies, under one of the suggested plans, is a good place to begin the search for answers.

Question Foci for Reflective Teaching

	Preparation	Interaction	Review
Perceptions	Was there anything in the way you set up the gym that could have alerted you to a potential safety problem?	What made you notice that some students were avoiding their turns by always standing in the back of the line?	I use several ways to remember to look for certain things in class so I don't forget. What are some of yours?
Interpretations	What do you suppose your students think when they come into the gym and see the equipment set up and ready to go?	Why do you think they were trying to avoid participating?	What do you think students feel about PE when a class has been a fun, stimulating, and positive learning experience?
Anticipations	(after viewing a lesson plan) What should you tell students to make that second transition simple and fast?	Based on student engagement during warm ups, what could you have expected later in that class?	What led you to think the student's weren't quite ready for that second extension task?
Reflections	You have planned to do the skill demonstration yourself. What other ways could you provide students with that information?	What could you have said to them during class to get them to participate sooner?	When you get to teach that lesson again, what will you change? What will you keep the same?

PART II

Implementing Physical Education Instructional Supervision

Good supervision, like good teaching, is highly context specific. One cannot determine whether a particular decision or action is appropriate without being reasonably familiar with the instructional setting and the teacher. This feature of supervision works against capturing tangible examples of effective practice. However, supervisors can begin to formulate a notion of what good supervision might look like when they are provided with some background information; this allows a supervisor to assess the situation and ask, "What would I have done or said if faced with a similar set of circumstances and information?" Part II presents a series of scenarios that illustrate how the PEIS Model can be applied in many different settings, by various supervisory personnel, and at various stages of a teacher's development. In fact, each chapter in this part is based upon the main contextual factor of teacher developmental stages, with one chapter for each stage: preservice, student teaching, induction, veteran, and classroom teacher as physical educator. Certainly, the many possible combinations of those key factors for supervision cannot all be represented in a few chapters.

Prior to depicting what supervision might look like in each stage, the chapters begin with some general characterizations of teachers within that stage and implications for supervisory practice. These descriptions are offered as starting points for supervision at that stage; certainly, not all teachers share the expressed characteristics and supervisory needs mentioned within a given stage. However, supervisors must consider a teacher's developmental stage and proceed from the resulting perceptions until those perceptions prove inadequate or erroneous. This allows for newer perceptions to be incorporated.

Readers are encouraged to not only look for similarities across the developmental stages but to search for ways in which each particular situation demands that supervision be approached just a bit differently to accomplish its ultimate goal.

The scenarios presented illustrate what supervision might be like when the model is implemented in different situations. Much of the content, in fact, was transcribed from videotapes of actual supervisory visits. I hope these scenarios answer some of the questions that might have arisen from Part I and provide a picture of effective, systematic supervision for physical education.

Chapter 8

Supervision for Preservice Teachers

The preservice stage typically comprises those years of formal teacher training at a college or university. Preservice includes all general studies, discipline studies, professional studies, teaching methods courses, lead-up field experiences, practice teaching, and related work that contributes to the development of teaching skills, subject matter expertise, early professional attitudes, and career dispositions. The key word at this stage is preparation, as the teacher training program must attempt to provide within a defined time and curriculum many skills and attitudes necessary for student teaching and induction. The preservice stage, as part of a developmental continuum, must strive not for a fully proficient and functioning teacher but rather for one who possesses a variety of beginning instructional skills, a reflective orientation, and a handful of coping strategies for surviving within schools as institutions.

Prospective teachers undoubtedly learn much about teaching prior to entering a formal training program at a college or university. These prospective physical educators learn many things about teachers, schools, curricula, and students as they progress through their own student years (Lawson, 1983). Feiman-Nemser (1983) estimates that future teachers spend as many as 10,000 hours observing their own teachers prior to entering the preservice stage. Many times, students regard practices and values demonstrated by their teachers as exemplifying physical educators in general, regardless of whether those narrow impressions are complimentary or not. Those early impressions often shape values, attitudes, and instructional skills as students begin their own preservice programs. Some of the things learned about physical educators prior to the preservice stage are beneficial and can promote a positive development through the preservice time. Often, however, students learn things that lead to the development of ineffective teaching practices and undesirable professional dispositions. The qualities that prospective teachers bring with them into the teacher training program form the backdrop for that training and must be considered throughout the preservice stage as the program strives to promote effective teaching skills and attitudes that might conflict with students' existing ones.

Characteristics of Preservice Teacher Supervision

When conceptualized as a process of changing instructional behaviors and professional attitudes, the preservice stage can be described as taking prospective teachers from their present skill level (entry) to a skill level needed for the start of student teaching (exit). Of course, this latter skill level depends a great deal on the preferred instructional skills promoted by the teacher training staff leading into student teaching.

Supervision for the preservice stage has three major goals: (a) to provide prospective physical educators with foundational pedagogical knowledge leading to the effective teaching of motor skills, cognitive content, and attitudes within school curriculums; (b) to reduce the influence of negative or ineffective skills and dispositions brought by students into the preservice program; and (c) to provide prospective physical educators with a functioning repertoire of effective beginning teaching skills that can be expanded and refined in subsequent stages of development.

Supervision at the preservice stage is more effective if it proceeds from several general assumptions about novice teachers and their needs relative to the acquisition of effective beginning instructional skills in the undergraduate training program. Even though not all preservice teachers have similar entry profiles nor progress at equal rates within the program, some observations do hold true for the majority of preservice physical education teachers.

Becoming Familiar With the Teacher Training Program

All physical education teacher training programs are not alike. They are housed in many different kinds of colleges and universities and attempt to prepare teachers in many different ways. Preservice teachers should become oriented to their program at an early stage; they must be informed about the goals, priorities for curricular selections, preferred instructional skills, and professional values and dispositions held by the program staff. This assumes that the teacher training staff has reached a consensus on the desired outcomes of the program and that students reflect those in their teaching and attitudes. These trademarks give each program's certified teachers a recognizable identity among other new physical educators in the region and provide the basis of future follow-up efforts. Ultimately, a program's expressed goals play a role in the conduct of supervision; preservice teachers should be made aware of this relationship.

Acquiring a Common Technical Language

Every profession has certain terms used commonly in its practice. Prospective teachers should acquire this language early and be able to apply it correctly. Learning such a repertoire can alert preservice teachers to the emphases and priorities of each program's instructional and attitudinal outcomes. This allows all persons in a program to speak a common language relative to teaching skills developed at this stage. The technical vocabulary for physical education can include descriptions of feedback types (e.g., general, specific, congruent, skill related), class management (e.g., waiting time, transition time), student engagement (e.g., motor engagement, cognitive engagement, academic learning time), curriculum foci (e.g., health related fitness, lifetime sports, team sports, new games), and various teaching strategies (e.g., mastery learning, direct instruction [Taggart, 1985]).

Observing Preferred Instructional Skills

Preservice teachers should have opportunities to observe models of preferred instructional skills and to understand how those skills differ from the preservice teachers' current notions of effective teaching. The observed samples of teaching must be carefully selected but can take many forms including

- videotapes,
- simulated laboratory applications,
- visits to schools, and
- pedagogical modeling.

Preservice teachers will probably not acquire a program's preferred teaching skills only by being told of these desired practices. In order to supercede previously learned attitudes about teaching, each program must acquaint students with planning, implementation, and evaluation techniques regarded by the staff as best practice. The staff must show preservice teachers the preferred skills being applied in actual situations by a variety of teachers. Members of the staff themselves should serve as models for these practices.

Practicing Systematic Observation

Preservice teachers' instruction skills should be monitored systematically often throughout the program. Prior to this monitoring, preservice teachers should have opportunities to learn systematic observation skills themselves, with instruments similar to those used to monitor their own teaching. These systems should focus on the program's set of preferred teaching skills, initially acquainting preservice teachers with them as observers. Coupling practice in systematic observation with opportunities to view preferred instructional skills is helpful. In this way, preservice teachers can relate observational data with positive examples of teaching/learning processes.

Sequencing Teaching Skill Development

Instructional skill acquisition experiences should progress sequentially in ecological complexity, length, and number of performance parameters being practiced. Teachers need to build up their skills to a point they can make effective decisions and take appropriate instructional action with large groups of students over full class periods. They should not be expected to handle the complexities of a full teaching context without careful development of the necessary knowledge and skills. A suggested progression includes (a) an initial demonstration of few and simple skills in ''low-context'' or ''no-context'' settings; (b) practice of one or a few skills in micro-teaching settings; (c) practice of several skills in extended laboratory settings; and (d) practice of several, more complex skills in controlled field settings that closely approximate student teaching.

Providing a Supportive Supervisory Environment

The practice, evaluation, and acquisition of preferred teaching skills should occur within a supportive supervisory environment. Supervision at this stage should accept most kinds of failures and provide preservice teachers with ample opportunities to master instructional skills. In fact, at this stage supervisors must work their hardest with eager young teachers who are bound to make mistakes due only to their lack of experience.

Individualizing Supervisory Processes

Even though many practice teaching experiences are based on common skills and contexts, supervision must strive for increased individual attention in the diagnosis and improvement of instruction. This implies that the teacher training program is structured to allow for adequate individual analysis and supervisory interaction on a regular basis. The complexity of the teaching environment and preservice teachers' need for in-depth communication with supervisors following instructional episodes make this component imperative. Extra efforts must be made at this stage to allow for teacher and supervisor to view, analyze, and evaluate practice teaching lessons.

Basing Progression
on Demonstrated Teaching Skills

Progression from the preservice stage to the student teaching stage must be based on consistently demonstrated preferred teaching skills. This requires establishment of preservice exit criteria related to the program's stated goals; the demonstration of these goals should be among the recognized prerequisites to the student teaching placement. One primary function of supervision at this stage is determining each student's readiness for continuation in the preprofessional program, based on observed instructional performance. This, of course, implies that students have been provided with ample opportunities to demonstrate preferred teaching skills.

In the preservice stage, supervision must perform two important roles. The first is to assure that teachers receive adequate knowledge, experiences, and guidance to acquire the program's preferred teaching skills. At the same time, supervision must be the key in evaluating each teacher's effectiveness, maturity, and readiness for the formal student teaching term. This places an important, dual responsibility on the supervisory staff.

Scenarios for Preservice
Teacher Supervision

The acquisition of physical education instructional skills takes many forms during the preservice stage. The university supervisor (typically a methods course instructor) plans most opportunities to learn preferred teaching skills; these opportunities can be numerous and varied. The following scenarios represent three ways preservice supervisors can foster the development of a program's preferred teaching skills repertoire.

■ *Scenario 1:* Using pedagogical modeling to introduce a ■ technical language and effective teaching practices

The supervisor in this scenario instructs a teaching methods course and has just finished implementing and videotaping a demonstration lesson. The experience is part of an introductory teaching skills course intended to familiarize preservice teachers with basic teaching terminology and instances of effective teaching/learning processes. The class will be asked to display these skills in an upcoming micro-teaching laboratory. The preservice teachers are sophomores and juniors.

The demonstration lesson's content concerns the tennis forehand, and the lesson simulates a complete 50-minute class period, with the 25 preservice teachers serving as the intact class group. The demonstration lesson took place on outdoor tennis courts and has just been completed; the methods class is now gathered in a nearby classroom. The instructor makes several preliminary remarks before the taped replay begins. (Some words are italicized the first time they appear. They represent terms discussed by the class previously and illustrate how terminology can be integrated into such an exercise.)

Instructor: We all know the situation for this demonstration lesson, so there is no need to cover it again. You were all informed about and were a part of the *context* of today's lesson, made up of class size, equipment, facilities, time, content, and, of course, students with varying degrees of tennis skills—in short, all those things that might make a difference in how well a teacher is able to plan for and reach stated *instructional goals*. You were all given a copy of my lesson plan for the demonstration class, so unless you have questions about the context, my lesson plans, or the *lesson content*, I'll start the tape.

Hearing no questions, the instructor starts the tape. The first part of the lesson shows the instructor posting a simple forehand practice drill; students' attention is directed to the poster. The students are expected to begin the day's first activity as soon as they see what it is. As they arrive, the instructor is shown reviewing her plans for the class. In a few minutes she asks four students to assist her with setting up the *practice stations* to be used in the class. The tape is stopped about 2 minutes into the lesson.

Instructor: You all saw and practiced the *preclass activity* I posted. Why do you think I did that? (Several students wish to respond.)

Dan: To keep us from lying around the courts before class began!

Jim: To help us get warmed up before the lesson actually began.

Marilyn: To let us know you meant business today!

Instructor: Actually, all three answers are correct, but let me rephrase them to fit some of today's teaching terms. Dan recognized that little tactic as *preventive management*, to keep you *engaged* in the lesson from the very start. This reduces students' tendencies to become *off task* before I even have a chance to formally begin the lesson. The reason Jim gave allowed me to incorporate an easy *warm-up activity* and provide students with an opportunity to *review* some things covered in a previous lesson. So, it had a double intention. Marilyn's statement that I was out to mean business is another way of saying I was trying to establish an *academic focus* immediately in the class, clueing you right away that we were here to learn motor skills in class today. So, without the class even knowing it, I had quickly established several *managerial*, *instructional*, and *class climate priorities* in those first few minutes. Did anyone notice what else I accomplished during that time?

Jerry: You mean with your gym aide . . . rather, your *instructional assistant?*

Instructor: Yes, what was Donna doing for me?

Jerry: Taking roll while we were in that preclass activity. I noticed her walking around asking some of us our names and recording them in your book. I guess that's what you mean by an *alternative roll taking method.*

The instructor replies affirmatively and starts the tape again. It plays until the demonstration class is brought together in the center of the tennis courts. On the tape, the instructor thanks the four students who helped set up the practice stations.

Instructor: Students need to know that their help is always appreciated by the teacher. That was an example of a *positive managerial feedback.* Did you notice that I gathered the class at the center courts to cut down on the time spent in *transition* from the preclass activity to the structured stretching period? Transitions are necessary in physical education, more than in any other school subject, because we usually teach in large spaces. While you can rarely eliminate them, you should plan for fewer and shorter transitions in your classes. Why?

Kathy: To allow for more practice time during class.

Instructor: Right, but let's call that *engaged time*, OK? Physical education involves two kinds of engaged time: *cognitive engagement*, in which the students are receiving information related to the lesson content, and *motor engagement*, in which the students are actually practicing or participating in drills, scrimmages, fitness routines, or games related to the lesson goals.

On the tape, the demonstration class goes through a planned stretching and warm-up period to prepare them for the tennis forehand lesson. The instructor keeps the tape playing through this segment, quizzing the methods class students on the proper selection and techniques of activities in the stretching period. The tape shows the instructor providing the demo class with information about the stations set up around the court area.

On tape, the instructor addresses the demonstration class: We've set up three stations for today's forehand practice time. Station 1 is on the far three courts, getting you to work on hitting down the line. Station 2 is over on the bounce-back wall; the task is to keep a forehand rally going by yourself, hitting only forehand strokes. Station 3 is on the near four courts, set up with target zones. You are to maintain a forehand rally with a partner as that task. Each station has its own posted *task card* for you to read when you get there. Notice that the card describes the *learning station task* and its purpose, the *organization* of the station with necessary *teaching devices* and *practice tips* for you to keep in mind as you work there, and several *task criteria* to shoot for. Begin by trying to reach *mastery* on the first criterion; when you can do that to the stated *consistency and accuracy goals*, proceed to the second one, and so on. Please do not change the station tasks from what is written.

If you finish all the tasks before we rotate, let me know and I'll give you something more advanced to practice.

Finally, a *student progress chart* is posted at each station. When you have completed each task to its criterion, write your name and today's date in the designated spaces. It looks to me like we'll have about 15 minutes for each station. Is this clear to everyone? (She quizzes Bob about the structure of the stations and how long they will last. He replies correctly, and others in the class nod in agreement.) OK (pointing to the demo class group), this third go to Station 1, this third to Station 2, and the rest to Station 3. I will *circulate* around to help you get going. Hustle up!

The methods class instructor stops the tape at that moment.

Instructor: Lots of things happening in that segment! Even though you saw everything earlier as the demo class, let's review them now. What is the advantage to having the task cards to begin with? Why take the time to write them up and post them before class?

Joan: So students can just go right to each station, read the information, and start to practice immediately. They don't have to depend on the rest of the class, or the teacher, to find out what to do.

Instructor: Right. No one ever said students must get their *task information* from the teacher.

Scott: The written descriptions also help to remind students of what they are supposed to be doing at all times. No one can say they forgot.

Janice: Doesn't that also contribute to *task accountability*?

Instructor: It sure does. The task criteria help in the same way; they keep students striving for more achievement at the stations, allowing them to get into it and become better players. Why should students progress through a *task sequence* in the written order? Why not just let them practice the ones they like best?

Diane: Because the tasks are based on *mastery learning* principles, and it looks like you did a *task analysis* to prepare for them. Students should not go on to more advanced learning tasks until they can perform *prerequisite tasks* first. As I went through the stations, I felt a sense of accomplishment at completing each task the way you wanted and was more confident that I could do the next task in the sequence.

Instructor: Great. It looks like you remember lots of terms we discussed in lecture and even some things from other courses! I'm going to let the tape run now and stop it periodically to point out some of the *teaching decisions and processes* I want you to notice.

(A few minutes later)

Instructor: On the tape you can see me *monitoring* the class as students work at the three stations. What should I be doing?

Bob: Making sure students aren't fooling around, I mean, being off task!

Phil: Watching to see if the students are doing the instructional tasks the way you had written them.

Randy: Checking to see if the tasks are OK for the students, that what they're doing is not too easy or too hard.

Instructor: Right, that's called *motor appropriate*. I'm looking to see little or no progress, or too rapid progress. What can I adjust if the tasks are too easy or too hard?

Donna: You might make changes in the tasks, or in their criteria.

Instructor: Right. Coming up you'll hear me on the tape give lots of different kinds of *instructional information* to various students in the demo class. Let me point them out as they occur. But first, what's the difference between cues, guidance, and feedback?

Harvey: *Cues* are those things you tell or show students before they try a task; things they need to know to have a better chance of succeeding at the task.

Paul: *Guidance* happens when the teacher gives information while a student is actually going through the task, sort of a concurrent cue to help the student finish the task the right way.

Sue: *Feedback* is information given to the student that tells how well the task was completed. We called it *knowledge of results* or *knowledge of performance* in motor learning class, but it's meant to let the student understand just how well one task was done and show the student how to use that information in the next task. To me, feedback and cues can sometimes sound pretty much the same; I guess it all depends on the teacher's use of them and how the student sees them.

Instructor: You're correct on that, Sue. Teachers do need to let students know whether the instructional information refers to a previous attempt, which is feedback, or is provided as a tip on how to do the next one, which is a cue. Sometimes a teacher will give one student several pieces of information in a row. What do we call this?

Harvey: Isn't that an *information chain*? I guess you could have a *cue chain*, a *feedback chain*, or even a *guidance chain* to give a student lots of each kind of information in a row. That sounds helpful to me!

Instructor: In your text, Siedentop [1983] explains that instructional information can be either *specific* or *general* and can have a *value content*. What does this mean?

Giselle: I'll use feedback to explain, but I think the ideas are the same for all kinds of information. Feedback is general if it only tells the student the outcome or makes an overall reference to the attempt, like "That wasn't a very good jumpshot, Jim." Feedback becomes specific when the teacher tells the student more detail about the attempt, like "You missed the shot because you did not follow through enough, Jim." It takes on more value content when the teacher explains the reasons why certain changes are needed, such as "When you follow through, it puts more backspin on the ball. With more backspin, you're likely to have the ball settle on the rim softly and go in on the second or third bounce."

Instructor: Thanks, Giselle, those were good examples, even if they weren't tennis ones!

The videotape is played through for all three station rotations. As a cue, guidance, or feedback is demonstrated, the instructor asks "What was that one?" and several members of the class respond out loud. When the responses are not all correct, the instructor replays the segment and clarifies the example for the class. The instructor stops the tape at several other times to ask "Why do you think I did that in the demo class?" or "What would you have done here if you were the teacher?" Occasionally, some of the students disagree with the instructor's decisions or rationales and are encouraged to discuss their viewpoints.

The demonstration lesson closes with the class gathered around the instructor for a review period. She examines the student progress records completed at each station and informs the class that 75% of them completed Station 1, 90% completed Station 2, and only 20% completed Station 3. She ends the review with a question-and-answer period, posing organizational, technique, and skill queries to the demonstration class. She asks several students for *managerial help* to gather equipment together; she then dismisses the whole class. This ends the videotape of the lesson.

Instructor: Let's discuss my *Q-and-A period*. As you noticed, only 20% of the students completed the tasks in Station 3. Why do you think that happened?

Scott: It was a completely different task than the other stations. Station 3 was a *dynamic task*, requiring that both partners rally adequately; the other stations were *static tasks*, and we were on our own to complete them. Station 3 was much more difficult.

Sue: And, we didn't have enough time for Station 3. Maybe you could have used a different *allocated time* schedule to give us more engaged time on Station 3 than on the others.

David: The task description for Station 3 wasn't very clear, either. I was in the first group on that one, and we couldn't figure it out until you came over to explain. I bet we lost nearly half of our time at that station because of the lack of *clarity*.

The instructor then leads the methods class through a discussion of ways to improve the demonstration lesson, especially the configuration of Station 3.

The methods class ends with its own review of the day's activities, including the main points covered in the demonstration class and related discussions.

■ *Scenario 2:* Systematic observation of selected skills ■

Many teacher training programs use micro teaching to promote the acquisition of just one or a few key instructional skills at a time. By limiting the number and complexity of skills, the supervisor draws close attention to those instructional skills in ways not possible when the class size is larger, the time is longer, the content is taken from actual curriculums, and the class is an intact group of students in an actual school setting.

Micro-peer lessons have

- 5 to 15 students (who are actually members of the same methods class),
- an instructional time from 10 to 20 minutes, and
- a limited instructional focus (one learning goal or task).

Making the learning task *novel* also helps reduce the impact of prior learning effects within the student group. Some good examples include juggling tennis balls, soccer instep dribbling in the air, hula hoop routines, and nondominant hand throwing. Each methods laboratory supervisor can devise his or her own set of novel tasks.

During a class meeting prior to the micro-peer teaching, the supervisor (course instructor) provides the class with all pertinent contextual information and performance parameters for the laboratory experience.

Supervisor: Each of you will have 10 students in your class. The micro-peer lessons will last exactly 15 minutes—I will time them. You will be provided with enough equipment for all students to practice at one time, and you will work in one half of the gym. Using as much of that space as you wish, you may set up your equipment and prepare any teaching aids and devices [Siedentop, 1983] before the time begins. Each of you has been given a novel learning task to teach your class. You must write a lesson plan for your class and let me review it prior to implementation. Remember, the purpose of this laboratory is not necessarily to get your students to master the task in 15 minutes; most of the tasks cannot be learned that quickly. Rather, you should design a 15-minute lesson that includes teaching and learning processes that would logically lead to student achievement if maintained long enough.

Another member of the methods class will monitor your teaching with the TA-IIS. All of you are familiar with the focus of this system and have been trained to use it yourselves. All of the lessons will be videotaped. In the event of observer error we will use the tape to recode your lesson correctly. You may also wish to recode it anyway as a reliability check, and I encourage you to do so. Several teaching and learning processes will be monitored during your lesson. Some focus on you as the teacher; others focus on how students spend time in the lesson. Let's review them and the performance criterion for each one:

Student time

 Management—less than 15%

 Instruction—less than 10%

 Practice—more than 75%

 Transitions—fewer than 5

Instructional information

 Overall feedback—2.5/min*

 Skill feedback—3.0/min*

 Nonverbal cues—3

 Kinds of guidance—2

 Use of student names—20 times

Supervisor: Remember, the asterisks indicate that only five uses of general feedback can count toward these rates. You can give more than five, but only the first five will be included in the computation of these rates. Each of you has been assigned to teach one of the novel learning tasks. Please write a lesson plan for that task, using the format we covered in this course, and be prepared to teach it the next time we meet. See you then, in the teaching gymnasium.

All of the methods class students teach a micro-peer lesson during the next scheduled meeting, and the lessons go as planned. Following is the postteaching conference between the supervisor and Bob, who was assigned to teach a three-ball juggling task in his lesson. The TA-IIS data sheet from his lesson is shown here and includes some notes made by the supervisor upon his review of the videotape between the lesson and this conference.

Supervisor: Bob, did you get a chance to review the tape of your lesson and make your own TA-IIS observation?

Bob: Yes, and my analyses came out the same as the observer's.

Supervisor: Good, then we can go on with no questions about your observational data. Let's focus first on how your students spent their time in the lesson. You kept their management time down to 10%, despite having six transitions. This indicated that you had them moving around a lot but planned for efficient changes between activities. What else did you do to help this?

Bob: I made sure they stopped the current activity promptly and made it clear what the next task was. I think this cut down on the time they needed to get going on the next activity, whatever it was. I also hustled them along, especially the slow ones like Jerry!

Time Analysis—Instructional Information System for Physical Education
(TA-IIS)

Date __5-20-89__   Teacher __Bob Weir__

Grade __N/A__   School __(EDPE 3714)__

Observer __Mike M.__   Content __PEER TEACH- JUGGLING__

Time Begin __10:15__   Time End __10:30__

Elapsed Time __15:00__   # Students __10__

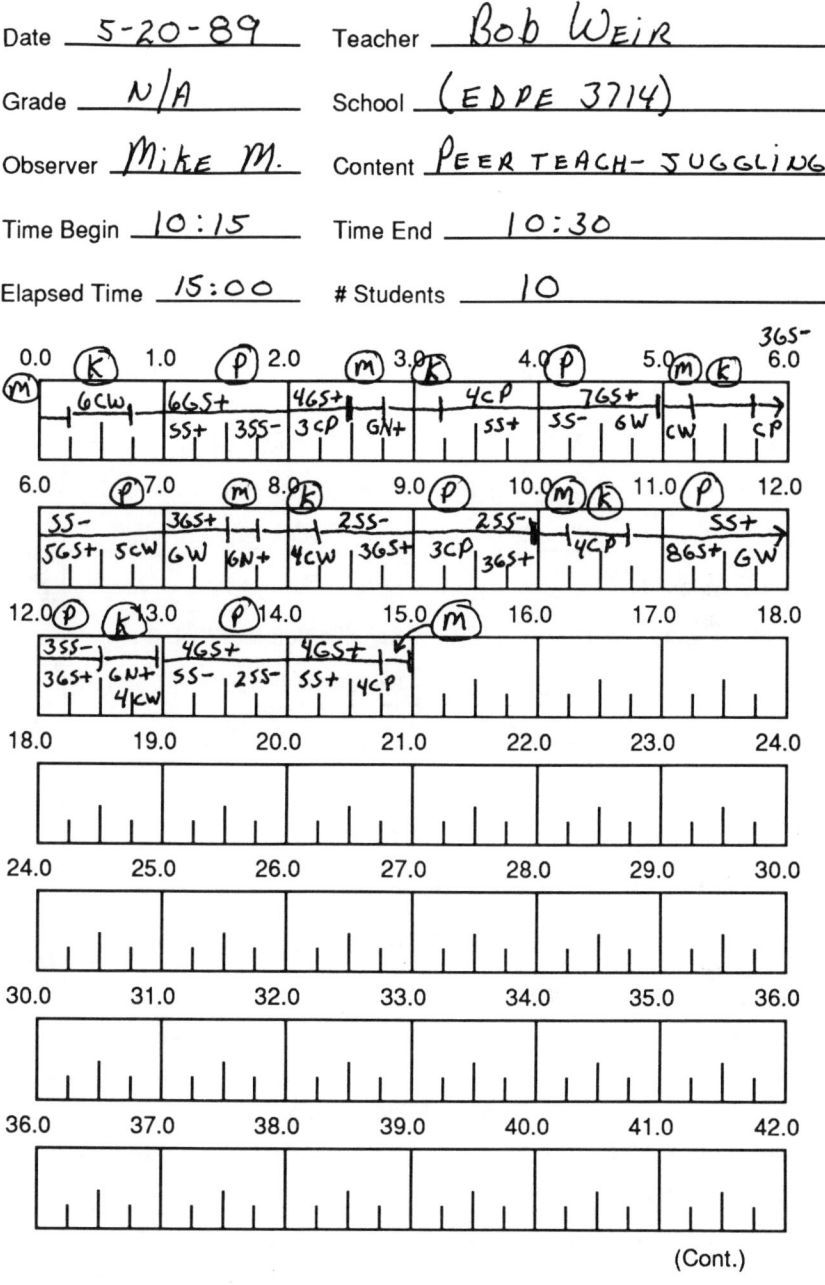

(Cont.)

TA-IIS (Continued)

Time Category (Code)	Feedback Category (Code)
Management (M)	General Skill (GS + or -)
Knowledge (K)	General Non-Skill (GN + or -)
Warm Up/Fitness (WF)	Specific Skill (SS + or -)
Skill Practice (P)	Specific Non-Skill (SN + or -)
Off Task (OT)	
Waiting (W)	Cues and Guidance [(Code)]
Resting/Break (R)	Cue [Whole (CW) or Partial (CP)]
Other/Undefined (O)	Guidance [Whole (GW) or Partial (GP)]

Category Calculations *Too mANY GENERALS-ONLY 5 cAN CouNT

Time Analysis	Min	%	Instructional Information	
Management (M)	1:30 = 10		+ General Skill (GS +) = 50	Total Feed-back
Knowledge (K)	3:00 = 20		+ General Non-Skill (GN +) = 3	
Warm Up/Fitness (WF)	___ = ___		+ Specific Skill (SS +) = 4	24*
Skill Practice (P)	10:30 = 70		+ Specific Non-Skill (SN +) = ___	
Off Task (OT)	___ = ___		- General Skill (GS -) = 3	Rate/min
Waiting (W)	___ = ___		- General Non-Skill (GN -) = ___	~1.5
Resting/Break (R)	___ = ___		- Specific Skill (SS -) = 15	
Other/Undefined (O)	___ = ___		- Specific Non-Skill (SN -) = ___	

SKiLL FEEDbAck — 24/10.5 miN.
2.3/miN. (ok)

Cue—Whole (CW) = 20		(cuES) Total
Cue—Partial (CP) = 15		
ONE GW wAs mANipulATivE— Guidance—Whole (GW) = 3		35
NicELy DoNE Guidance—Partial (GP) = ___		

Notes and Comments

- Time mANAgEmENT wAs GOOD, EvEN w/LoTs oF M→k→P SEQuENcES
- CAN you thiNk of wAys To coNvERT GENERAL Fb's To SPEcific? (TELL ThEm w<u>hy</u>)

Supervisor: So I noticed, and that's a good thing to do. Sometimes you need to take control of the pace of the lesson when students want to take their good old time. Now, take a look at the 20% of class time they spent listening to you instruct. That's 3 minutes of a very short lesson in which they did nothing but listen or watch you demonstrate.

Bob: But I had to make sure they got to see and hear about the whole juggling task and that they saw each new activity before practicing it.

Supervisor: Were you remembering *active demonstrations* from our class discussions? Sometimes students do not have to be watching passively as the teacher gives information; they can be practicing along with the teacher as they listen. I know this isn't always possible, but in this lesson I think you could have used active demonstrations often and effectively, especially for the simpler tasks. Remember, even though students are listening and practicing at the same time, the TA-IIS counts it as practice time, which encourages you to find ways to implement active demonstrations whenever possible. So, if you had done that, it would have reduced students' instructing time by about half, shifting those minutes to practice time and putting you well within the criterion range for both kinds of student time involvement.

Bob: I see now. Making adjustments in one kind of time affects how students spend their time in other ways. In this case, if I give them more practice minutes with the active demonstration, it automatically reduces the number of knowledge minutes, while still providing them with the necessary information and demonstrations.

Supervisor: That's the idea! Now, let's take a look at your own teaching processes in the lesson. You gave lots of verbal cues to students, nearly 35 in just 15 minutes of teaching. Nice job on that.

Bob: Thanks. The night before the lesson I reviewed the several juggling tasks I wanted to cover and made a list of things to tell students on each one— *teaching tips* I think you called them in class.

Supervisor: Right. I find it helpful to jot them down on my lesson plan and take a quick look at them just before I start a lecture/demonstration. Sometimes I'll even look at them again just after the lecture/demonstration, when the students are usually getting started on a task. You also did a nice job of using nonverbal cues and two types of guidance in the lesson. Overall, this was the strongest part of your teaching. You seemed very much at ease when delivering those kinds of information, and students seemed to make good use of what you told them. I noticed Janice got the two-ball juggle right away after you reminded her not to follow each ball with her eyes directly.

There is one part of your lesson that needs some attention, and I think I know the reason why. You did not make the criterion with your overall feedback rate of 1.5 per minute or your skill feedback rate of 2.3 per minute. The problem is clearly in the number of general feedback comments you gave in the lesson. You gave almost 75 different feedback statements, which is quite a few (and well over the criterion rate), but nearly two thirds of them were general. Remember, only five of those general feedback statements could count toward the criterion rates. You had an obvious reliance on "Good job," "Nice try," and "That's it" in your feedback statements to students.

Bob: I realized that quickly when I reviewed my tape. I guess I was trying to say something that sounded like feedback, but paid no attention to what came out of my mouth—kind of talking to myself! During the lesson I also thought many of my cues were really feedback, but I found out that wasn't the case.

Supervisor: Many inexperienced teachers will do and say things that make themselves appear busy in class, but some of those things don't contribute to student learning in any meaningful way. It's almost as if the teacher is talking to himself, like you just described. But, on the positive side, at least you made active mistakes. I think it's much easier to reshape verbal teaching patterns than it is to increase low rates of them. I'd suggest that you still strive for high rates of verbal interaction with students but begin to think of the purpose and value of what you say. Rather than just say, "Nice job," try to attach some specificity and content, like adding "with the timing of your tosses. See how much easier it is to catch the ball to start your next toss when the tosses are consistently in the correct place?" Students can really use statements like that one to improve their skills.

Overall, I was very pleased with your micro-peer lesson. I saw lots of good planning evident in your lesson and lots of effective teaching/learning processes in action. Your TA-IIS data sheet verifies that. Try next time to work on the things we just noted for improvement, and I think you'll teach an even better micro lesson. Here is a copy of your TA-IIS data sheet with a few notes I made on it as I reviewed your tape. Any final comments or observations?

Bob: No, we've covered everything I saw in my lesson.

■ *Scenario 3:* **Using small groups for reflective teaching** ■

As discussed in chapter 7, reflective teaching can be used to help teachers discuss, analyze, and determine the effectiveness of their decision making and instructional processes in retrospect (Cruickshank & Applegate, 1981; Gitlin, Ogawa, & Rose, 1984). As lessons are discussed after they conclude, the real purpose of reflective teaching is to help teachers make faster, more informed, and better decisions the next time they are faced with similar circumstances (similar to those that occurred in the completed lesson). Reflective teaching works especially well in combination with peer teaching and can be designed for small group interactions to benefit the teacher as well as the several other observers.

The following scenario outlines how small group, reflective teaching might be used as an effective strategy for instructional supervision in the methods class described in Scenario 2. To review, each micro-lesson teacher had 10 students and 15 minutes of instructional time in which to teach a novel learning task. The teacher was to prepare a written plan prior to the lesson and give it to the supervisor. All lessons were systematically observed by another member of the methods class using the TA-IIS, which focuses on how students spend time in class and how the teacher provides a variety of instructional information types. All lessons were videotaped.

Mickey taught the lesson discussed in this scenario. His assignment was to teach his students how to throw a softball through a small target at a distance of 45 feet, using the nondominant throwing arm. The supervisor has asked several other members of the methods class to observe Mickey's tape and to form his reflective teaching group. Each has received a copy of Mickey's lesson plan and his TA-IIS data sheet. The data sheet appears on pages 190 and 191. Mickey is designated in the scenario as the teacher. Other members of the group are Phil, Randy, Janice, Brent, and Donna. Each of them has recently taught a micro-peer lesson as part of the methods class. The supervisor leads the group but attempts to assume a low profile during discussions.

Supervisor (to Mickey):   Now that we have all reviewed your tape and TA-IIS data sheet, is there anything you'd like to tell the group about your lesson to start the discussion?

Teacher: Yes. First, I have to say this was a unique task to prepare for. We all throw to targets a lot but are rarely asked to use the nondominant arm. It was like learning to throw all over again, even though all the students knew how to throw! I debated for some time whether to take a biomechanical approach by reviewing basic throwing patterns or a task sequence approach by assuming you already knew the mechanics and just needed to get into a series of progressive mastery tasks. I finally chose the first approach, and it showed in the data.

Randy: Yes, we spent lots of time listening to the standard biomechanical aspects of throwing. At least for me, that wasn't terribly helpful. I don't think of them much when I use my dominant arm and couldn't relate them to using my other one! I felt somewhat uncomfortable having to get the same information you'd provide for a class of first graders! And to spend nearly 25% of the lesson getting it!

Teacher: I sensed that, and soon I felt uncomfortable passing it along to you. Phil seemed either bored or upset that he had to get that simple information laid on him again.

Phil: Bored. I know how to throw well enough; I just wanted to get on with practicing with my left arm!

Teacher: Maybe I should have just started you off throwing right away from a short distance and correcting only those things that needed attention.

Phil: Good point. Some of us actually could throw quite well with our nondominant arm and didn't need a biomechanical review. However, you did

Time Analysis—Instructional Information System for Physical Education
(TA-IIS)

Date __5-20-89__ Teacher __MicKEY HART__

Grade __N/A__ School __(EDPE 3714)__

Observer __MiKE M.__ Content __ThRow w/NONDOM. ARM__

Time Begin __10:40__ Time End __10:55__

Elapsed Time __15:00__ # Students __10__

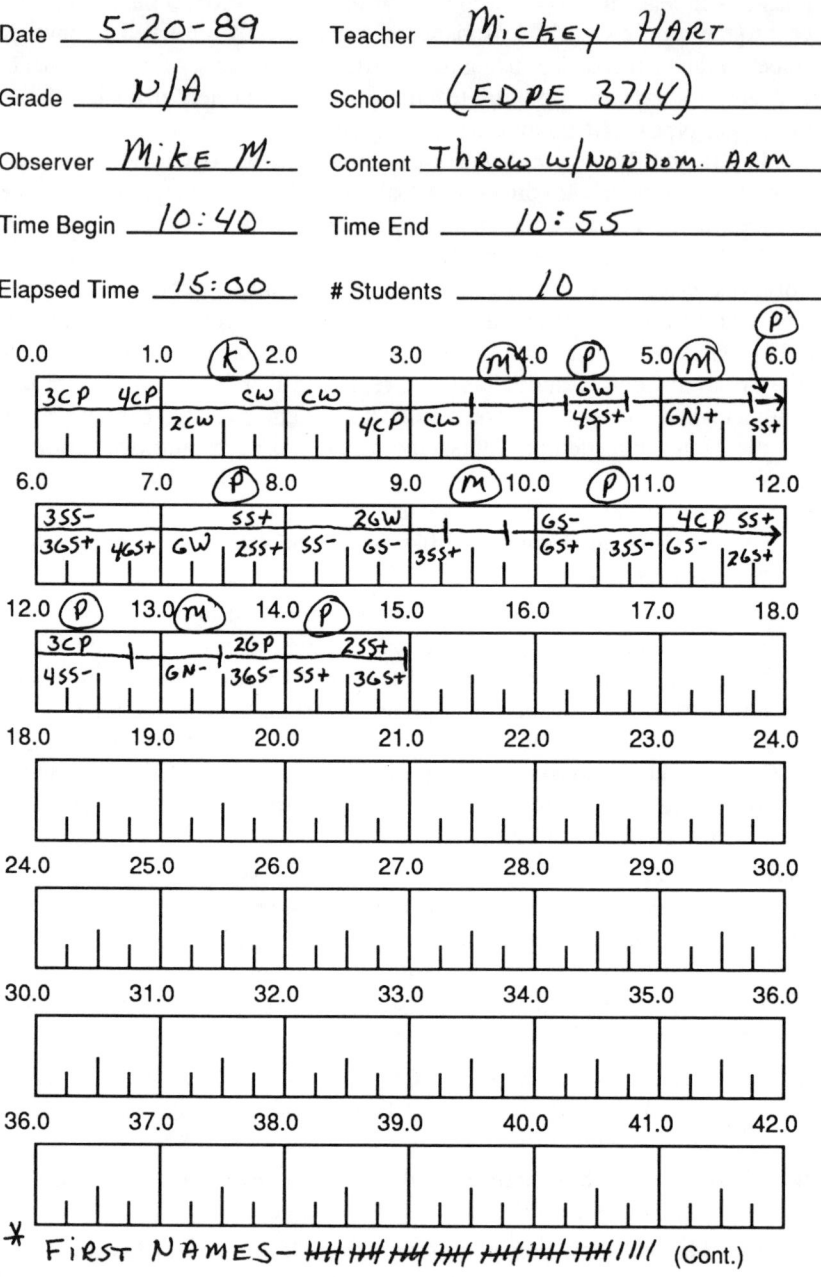

✱ FiRST NAMES— ####### ##### ##### ##### ##### ##### ##### //// (Cont.)

TA-IIS (Continued)

Time Category (Code)	Feedback Category (Code)
Management (M)	General Skill (GS + or -)
Knowledge (K)	General Non-Skill (GN + or -)
Warm Up/Fitness (WF)	Specific Skill (SS + or -)
Skill Practice (P)	Specific Non-Skill (SN + or -)
Off Task (OT)	Cues and Guidance [(Code)]
Waiting (W)	
Resting/Break (R)	Cue [Whole (CW) or Partial (CP)]
Other/Undefined (O)	Guidance [Whole (GW) or Partial (GP)]

Category Calculations   *ONLY 5 GENERALS CAN COUNT

Time Analysis	Min	%	Instructional Information		
Management (M)	3:00 = 20		+ General Skill (GS +)	= 13	Total Feed-back 28*
Knowledge (K)	3:30 = 23		+ General Non-Skill (GN +) = 1		
Warm Up/Fitness (WF)	___ = ___		+ Specific Skill (SS +)	= 12	
Skill Practice (P)	8:30 = 57		+ Specific Non-Skill (SN +) = ___		
Off Task (OT)	___ = ___		- General Skill (GS -)	= 6	Rate/min 1.9
Waiting (W)	___ = ___		- General Non-Skill (GN -) = 1		
Resting/Break (R)	___ = ___		- Specific Skill (SS -)	= 11	
Other/Undefined (O)	___ = ___		- Specific Non-Skill (SN -) = ___		
			Cue—Whole (CW)	= 4	
			Cue—Partial (CP)	= 18	Total 28
			Guidance—Whole (GW) = 4		
			Guidance—Partial (GP) = 2		

Notes and Comments

- I'LL LEAVE THIS FOR THE REFLECTION GROUP TO DISCUSS

provide lots of verbal and modeling cues; they just weren't all necessary in that lesson. By the way, you called me "Phillip" all through the lesson, and I prefer to be addressed as "Phil."

Teacher: Sorry. I'll try to remember that the next time.

Supervisor: Phil's point is a good one. Students do have preferences for how they are addressed and they feel uncomfortable when a teacher uses a different name for them. At least Mickey used lots of first names in his lesson; that's much better than pointing at students and saying, "Hey, you!"

Brent: Why did you have us go one at a time when we finally got to throw to the target? It seems to me that we spent lots of time waiting our turns. Our management time amounted to almost 20% in that lesson, most of it due to waiting during practice segments.

Teacher: I wanted to get clear and uninterrupted views of your throwing. You know how everyone gets in the way of each other when there is no control.

Brent: But aren't there other ways to let students keep practicing that allow you to see each one throw? (Several members of the group nod in agreement.)

Teacher (after a pause): I guess I could have taken each student aside while the others worked at individual targets. But that seems like a lot of extra effort.

Brent: But for us students, that effort would have meant much more engaged time and eventually more improvement. Your task organization seemed quite inefficient to me, and it showed in the excess management time percentage.

Teacher: I'll need to remember that the next time I make lesson plans. That was definitely a weakness in this lesson.

Donna: Don't be so negative about that decision. Focusing on one student at a time allowed you to give lots of specific verbal feedbacks and manipulative guidance. You actually had lots of nice information chains for those of us who needed that extra attention at one time. For me, that was very helpful.

Supervisor: I see Donna's point and hope all of you realize that many planning and interactive decisions can have two or more likely outcomes. Sometimes as teachers, you must call them as you see them. The important thing is that you are able to account for your decisions with a good rationale. Many times, circumstances call for trade-offs by teachers on students' behalf; by doing something right for some students, you run the risk of doing something wrong for other students at the same moment.

Janice: I'd like to switch the topic for a moment. My impression of Mickey's lesson was based on his enthusiasm. While it doesn't surface directly from his data, he was obviously animated during the lesson; his high rate of feedback and his many cues and guidance statements gave me the message that he was psyched to teach that lesson. Even though we did stand around during his lecture/demonstrations, at least we saw him go for it and provide interesting, clear, and correct models of the skills. His frequent use of students' first names also contributed to his enthusiasm, I thought.

Teacher: Thanks, Janice. I really worked on ways to make the lesson interesting and my teaching enthusiastic. I felt good about those parts of my lesson. I guess I just need to find ways of translating that enthusiasm into more student engagement. Physical education can be interesting for students in other ways besides watching an entertaining teacher provide demonstrations. After a while, entertainment is less exciting than doing and learning. There must be a way I could balance the two better to make my teaching interesting *and* more effective.

The supervisor ends the reflective teaching group discussion by asking each member of the group to note one positive aspect of Mickey's teaching. This completed, the supervisor ends the reflective teaching session by saying how much he appreciated the supportive tone and constructive comments expressed by all members. It is apparent that everyone in the group benefited from the group's reflection and interaction.

Summary

Preservice teachers typically have only their personal perspective from which to base early professional and instructional development. This is certainly important, but they must soon learn that there is a difference between knowing about teaching and knowing how to teach (Siedentop, 1983). Supervision in this stage must make strong efforts to acquaint young teachers with the existing knowledge base on effective instruction and prepare them for upcoming field experiences. This is a difficult dual task, yet one that can be accomplished by considering the characteristics of the preservice stage and by providing adequate amounts of individual attention as teachers struggle for the first time with learning how to teach.

All of these scenarios depict the emergence of one important aspect of the supervisory process necessary for all stages of teacher development—a lively, open interchange between the supervisor and teacher. This interchange is based on the notion that teachers can begin very early to discuss and reflect upon effective practices for physical education. Eventually, they will be able to expand from just discussing them to taking an active part in identifying, choosing, and implementing preferred teaching skills in the gym. This communication must be developed early in the program and be nurtured in a supportive, open atmosphere typified in these three scenarios.

Chapter 9

Supervision for Student Teachers

The formal student teaching term has long been the focal point of supervisory efforts, for justifiable reasons. It is the major opportunity for teachers to showcase the skills they have acquired in their preservice program in a context quite similar to school ecology as it exists for most teachers. If a teacher is effective during student teaching, he or she is viewed as reasonably able to carry out the responsibilities of a full-time teaching position. As such the student teaching term is uniquely characterized as both an exit and an entry experience; it signals a teacher's readiness to progress from the preservice stage to a situation very much like that of an in-service teacher.

From my own perspective, a person enters the experience as a *student first–teacher second* and leaves it as a *teacher first–student second*. What happens during that transformation, and how it occurs for each individual, is one of the most important metamorphoses on the developmental continuum. Very few induction teachers look, feel, instruct, and think the way they did when the student teaching term began; the changes are profound, as is the role supervision must play at this pivotal time in a teacher's development.

The student-to-teacher transformation will probably occur just by the structure and nature of the student teaching experience itself; the crucial function of supervision at this time is to promote a positive and successful transformation. That transformation occurs in the areas of professional growth, professional and personal socialization, and, of course, instructional skills. While acknowledging that all three areas ultimately contribute to this ongoing development, this chapter focuses on how supervision can help physical education student teachers carry preservice skills into and through the student teaching stage.

Characteristics of Student Teacher Supervision

As in the preservice stage, effective supervision for student teachers takes on some general characteristics. Some of these are based upon assumptions about student teachers' needs, their prior experiences, the contexts in which they practice, and their instructional skill competencies. They can be considered starting points for supervisory practice in this stage; specific contextual factors of the field placement and individual differences among teachers naturally reduce one's ability to make accurate predictions for all supervisory applications at this stage.

Entering Student Teaching

Preservice teachers should not become student teachers until they have demonstrated consistent performance of the teacher training program's preferred instruction skills. The contexts of most student teaching placements do not allow for the acquisition of basic instructional skills, nor should supervision at this stage focus on introductory pedagogical procedures that should already be part of a teacher's repertoire. This stage should focus on how to apply existing skills in more complex contexts and on a regular basis.

Learning the Context of the Placement School

Student teachers need essential contextual information for the placement term. This includes information about their placement school, their cooperating teacher, and the curricular units they will be expected to teach. The supervision program must provide ways for student teachers to learn the context in which they will teach for the next several weeks. The university supervisor can help by maintaining files on all placement schools and providing that information to student teachers who will go to those schools. The supervisor can also arrange for student teachers to visit their assigned schools and meet with their cooperating teacher prior to the start of the placement.

Understanding Criteria for Performance

Student teachers need explicit criteria for instructional skill performances during the term. Student teachers, like preservice teachers, must have a clear understanding of instructional performance standards prior to the start of the placement. This does not mean that specific performance criteria should be set but rather that student teachers are made aware of what is important during their current experience.

Specific expectations for each student teacher should reasonably reflect all contextual features of the assigned placement, units that will be taught, and potential impediments to effective teaching. All student teachers will probably not have equal opportunities to display the university program's preferred instructional skills in the field; some placement schools clearly are better than others in promoting those skills. This requires that supervisors also become familiar with the various contexts in which they monitor teachers' skills.

Learning Specific Applications for Teaching Skills

Student teachers must strive for specific and ecological applications of effective teaching practices in their instructional skill performance. They must be guided to make and implement instructional decisions *in situ*, not generically. Recognizing the effects of context and making proper decisions while considering those factors are important developmental steps for young teachers. The identification of quick fix strategies that work immediately is important but should not displace more stable practices that have the potential to remain effective over time and within the context of the placement.

Exploring Alternative Instructional Approaches

Student teachers should be allowed (even encouraged) to explore alternative instructional decisions and processes using several different approaches to a similar situation. Through experimentation, using systematic data for comparison, teachers can test the relative effectiveness of various instructional strategies. A corollary to this assumption is that it is acceptable to experiment and fail, as this allows student teachers to learn firsthand why some decisions and actions should be avoided. Student teachers, under the constant monitoring of a cooperating teacher, enjoy a somewhat safe environment in which to try new instructional ideas; supervision at this stage should support attempts to explore new and unique ways to apply teaching skills.

Providing Frequent Supervisory Feedback

Supervision should provide maximum monitoring and performance feedback for student teachers. Supervisors, presumably clinical supervisors, should provide student teachers with some supervisory functions on a daily basis. When clinical supervision is not possible, university-based supervision should occur at least once a week. Possibly the most common complaint from student teachers is that they are not visited often enough by their supervisor—another good reason to promote the clinical supervision approach in this stage.

Phasing In

The amount, complexity, and degree of individual responsibility of instruction should be phased in for student teachers. Student teachers should assume instructional roles over a period of time, to ensure they are prepared and able to eventually take on a full schedule of classes. A sink-or-swim approach is inappropriate for a positive and successful transition from student to teacher.

The supervisor should communicate with the cooperating teacher early in the term, to establish a plan for phasing the student teacher in to the full set of expected responsibilities. Adjustments can be made to this schedule to accommodate student teachers who need more or less time than originally planned.

Increasing Performance Expectations

The supervisory focus and teacher performance expectations should gradually increase throughout the student teaching term. Supervisors should not expect new student teachers to demonstrate a complete repertoire of highly effective, contextually appropriate instructional skills right from the start. Student teachers need to demonstrate an ability to perform a few, simple instructional skills in this new setting before progressing to more complex and demanding ones.

Demonstrating Performance Outcomes

The primary purpose of instructional supervision at this stage is to document by the end of the term consistent performance of the program's (and some other) preferred teaching skills. Such documentation indicates a teacher's preparedness for certification and entry into the teaching force as a physical educator.

Scenarios for Student Teacher Supervision

Unlike the preservice stage, supervisory activity in the student teaching stage takes place mostly in the placement school. Many features of placement schools can differ (location, size, grade level, and staffing), but they all share one thing; they are all *field based* and require student teachers to make and act upon decisions with real students, experienced colleagues, and undeniable consequences.

Supervisors, too, must recognize the realness of these settings, be familiar with the contextual features of each placement, and be prepared to offer student teachers tangible assistance on the spot. Many of the problems faced by student teachers cannot wait for the few or irregular visits typical of university-based supervision.

The following scenarios depict student teaching supervision by two different kinds of supervisors. The first is traditional university-based supervision, carried out under the PEIS Model. The second represents an interchange between a student teacher and her clinical supervisor. It is likely that the two scenarios will sound quite similar, even with the different personnel. That illustrates the point made in Part I about providing effective supervisory processes across many kinds of personnel. The key message here is that a well-trained clinical supervisor and a well-trained university supervisor, both following the PEIS Model, should pursue student teaching supervision in many similar ways.

■ *Scenario 1:* Monitoring content development ■ for physical education

This scenario depicts a supervisory observation typical of the early weeks of the student teaching term. The student teacher has only recently taken responsibility for her own classes, and the supervisor wishes to monitor just one aspect of her teaching—how she plans for and implements instruction with logical progressions through learning tasks. The teacher's name is Susan.

Supervisor: Hello, Susan. How are you today?

Susan: Mostly fine, but a bit tired. I haven't become used to these long days on my feet, but it'll get better.

Supervisor: I'm sure it will, but that's easy for me to say! We have some time before your next class, so I'd like to ask you some questions about what you'll be doing in it. Can you describe the class for me, Susan?

Susan: Sure. They are all fourth graders, 30 of them. About an equal number of boys and girls. Four of them are mainstreamed for PE; I'm not sure yet why they take PE with this class. But so far it hasn't been a problem; I just treat them like the others, and they respond! The class will last for 35 minutes and be held here in the gym. As you can see, I already have my equipment set out and ready to go.

Supervisor: Great. May I see your lesson plan for the class?

Susan hands the supervisor a written lesson plan that uses a planning format learned at the university. The plan identifies a basketball dribbling skill theme (Graham, Holt/Hale, & Parker, 1986) to be covered in the lesson. Susan has carefully outlined several learning tasks as well as the necessary management, equipment, sequencing, and time allocations for each one. The supervisor chooses to focus on Susan's content development decisions in the class, using the CDPE system.

Supervisor: Susan, do you remember the content development system we used in your elementary methods class last semester?

Susan: Yes, that's the one that looks at how a teacher sequences learning tasks to help students progress in a logical order.

Supervisor: Exactly. Since you have planned several different learning activities for this lesson, I'd like to take a look at them with that same system. It should give us a good picture of how you help students become more skilled, at dribbling in this case. The gym isn't very large, so I'll just sit on the stage and stay well out of your way. Is there anything else to discuss before you begin?

Susan indicates that she has no questions. The fourth graders file in a few minutes later and the lesson begins. The supervisor completes the observation for content development and makes some notes as the lesson progresses. The resulting CDPE observational record appears on page 201.

When the class has ended and the children have gone back to their classroom, the supervisor meets with Susan to share the results of the observation.

Supervisor: Did the lesson go pretty much the way you planned it, Susan?

Susan: Yes, it did. There were no major disruptions or other events to make me change what I wanted to do. As always, the time seemed to slip away and I got rushed at the end. But, I can start their next class with a quick review and go into the keep away game a bit sooner.

Supervisor: That's a good idea. (She shows Susan the content development sheet, with its graph.) As you can see, you made seven content development statements and learning tasks for the children in that class. That's why it went by so fast: you were very busy! Your initial *informing* episode was just right. They needed to know the basics up front and be aware of rules on traveling and proper advancement of the ball. The following two *extensions* were appropriate as their first learning tasks. They are basic skills, but you needed to know the children could do those simple things before moving on to harder stuff.

Susan: Right. I do think I could have shortened those two extension tasks a bit, because the children could do them so easily. I'll try that with my next fourth grade class.

Supervisor: OK. Now, let's focus on the fourth task, the *refinement* task of moving in their general space using alternating hands and looking up at you at the same time. Why did you go to that one so soon?

Susan: Well, when I saw they could do the first two so well, I thought I could take a chance by advancing them along a bit faster.

Supervisor: Wanting to experiment at times is a good thing to do, but in this case it was a bit premature for those children. The combination of a new

Content Development for Physical Education System (CDPE)

Date __5-7-89__ Teacher __Susan G.__

Grade __4__ School __Shady Hollow Elem.__

Observer __D. Sebolt__ Content __Basketball - Dribbling__

Time Begin __8:45__ Time End __9:20__

Elapsed Time __35 mins.__ # Students __30__

Write down the statements the teacher makes to the entire class when students are stopped—not to individual students. Classify each one related to the motor skill content of the lesson as either Information, Extension, Refinement, or Application. Graph the statements at the bottom in the order they occur.

1. You must dribble the ball - no carrying allowed (I)
2. "Air dribble" w/out the ball (E)
3. Dribble the ball, catch it after each bounce (E)
4. Move in Gen. space, use alt. hands, don't watch ball (R)
5. Move in Pers. space, use alt. hands, don't watch ball (E)
6. Pers. space, alt. hands, dribble 10 in a row (A)
7. (In pairs, w/one ball) - "keep away" f/your partner
8. for 15 seconds (A)
9.
10.
(Continue on back if needed)

#4 was too hard - good choice to change to next (E)

Content Development Series

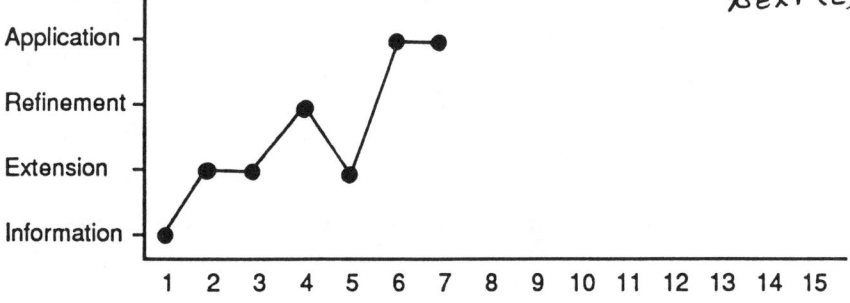

#Information __1__ #Extension __3__ #Refinement __1__ #Application __2__

task of alternating hands to dribble and looking up, not having to catch the ball every time, and the opportunity to travel in the general space made for a big jump in task difficulty. Did you notice what happened?

Susan: Yes, the children were either bouncing the balls off their feet or looking down and bumping into one another! I thought they might get it after a while, but most of them never were able to do that task well. So, I decided to go back to another *extension* task to simplify it for them.

Supervisor: That was a good decision, even if it was made a few minutes late. Just restricting them to their personal space made all the difference. They were then able to do the task well. I saw all of them looking up at you while maintaining enough control to use alternating hands to dribble. What does that tell you?

Susan: It seems like just reversing the order of those two tasks would have made a big difference. And, I should be more careful in generalizing from a simple to more complex skill performance.

Supervisor: Right. But, lots of times you just have to try something to see how it will work. To your credit, you were thinking on your feet and that's encouraging for me to see. And, as the content development graph shows, you didn't repeat the mistake. The rest of the learning tasks were appropriate for the children and presented in a logical sequence. Except for the misplaced refinement, the learning tasks represented a nice progression for the children to have. I saw lots of children performing all the other tasks you gave them, even the keep away game at the end. This was a good lesson for the things I was monitoring today. Next time, depending on your lesson focus, we'll take a look at some other aspect of your teaching. In the meantime, why don't you make a list of things you think need attention, and we can work on them the next time I visit.

Susan: OK, and thanks.

■ *Scenario 2:* Clinical supervision with MOST-PE ■

This scenario depicts an interaction between a student teacher in the last weeks of her placement and her clinical supervisor. The clinical supervisor has been trained in teaching analysis and the delivery of all functions outlined in the PEIS Model (see chapter 3). He has made systematic observations of the student teacher throughout the term and is familiar with Regina's progress and development thus far. The scenario takes place as they prepare for another supervisory observation in an upcoming class.

Clinical Supervisor: Before you begin this next class, can you describe your plans to me, Regina? Start with a description of the student group and the lesson content you are going to cover.

Regina: Sure. As you know, we're about halfway through a tennis unit. Today I'd like the students to work on their serving skills and the return of service. All of the students are 10th graders. The class will have 27 students in it; only about five or six are girls, so it's not balanced that way. But, with tennis it doesn't really make a difference, so I don't need to worry about it. All of the students will have their own racquets, which is good. But, we only have about three balls per student to start with and usually fewer as the class goes along.

Clinical Supervisor: Why is that?

Regina: Because they hit lots of balls over the fence, and I have them wait until the end of class to retrieve those balls. It's kind of a trade-off, I think. They either lose practice time getting the balls after every shot that goes over the fence or they have fewer to practice with as the class goes on. By doing it this way, at least they can't hit the ball over intentionally to get out of practicing!

Clinical Supervisor: Good idea! With the students you have in that class, that kind of preventive management is good thinking! What facilities are you going to use for this class?

Regina: There are six courts and two hitting walls outside. As you know, we don't have any ball tossing machines. Would you like to see my lesson plans?

Clinical Supervisor: Sure, but first let me see the ones from your last three lessons with this group. I need to catch up on what you've covered so far.

The clinical supervisor quickly reviews the previous plans, noting the recent task content and learning progressions. Satisfied that the students are now ready for serving and return skills, the upcoming plans are reviewed carefully. Regina has written her plans neatly with much attention paid to detail. The class will meet for 50 minutes with 5 minutes allocated on both ends for changing clothes (a school policy for physical education). She has prepared two drills for the serve and two for the return, preceded by her demonstration of each skill to the whole class. She has carefully drawn diagrams of how each drill will be arranged and made a time budget for all class activities. Next to each drill she has jotted down some notes for herself to keep in mind and a few teaching tips to emphasize with students. The clinical supervisor hands the plans back to Regina.

Clinical Supervisor: This seems like an ambitious plan for just one class period. Do you think you'll be able to get through all four drills in your 40 minutes of teaching time?

Regina: Yes. My second period class managed just fine.

Clinical Supervisor: But that class has only 14 students in it, and they are a good group. You may want to be prepared to adjust your plans for this larger class, just in case they don't progress so quickly. Do you have any ideas for changing your plans if things get behind?

Regina: Not really. But you might be right, so I'd better think of something between now and class time!

Clinical Supervisor: Fine. Is there anything else I need to be aware of before this class begins?

Regina: Not that I can think of.

Clinical Supervisor: You seem to be doing quite well in many areas of your teaching, according to my previous observations. Your progress has been very good to this point, and I see no reason why things shouldn't remain that way. Do you have any particular aspects of your teaching you want to work on in this class?

Regina: Well, you've made lots of specific observations of feedback and other things so far. I'm getting far enough along that I should be able to put it all together in a single lesson, trying to put all the pieces of the puzzle in place at once. What do you suggest?

Clinical Supervisor: Do you remember the MOST-PE recording sheet from your secondary methods classes on campus?

Regina: I think so. Isn't that the one that looks at several different areas of student and teacher behavior in class?

Clinical Supervisor: Yes, it's good for getting a comprehensive picture of teaching, just as you indicated you wanted. Remember, the MOST-PE system looks at teachers and students, each in different ways, so you'll need to pay attention to lots of things at once. How about if you try to reach the following teaching and learning process goals in this lesson.

Management time—less than 15%

Lecture/demo time—less than 15%

Practice time—more than 80%

Overall feedback rate—2.5/min

Skill feedback rate—3.0/min

Use of student first names—25 times

Motor engagement during learning tasks—80%

Motor appropriate during learning tasks—70%

Content development—a logical sequence

I'll also be monitoring planning, enthusiasm, task orientation, and the clarity and correctness of information you give to students. Do those goals seem fair to you, since this is the first time having so many things monitored at once?

Regina: Well, I can't say for sure, but I guess I'm going to find out soon! I understand all of those except task orientation. What is that?

Clinical Supervisor: That's nearly the same as motor appropriate; it's how well you plan learning tasks that take into account your students' current skill levels. Can I explain anything else for you before the lesson?

Regina: No, those goals do sound fair to me, and I already have reached many of them individually. I'll have to work hard to keep all of them in mind at once, but I'm ready to go.

Clinical Supervisor: One last item. I'll need to walk around the courts to watch and listen during class. I'll try to stay out of your way, but if you see me in a bad spot, just let me know. Good luck and I'll see you after class, once the students have been dismissed.

The clinical supervisor completes the MOST-PE observation during Regina's tennis lesson. The supervisor makes the calculations while Regina stores the tennis equipment back on the shelves. A copy of the recording form with data calculations and notes is shown on pages 206 and 207. Regina has the next period free, so they find a quiet spot and the postteaching conference begins.

Clinical Supervisor: Did anything happen in the class to keep you from teaching the way you had planned?

Regina: Just one. Those boys returning from their senior pictures came in very late, so I had to sign their late slips and get them going on the lesson. That put me behind a little, which made me uncomfortable. I wanted everything to go perfectly for this lesson!

Clinical Supervisor: Well, it was announced that they would be late, so you could have anticipated the problem and adjusted accordingly. However, you handled it well and I don't think it evolved into a major problem. Any other problems?

Regina: No, everything else went about the way I had planned.

Clinical Supervisor: OK, then let's take a look at the way your students spent their time in that lesson. They had 20% management, 10% lecture/demonstration, and 70% practice time. Some of the management time occurred when you had to handle the group of late students; that cost them about 3 or 4 minutes. Could that have been handled any differently?

Regina: Probably. I guess I could have told the rest of the class to begin their warm ups while I checked off those boys, instead of having the whole class wait until I was ready. I didn't think of it at the time, though.

Clinical Supervisor: Yes, remember that class time cannot be split between two separate activities; at least not the way we looked at it for that class. Every minute lost to management stays lost in terms of practice time. You must be constantly aware of how the time is being spent and be extremely protective of those practice minutes. You did do a nice job of reaching your lecture/demonstration goal, right at 10%. It was obvious to me that you planned

Multiple Observation of Student Teachers in Physical Education (MOST-PE)

Date __4-20-89__ Teacher __REGINA YOUNG__

Grade __10__ School __PATRICK HENRY HS__

Observer __G. KANODE__ Content __TENNIS - SERVE + RETURN__

Time Begin __9:05__ Time End __9:45__

Elapsed Time __40 mins.__ # Students __27__

Management	Lecture/Demonstration	Skill Practice
		WARM-UP
1 9:05 - 9:09 = 4	1 9:12 - 9:13 = 1	1 9:09 - 9:12 = 3
		SERVES
2 9:14 - 9:15 = 1	2 9:26 - 9:27 = 1	2 9:15 - 9:26 = 11
		SERVES
3 9:33 - 9:36 = 3	3 9:36 - 9:37 = 1	3 9:27 - 9:33 = 6
		W/ RETURNS
4 ___ - ___ = ___	4 9:41 - 9:42 = 1	4 9:37 - 9:41 = 4
		W/ RETURNS
5 ___ - ___ = ___	5 ___ - ___ = ___	5 9:42 - 9:45 = 3

__8__ mins = __20__% __4__ mins = __10__% __27__ mins = __70__%

Was management appropriate? Yes (No) Explain START ON TIME!

Feedback

	General	Specific (27)		Cues	Guidance
(43)				P P P P	
+ Skill	111 ₩₩ ₩₩ ₩₩ ₩₩	₩₩ ₩₩ 11	Verbal	WW PW W	PW P P WW
	₩₩ ₩₩ ₩₩	₩₩ ₩₩ (20)		W W W W W	
- Skill	(30) ₩₩ ₩₩ ₩₩	₩₩ ₩₩	Modeling	WW P P PW	W W
+ Non-Skill		111 (3)	Manipulative		P P P P P
- Non-Skill			Mediated		
+ Management		111 (3)	Other		
- Management		11 (2)		Whole (W) or Partial (P)	

GOOD RATE, but TOO MANY G's

__128__ Feedback = __3.2__ /min # __34__ Cues + Guidance = __~.8__ /min

First Names ₩₩ ₩₩ ₩₩ ₩₩ ₩₩ ₩₩ ₩₩ ₩₩ 111 (43) GREAT!

(Cont.)

MOST-PE (Continued)

PLACHECK 1 *SERVE DRILL 1*   PLACHECK 2 *SERVE DRILL 2*

1	2	3	4	5	6
E/A	E/A	E/A	E/A	E/A	E/A
23/21	25/22	21/21	27/24	21/21	23/23

1	2	3	4	5	6
E/A	E/A	E/A	E/A	E/A	E/A
25/20	25/19	25/21	21/20	21/20	21/21

PLACHECK 3 *W/RETURN*   PLACHECK 4 _____

1	2	3	4	5	6
E/A	E/A	E/A	E/A	E/A	E/A
24/22	22/20	22/19	24/21	23/22	23/23

1	2	3	4	5	6
E/A	E/A	E/A	E/A	E/A	E/A

% Motor Engaged = **86**   % Motor Appropriate = **80**

CONSISTENTLY HIGH MA AND ME - NICE JOB ON THIS

Content Development Graph

#_3_ Application

#_3_ Refinement

#_3_ Extension

#_1_ Information

NICE PROGRESSION - EVEN W/ SHORT PRACTICE SEGMENTS

Clarity of Information	1	2	3	4	5	6	7	8	(9)	10	NA
Task Orientation	1	2	3	4	5	6	7	8	9	(10)	NA
Enthusiasm	1	2	3	4	5	6	7	(8)	9	10	NA
Planning and Preparation	1	2	3	4	5	6	7	8	(9)	10	NA
_____	1	2	3	4	5	6	7	8	9	10	NA

Notes and Comments

- *PRACTICE SEGMENTS WERE A BIT SHORT (3-11 mins.)*
- *FB RATE WAS HIGH - MOSTLY GENERAL*
- *GET CLASS GOING, THEN DEAL W/ LATE-COMERS*

your demonstrations well and knew just what and how you wanted to show the students related to those four skills. To do four lecture/demonstrations in just 10% of class time is quite good. As you can see, I also rated you high on clarity; I saw students getting into the drills quickly, which is management information, and doing the tasks correctly from the start of each one, which is task information.

Regina: Yes, I really worked hard on that part of my lesson. It's something I can control totally myself, so getting ready is a bit easier.

Clinical Supervisor: Good point! Now, because you didn't meet your goal for management time, the student practice time had no chance to make the criterion, either. As we discussed, each kind of class time affects the other directly; you can't take back unproductive minutes and redistribute them in more effective ways! Had you made just one different management decision, you could have reached the students' practice time goal.

You overall feedback rate was 3.2 per minute. You exceeded the criterion goal of 2.5 per minute, but many of your feedback statements were general in nature, like "good job," "nice try," or "you missed." What were you thinking when you were giving students feedback in the class?

Regina: I wanted them to know I was paying attention to their shots, and I wanted to give them encouragement. I saw lots of students doing the skills well and I didn't want to overuse the same few feedback comments. After a while it sounds a bit phoney, so I just wanted to acknowledge their successes.

Clinical Supervisor: Your intentions were admirable, but I think you came to the wrong conclusion and course of action. You based that decision on your own perceptions of how it sounded rather than on some well accepted teaching theory about what students need in order to improve their performance. It might have sounded repetitious to you, but each individual student hears a certain kind of feedback much less often in a class! With about 100 feedback statements spread across 27 students, you can see that there is little chance of any one student hearing too many comments!

Regina: You are right. I should have been a bit more careful in my decision making. I never really thought of it that way.

Clinical Supervisor: To your credit, you made a conscious decision about your pattern of teaching; a decision that can easily be changed the next time you teach. All you need to do is change those generals to specifics and maintain the same overall rate. Moving on, your use of cues and guidance was quite good in the class. You did a nice job of varying the types of information you gave to students. You also circulated around the courts well, giving some information to nearly every student in the class. You provided them with good demonstrations and made clear explanations of how to do the skills, giving them nice models for all four skills. Keep that up.

Regina: Thanks. I guess that was related to the effort I made to plan my demonstrations carefully. I felt really comfortable with the content of the lesson. Also, that's the strongest part of my own tennis game!

Clinical Supervisor: Yes, that was apparent in every aspect related to presenting, demonstrating, and sequencing the learning tasks. Your content development progression looked nice, too. So, when the students got to practice the four tasks, they had a good chance to perform them well. That shows in the PLACHECKs for motor engagement, which were 86%, and motor appropriate, which were 80%. Those percentages indicate the *average percentage* of students who were actually practicing during drill segments and who were able to perform the tasks as you described, respectively. Those percentages are very high, especially for a tennis lesson.

Regina: Yes, they did work extremely hard today. Like I said a minute ago, I was confident I could give them a good picture of the skills, to help them get going faster and to perform the drills. It was neat to see so many of the students learning and enjoying themselves in a physical education class. It was a good feeling to watch it happen. I hope things go as well with my eighth period class!

Clinical Supervisor: Just remember that it went well for many reasons, mostly because of your planning and preparation. As you can see, I rated you very high on that item. Since we don't have time to cover the entire MOST-PE sheet, I'll leave it with you to read over the data and my notes. I assume you know how to interpret what's there.

Regina: Yes, I remember it from campus lab classes. I'll look it over when I get a chance; I'd really like to compare several of the items with performance from previous lessons you have monitored. I know I can always find places for improvement in my teaching.

Clinical Supervisor: When you're finished looking over it, I'd like you to do a little assignment for tomorrow. Using the same nine items of teaching we set goals for today, I'd like you to project your own set of goals for the same period tomorrow. I think you have an idea of what's possible in that class, now let's see if you can meet your expectations, not mine!

Regina: That sounds like a good challenge. I'll think about those goals and even more about how I can meet or beat them. There is always room to get better! The area that comes to mind right away is my feedback to students.

Clinical Supervisor: Even though you've done well in almost every area so far, that is a good attitude to have. Any final comments?

Regina: Just one question. When does good teaching start to be easier to do consistently? I know I'm doing well, but it's really hard work at times.

Clinical Supervisor: I was well into my second year of full-time teaching before things became more automatic. Usually, it gets easier and more enjoyable in small steps, until one day you realize you have been doing a good job without struggling over so many of the decisions and actions you make now. I think you are well on your way to that point but do know that it will take time to get there.

Regina: Well, I can't wait for that time to arrive! Thanks for the help.

Summary

The student-to-teacher transformation is the central goal of supervision during the student teaching stage. For teachers, it is marked by a clear change in environment (i.e., from campus to school) and a growing set of expectations and responsibilities. This is often their first extensive opportunity to display the effective teaching skills they have learned in the preservice stage. Supervisors need to keep in mind that this is a developmental experience as well as a culminating one—student teachers are just beginning, and like other beginners, they need to progress gradually in this new setting.

These scenarios illustrate the beginning of a shift in the supervisor/teacher interaction. In the early part of student teaching, the supervisor takes a somewhat more direct approach, making most of the decisions that guide the focus and conduct of the supervisory visit. The later interaction depicts much more involvement by the student teacher in what will be monitored, what the observation data mean, how to improve in areas of need, and what future performance goals will be. The supervisor still makes many decisions, but they are more subtle and almost always involve asking the student teacher for opinions. This shift becomes somewhat evident during the student teaching stage but needs to be even more pronounced as the teacher advances into the induction years.

Chapter 10

Supervision for Induction Teachers

Although the induction stage is sometimes considered to begin during the formal student teaching experience (Feiman-Nemser, 1983), this book treats this stage as starting with a teacher's first full-time position. The end of the induction period is more difficult to pinpoint and is generally defined in terms of one's preparedness to comfortably assume the complete range of instructional, professional, and socialization responsibilities expected of an effective and autonomous teacher. For a few teachers that time comes early in their first year; for a few other teachers that time never arrives. Most teachers who remain in the teaching force achieve this high degree of comfort and effectiveness by the end of their second or third year. But it is important to recognize the end of the induction period in terms of effectiveness and abilities, not merely accumulation of experience and time. For a long time teacher educators assumed that survival of the first year or two was tantamount to full induction, and that a teacher who achieved this needed less instructional and professional support; supervisors today should not make that same mistake.

Teaching during the induction stage can be described in many ways; the most appropriate labels reflect *learning* and *autonomy*. New teachers learn much as they progress through their induction period. They learn about teaching as both a profession and a way of life, plus they learn how to teach in ways that address specific contexts molded by community, school, department, colleagues, curriculum, administrators, and, of course, students. This stage is a time when performance affects attitudes toward teaching, career enjoyment, and many professional choices, while the idiosyncracies of one's environment greatly influence teaching effectiveness.

Effective supervision for induction cannot ignore the role context plays; indeed, effective supervisory strategies must be highly context specific at this stage. However, supervisors cannot anticipate what a specific context might be or how it will influence supervision for an individual teacher. So, this chapter suggests general approaches to instructional supervision appropriate for the induction stage itself.

The second feature of the induction stage is teacher autonomy. Very early in the induction, a teacher realizes how this stage differs from student teaching, when a cooperating teacher, clinical supervisor, or university supervisor observes nearly everything the young teacher does. Student teachers do teach independently to an extent but are almost always monitored in some way. Several sources of support are always close by in case of questions, problems, emergencies, or successes! The scrutiny and its accompanying security are constant.

Neither monitoring nor support are available with such regularity during the physical educator's induction period. Much of what induction teachers learn and experience occurs within isolation, demanding that new teachers function on their own almost regardless of the situation. Induction teachers must learn to make autonomous decisions and to take instructional actions; rarely do they teach under a watchful eye. So new teachers must learn ways to improve their instructional skills largely on their own. They receive instructional supervision from others only infrequently, even in the best of mentoring programs.

Characteristics of Induction Teacher Supervision

While no two induction teachers proceed through this stage in the same way, some general observations about induction physical educators and the role supervision must play for them can be drawn. Because of the great variety of situations in which new teachers find themselves, these characteristics do not hold true in every case. But, they can provide supervisors with some general viewpoints on which to base their role until the specifics of each teacher's situation become more apparent.

Experimenting With Instructional Strategies

Supervisors should encourage induction teachers to continue experimenting with various instructional strategies. In order for a teacher's instructional skill repertoire to continue to develop, the teacher must perceive the process of learning how to teach as ongoing. New teachers should constantly explore viable patterns of effective teaching and learning practices from which to choose the best one in given situations. This process of exploration can help to break the debilitating cycle of teachers teaching the way they were taught.

Supervisors should discourage induction teachers from seeking and adopting expeditious strategies with only limited effectiveness over time and situations. The acquisition of a lasting repertoire of instructional skills is a lengthy process; the teacher should not adopt the first technique that works, just to save time.

Selecting and retaining the very first practice from any group of potential choices risks molding a highly inflexible pattern of instruction that may prove detrimental across time and changes in context. Supervisors should encourage new teachers to find many different ways to instruct effectively rather than settle for a single way to accomplish their goals.

Induction teachers should be able to make informed decisions about effective patterns of instruction based on available data, feedback from students, and interactions with colleagues and mentors. The supervisory process at this stage should be a part of, and should facilitate, efforts to provide teachers with many sources of information about their effectiveness. Having such information, induction teachers can be better apprised of their performance in meaningful and diverse ways.

Learning Their Context

New teachers should learn quickly the context in which they teach and those factors that will impact their instructional program. They need to learn how context influences their potential effectiveness as a physical educator and how to formulate sound decisions and patterns within that context. In addition, induction teachers should be advised to recognize the difference between *alterable* and *unalterable* contextual features in their programs. Knowing what is within and outside one's power to change can help new teachers make realistic assessments of their situations and channel their energies in a productive way.

Learning Routines

Induction teachers should establish routines that promote effective teaching while reducing cumbersome managerial requirements. Effective, experienced teachers have learned how to function in their school and program with a minimum of wasted time and energy. This often means they know how to simplify, organize, economize, and sometimes even ignore managerial tasks that reduce their available attention for instructional tasks. Supervisors should play a key role in this process by combining viable suggestions from personal experience with common professional practices.

Designing an Instructional Supervision Plan

Each new physical education teacher should have an instructional supervision plan. Such a plan is the responsibility of the new teacher and the person charged with his or her instructional supervision—mentor, building administrator, curriculum supervisor, or colleague. This plan should include an outline of known strengths, areas in need of improvement, criteria for identified performance parameters, and the necessary supervisory support to help the teacher reach those goals. The development of a new physical educator's instructional skills should not be left to unsystematic efforts; too often, that means skills will not be developed at all.

Using Several Supervisors

Plans for instructional improvement should be based on a combination of supervision from self, peers, administrators, and mentors during the first 2 years of teaching. The systematic development of teaching skills must be viewed as the responsibility of several people through a concerted effort. All of the personnel just mentioned have much to offer the supervisory process for induction teachers; those supervisory personnel resources should not be underused or ignored.

Continuing to Develop Teaching Skills

Teaching performance in the induction stage should reflect a continuation of the skills acquired in the preservice and student teaching stages, as well as those skills necessary for successful performance and retention within the state and district. States and school districts in increasing numbers are delineating a set of their own *preferred teaching skills* from which to base important decisions on teacher retention and promotion. New teachers must be fully aware of all performance criteria and be provided with opportunities to practice those skills prior to formal assessment. New teachers should be assisted to identify contradictions between the skills they learned in the preservice stage and evaluation/assessment items outlined by their local or state agencies; a new teacher accomplishes little by displaying teaching practices not preferred by those who evaluate him or her for retention or renewed certification. Supervisors (peers, mentors, or administrators) should become acquainted with the focus, instrumentation, and standards in place for new teachers and should periodically monitor those instructional skills for induction teachers.

Scenarios for Induction Teacher Supervision

Supervision for induction teachers faces a serious dilemma; while most people accept that new teachers need lots of assistance in those first 2 or 3 years, few schools provide such assistance. Ironically, new teachers are surrounded by teachers and administrators who know much about teaching and would make excellent supervisors. The problem is getting those experienced and expert people in meaningful contact with the new teacher.

Instructional supervision for the induction stage most likely needs to be performed by personnel already in the teacher's school. Central office personnel or university personnel cannot provide the necessary frequency and interactions needed for this stage. So, supervision must be provided by another teacher in the building or by the induction teacher himself or herself. The first scenario depicts how a neophyte can work independently to improve his teaching skills, keeping the focus and analysis simple and limited. The second scenario involves a mentoring arrangement for a new teacher; this is actually a conversation between the mentor and new teacher, who are discussing how the teacher can improve her teaching. It illustrates that much of the assistance provided by the mentor will be *indirect* because mentors have their own classes to teach as well. However, the topics raised and the mentor's willingness to show the teacher that her struggle is a common one can help to improve her teaching.

■ *Scenario 1:* Self-supervision of verbal instructional processes   ■

Even though systematic self-supervision represents a direct and promising way for teachers to improve their instructional skills, it must be practiced under many limitations. The most serious limitation stems from the fact that a teacher cannot actively instruct during a class and successfully monitor complex teaching/learning processes simultaneously. In addition, new teachers do not have much time away from class to devote to extensive data analyses. However, periodic attention to just one or two performance aspects, combined with some personal analyses and reflection, is both possible and beneficial for new teachers.

One self-supervision technique centers around the use of a small, audiotape recorder, which is belted to the teacher's waist to record verbal statements made in class. Such tape recorders are small enough to be worn comfortably without distracting the teacher or students. The teacher starts the recorder at the beginning of class and lets it run for the duration of the period. After class the teacher plays back the audiotape and monitors his or her verbal statements with the PEIIS. Some statements will not be understandable from the audio recording and will be lost for PEIIS coding; this is to be expected and presents no serious obstacle to the success of this technique.

A PEIIS data sheet coded from an audio tape is shown on page 216. The verbal statements were made in a 40-minute seventh grade archery lesson in a class with 24 students. The teacher, Greg, had 12 targets, 12 bows, and about 60 arrows available. The lesson took place near the end of the archery unit, with the students attempting to hit balloons attached randomly on each of the targets. All of the students stood 40 feet from the targets for shooting. The students relocated to the physical education field, warmed up, inflated four balloons each, and began practice. Two students shot at each target simultaneously, with each group of 12 rotating for turns. Greg gave the signals for starting each end and for retrieving arrows when all students at the line were finished. Students were allowed to shoot at their own pace after each end began. Greg kept this simple rotation pattern throughout the class and circulated freely during each end to provide students with ample skill instruction.

Physical Education Instructional Information System (PEIIS)

Date __1-21-89__   Teacher __GREG HARTMAN__

Grade __7__   School __MOUNTAIN LAKE JR. HS__

Observer __SELF__   Content __ARCHERY-Balloon TARGETS__

Time Begin __8:40__   Time End __9:20__

Elapsed Time __40 MINS.__   # Students __24__
__(25 min. PRACTICE TIME)__

Type	Cues Whole	Partial	Type	Guidance Whole	Partial
Verbal	₩ III	II	Verbal	IIII	₩ / ₩ ₩
Model Before		₩ ₩ /	Model Along		II
Manipulative			Manipulative		III
Mediated			Mediated		
Other			Other		
Totals	8	13	Totals	4	20

Feedback [Code Verbal (V) or Nonverbal (N)]

	Skill Attempt	Non-Skill Attempt	Totals
+ General	₩ ₩ II (37) ₩ ₩ ₩ ₩ ₩	∅	37
- General	₩ IIII (9)	∅	9
+ Specific	IIII (4)	∅	4
- Specific	₩ ₩ ₩ III (18)	∅	18

Total Feedback __68__ / __40__ Elapsed Time = Feedback Rate __1.7__ / min

Skill Feedback __68__ / ~__25__ Practice Time = Skill Rate ~__2.7__ / min

Use of Student First Name __DIDN'T COUNT THEM__ = ____ Times

While examining the PEIIS record made from the class and its resulting analyses, Greg proceeds through several sequences of

$$Question \rightarrow Evidence \rightarrow Self\text{-}Analysis$$

for his verbal instructional statements in that lesson. This sequence allows him to self-supervise by asking the kind of questions another person supervising his classes might have asked.

Question: What was the total frequency of instructional information in that class, including cues, guidance, and feedback?

Evidence: The total was 68, a rate of about 1.7 per minute.

Self-Analysis: It sure seemed like I was giving more information than that in class! And if I count just the instructional minutes which total about 25, that rate goes to 2.7 per minute, which is still below the range I'd like to have in my teaching.

Question: What was my skill feedback rate, and how were my feedback statements distributed across generals and specifics?

Evidence: My skill feedback rate was 2.7 per minute, with 68% general comments and only 32% specific ones.

Self-Analysis: Even though I tried to provide more specific feedback, I fell into a bad pattern of just acknowledging where the arrows went rather than why students got certain results. I need to reduce that tendency and change many of those to specifics. Maybe I can keep asking myself, "Now, what was good or bad about that shot I just saw?" and then just tell the student that information.

Question: How many non-skill feedback statements did I direct to students?

Evidence: None.

Self-Analysis: I was so busy trying to keep the class moving along that I forgot to interact with them in any other way! They were behaving very well that period, and I should have taken the opportunity to acknowledge that to the class. Yes, especially to that group of do-nothings who actually dressed out and participated today. I must remember to do that tomorrow, if they behave as well again. I really missed a chance to communicate with them about good behavior; better make a mental note for next class.

Question: What was my pattern for providing cues and guidance to that class?

Evidence: My cues were mostly modeling of partial tasks, and my guidance was mostly verbal statements on partial tasks.

Self-Analysis: That was pretty much the way I have planned them, to demonstrate certain features of the shot in isolation for individual students and to then make *adjustments* while they were in the shooting position. It doesn't seem to be helpful to let them finish a shot before making adjustments. I think it's best to get them into the correct shooting position before releasing the arrow, even if they must hold it for a few more seconds. That seemed to work well; the students I spent time with had a good success rate on those shots because they got the proper feel before the release. I should remember to do that all the time.

Question: What do I need to work on from here?

Evidence: Increased skill feedback, along with a reduction in general statements.

Self-Analysis: Maybe writing down a few specific feedback examples on my lesson plan will prompt me to give more feedback, especially more of the right kind of feedback. I think I'll also monitor my content development the next time I get a chance to audio tape a class.

■ *Scenario 2:* Supervision from a mentor ■

Some states and local school districts have in recent years initiated mentoring programs for new teachers. Early indications substantiate both the need and the value of assigning a new teacher directly to a model, veteran teacher. In a unique approach, New York City schools have successfully trained and deployed retired teachers to serve in this capacity, recognizing them as an untapped resource for this important function (Pepin & Sardy, 1987). Even though retired teachers might not know the specific context for each new teacher, they do have the time to spend observing both the school and the induction teacher more often than in-house mentors who must teach their own classes during the school day.

Regardless of who the mentor is, that person must be trained to deliver a complete range of supervisory functions and be available to carry them out on a regular basis. Mentors must help new teachers through many problems, both personal and professional. They must also be trained to help new teachers improve their instructional effectiveness. Both roles are important, and mentors must find ways to identify and resolve problems that stem from learning to teach and learning about teaching.

In many cases, mentoring for instructional improvement in this stage can be pursued in ways similar to those described for preservice and student teachers; the diagnostic and prescriptive processes of supervision do not vary. Rather than repeating those familiar scenarios, the following one depicts a conversation between a first year teacher and her mentor, who is trying to uncover some general problems contributing to ineffective instruction recently observed. The teacher, Marian, is a certified 9-12 physical educator, in the fifth month of her first school year. Her mentor, Jerry, teaches physical education in the same school; he is a 12-year veteran who has been formally trained as a mentor teacher. They teach in a middle-class, suburban high school with a racially mixed population of 1,200 students.

The need for this conversation has arisen from Marian's recent inability to demonstrate adequate control in her classes. The problem has not reached crisis proportions; however, the mentor has expressed his concerns and comments to alert her that continued failure may lead to much more serious problems in the future. This is not intended to be a formal supervisory interaction but rather a hallway conversation that might help the new teacher.

Mentor: I'm glad we could get this free period to talk a little. Do you mind if we spend some time discussing how things have been going recently? As you know, my last four or five observations of your teaching indicated a few mounting problems, and I don't want them to get out of control.

Marian: I don't mind at all. In fact, I was hoping we could discuss some of those same things myself, lately. Where would you like to begin?

Mentor: Let's start with some general observations I've made about your teaching. It seems to me that you've been very uncomfortable in class lately. I have observed this from the beginning of the year, but really thought you'd be over it by now. Do the students make you nervous?

Marian: No, it's not that. In fact, so far I've had a lot fewer discipline problems than I expected; after all, this is not the best school in the district! My discomfort comes more from not being able to anticipate during class; it seems like I'm not getting the feel of things yet. Sometimes I don't see potential managerial problems until they happen; other times I lose track of how the time is going and class ends before I want it to. It seems like I'm always one step behind, no matter how hard I try to keep up.

Mentor: How much time do you spend planning for each class?

Marian: About 10 or 15 minutes.

Mentor: I know we're supposed to hand weekly lesson plans to the department head. Do you plan more than the brief outlines most of us turn in?

Marian: Not usually. I don't have much time to write formal lesson plans, so I typically just expand my weekly entries and make some notes on a card before classes. Isn't that what everyone else does?

Mentor: Yes, but the rest of us have been teaching those units for several years! I think it would be helpful to increase your planning time, make more complete plans, and carry them with you into classes. The time you take to do that will easily be gained back in productive class time and should reduce many of your frustrations. If you like, I can review your lessons at night, if you get them to me the day before. Will that help?

Marian: Yes, I'm sure it will. I hope some of my mistakes and omissions will be obvious so you can alert me to them before I use the plans in class.

Mentor: Okay. Let's try that. My recent observations of your teaching have also detected a sort of good and bad pattern emerging in your instruction. The positive part is that you circulate around the gym quite well and get to nearly every student at some time during class. You really motor around!

However, this has resulted in a sort of hit-and-run tendency for providing students with instructional information. Do you know what an *information chain* is?

Marian: No, I don't.

Mentor: It's a sequence of related pieces of information provided to one or more students who need some extra attention. A typical chain begins with *cues* on important features of the skill being practiced; cues can be verbal or nonverbal. Once the student has received a sufficient number of cues, he or she tries the task while the teacher watches specific parts related to the previous cues. If the teacher sees something that needs adjusting during a task, she gives *guidance* information to help the student right when the task is being attempted. Following each attempt, the teacher provides *feedback* to help the student know how well the task was done. If necessary, the teacher provides more cues and the student makes more monitored attempts at the task. The idea is for the teacher to stay with that student until the task is performed correctly.

Marian: If I use that kind of pattern, I would then be ignoring the rest of the students for the benefit of a few, or just one! Is that right for a teacher to do?

Mentor: That's a legitimate question! My own feeling is that the hit and run approach helps no students improve their skills; at least information chains have a better chance of helping a few students during each class. It's a tough call, Marian, but sometimes we need to make those kinds of decisions. I feel more comfortable paying increased attention to students who really need it rather than trying to get around to the whole class in a superficial way. How do you feel?

Marian: I like the idea of information chains but would rather search for ways to use them and still let my students know I am aware of them all during class. Maybe the answer is better use of my gym aides. I could teach them to take more than just managerial responsibilities, and they could work with those students who need the extra attention. That would free me from having to motor around, as you put it, and allow me to work on providing students with some information chains.

Mentor: Great idea! I think that will work well and make noticeable improvements in your classes right away. Can we discuss just one more thing before you must go to hall duty?

Marian: Sure, but I'd gladly get someone to cover it for me!

Mentor (Jokingly): You don't like hall duty? It's the highlight of some teachers' day!

Marian: Actually, it's another one of those things that put me behind during the day. I rarely get a few quiet moments for myself to collect my thoughts and grab a bit of mental R and R. Hall duty is so loud and public. It is the part of the school day I dislike most of all. Even in-school suspension is better;

at least I can sit down for a few minutes. And, because most of the students are asleep during it, it's pretty quiet!

Mentor: I realize those extra duties are taxing and distracting, but we all share them equally. If someone is relieved of those duties, another person on the staff must make up for it. I'm afraid there's not much we can do; all I can recommend is that you hang in there and try not to make the assigned duties any more aversive by complaining too much.

Marian: OK, I'll try. Getting back to your final point, what was that about? Hall duty awaits!

Mentor: Just a few comments, actually. I have enjoyed watching you teach so far this year. You came highly recommended and show signs of having solid teaching skills. Obviously, you learned much in your university program and in student teaching. Part of my job as your mentor is to help you maintain those skills in order to strengthen our own program for the students' benefit. From time to time I'll tell you things you don't like hearing, but that's part of my job, too. Right now I think you need to know that you are in a critical period; after a strong start with your teaching I have observed some troublesome signs of washout in your instructional skills. We can work together to reverse this trend, to get you over this hump in a way that will allow you the enthusiasm and desire to be a consistently good teacher. I think that teaching physical education effectively is the hardest job in any school; doing it poorly is among the easiest. I am confident that you want to be an effective teacher, but that you are a bit overwhelmed by it all right now.

Part of becoming more comfortable as a teacher is teaching better. Lots of problems take care of themselves when you feel good about your teaching and when you see your students achieving regularly. Most of us started out hoping to help students learn more; unfortunately, few end up staying for that same reason. I'd like that to be your reason for a long career as a physical educator, and I'll do my best to see that you get the support, advice, and supervision necessary for a good start. I just wanted you to know that, and to remind you once again to let me know when I can help with anything. OK?

Marian: Thanks. Please know that I appreciate your efforts so far, and I do look forward to a long career as a teacher, a coach, and even a hall monitor! It's just so difficult at times. But, I will take you up on your advice and work on those things we discussed to improve my teaching. Got to go.

Summary

It seems very easy to let induction teachers slip through the cracks of even the best-intentioned supervisory efforts. Everyone knows who they are and where they teach and acknowledges the isolated struggles they must endure in those early years in the profession. However, providing these teachers with good supervisory personnel and support in most situations is not an easy task. Schools are great places for learning about teaching and about how to teach; the irony of that statement is that little of what teachers learn is acquired systematically or through much direct participation with the best available resource—other teachers! Supervision for the induction stage must work on two fronts at once: to help teachers become more independent in their attempts to instruct better and to have in place the support mechanisms needed when self-supervision is not adequate.

These two scenarios depict both of these key functions of supervision at this stage. Even though the potential is somewhat limited, self-supervision is likely to be the kind most often available to new teachers; they cannot always wait for others to help them learn the early lessons of teaching in schools. The second scenario shows the importance of an experienced teacher working with a new teacher when one of those rare opportunities does happen. The common tie between both scenarios is the use of a systematic plan for improving teaching skills, regardless of who implements it. New teachers need to have some direction for their efforts to improve instructional effectiveness, that direction is best provided by another, experienced teacher. However, the reality of life as a teaching professional will often place that responsibility with the new teacher alone, and can play a significant role in his or her development.

Chapter 11

Supervision for Veteran Teachers

Differing from other stages on the developmental continuum, the beginning of the veteran stage is an elusive point and should not be defined merely by the number of years of teaching service. Entry into the veteran stage is marked by the establishment of mostly stable professional attitudes, dispositions toward teaching, and patterns of instructional skills. Experienced teachers have learned both the positive and negative aspects of teaching, schools, and life as a teacher.

Entry into the veteran stage is typified more by constancy than by uniformly beneficial learning experiences. For some physical educators at this stage, the primary motivation for remaining in the teaching force is not teaching at all (Lawson, 1983); rather, advancement as a coach or aspiration to administrative appointments keep them on the job. This reality must figure into the delivery mechanism of any physical education supervisor who wishes to work with veteran teachers for improved instructional skills.

The most obvious characterization of veteran physical educators is their constancy; over the years they have typically narrowed their patterns of instructional behavior considerably and can be quite resistant to some suggested changes. If their performance has gone for many years without analysis and comment of any kind (especially negative), veteran teachers can interpret supervisory suggestions as indicators of inadequacy. Most veteran teachers have honed a repertoire of instructional behaviors over the years. These repertoires seemingly have served them well, helping them survive the induction years and winning them some degree of respect from students, administrators, and colleagues. If a teacher's patterns have served well enough to allow entry into the veteran stage, these patterns have passed a test of time that is strong enough to foster indefinite continuation of them. The fact that most current veteran teachers had little systematic assistance from others in the acquisition of those skills further adds to this constancy.

Throughout this book, the overriding rationale for identifying, diagnosing, and making prescriptions for physical education teaching/learning processes has been the relationship to student learning. Teachers are considered more effective when they perform certain instructional functions that allow students to interact with the subject matter in specified ways. Therefore, instructional supervision should attempt to develop those effective teaching patterns in physical education classes. However, some evidence indicates that teachers, especially veteran teachers, do not view effectiveness as the most important criterion for determining good teaching and good teachers. When asked, "What, in your mind, describes a good physical education teacher?" most veteran physical educators will probably list personal characteristics as more important than effective teaching/learning processes cited by teacher educators, researchers, and supervisors (Metzler & Reif, 1986). The dilemma for the supervisor is apparent; while the supervisor prepares to monitor and focus upon a discrete set of teaching skills recognized in the literature as being important, veteran teachers often expect to be monitored for and to later discuss quite different things!

Characteristics of Veteran Teacher Supervision

Undoubtedly, supervisors face their biggest challenge in promoting changes with veteran teachers. This is not meant to be a criticism of veteran teachers; few of them have had opportunities to become acquainted with the constructs of effective teaching for physical education, and few of them have ever needed these skills for advancement in their professional careers. So, in many instances veteran teachers lack adequate motivation to be supervised and to alter their instructional practices.

If supervision for veteran physical educators is to be effective, those involved must recognize some common characteristics between veteran teachers and supervisors as well as the uniqueness of this developmental stage. With fewer teachers remaining in the teaching force past the initial 5 years of service, this cadre of physical educators represents an ever-diminishing and ever-important human resource for our school programs. We cannot afford to ignore their completed years of service or their needs and wishes to improve instructional skills, despite the formidable obstacles hindering supervision at this stage.

Dealing With Existing Instructional Patterns

Veteran teachers generally possess a narrow and highly pragmatic set of instructional skills. The supervisor must recognize that patterns are a mostly fixed part of a teacher's instructional repertoire. In some ways it is easier to work with new teachers, who are acquiring certain teaching patterns for the first time; veteran teachers must not only learn new patterns but must give up existing patterns as well. Effective supervision at this stage must take into account those existing patterns of teaching skills. Attempts to radically restructure a teacher's entire instructional repertoire are not necessary; many veteran teachers who wish to improve merely need updating and refinement of instructional skills.

Resisting Supervisory Assistance

Veteran teachers may resist supervisory efforts that ignore or challenge instructional repertoires already in place. Therefore, supervisory changes must take place within the existing framework of how each teacher instructs rather than by externally imposing entirely new patterns. Veteran teachers are less likely than younger teachers to change schools and contexts often. Much of what they know about teaching has been learned in their school; therefore supervisors must base interactions and suggestions on that context in order to increase supervisory effectiveness.

Becoming Familiar With Effective Teaching Practice

Veteran teachers are not likely to be familiar with the literature on effective teaching in general and particularly in physical education. More likely, their personal opinions about good teaching are radically different than those held by supervisors who are acquainted with and work to develop effective teaching/learning processes in the gym. Further, supervision will probably not be successful in changing veteran teachers opinions about good teaching but may affect their willingness to implement a few new practices.

Establishing Credibility

Veteran teachers are sensitive not only to supervision in general but also to the source of supervision. Supervisors must hold demonstrable credibility in the eyes of veteran teachers; often this credibility is based on actual teaching experience in or familiarity with public school contexts. Supervisors should not automatically assume that veteran teachers will wish to work with or cooperate with them; that willingness must be established before any supervisory interactions can be meaningful and effective.

Sharing the Supervisory Responsibility

Supervisors and veteran teachers must share responsibility for making meaningful changes in instructional skill patterns. Efforts to improve instructional skills will be more successful if the veteran teacher identifies and values the need for assistance personally and becomes a full partner in the process.

Through their many years in service, veteran teachers recognize aspects of their performance that need supervisory assistance; supervision must facilitate teachers' efforts to improve selected parts of their instructional repertoires.

Most veteran teachers hold strongly positive perceptions of their teaching; for many reasons, they believe themselves to be good and effective. By virtue of their experience and their comfort in the teaching role, veteran teachers probably have a greater opinion of their abilities than do other teachers. Supervision must construct a framework for improvement that does not diminish or contest those notions of efficacy. Successful supervision does *not* have to tear down in order to build back up.

A Scenario for Veteran Teacher Supervision

Because many veteran teachers are sensitive to the reasons for supervision and to the supervisor as well, the use of peers in systematic efforts to improve instructional skills is often helpful. By virtue of their own experience, familiarity with contextual factors, and acquaintance with the teacher, peers have a unique position from which to monitor, diagnose, and prescribe patterns for instructional improvement. Of course, this implies that the peer supervisor has been sufficiently trained to deliver the necessary functions for maximum impact; merely having one teacher watch another will not likely result in any significant change for either one.

The following scenario depicts a series of events in which two colleagues from the same high school physical education department work together in a teacher-supervisor capacity. The designated teacher and supervisor roles they play are temporary and can be reversed at another time. This role reversal feature of peer supervision provides unique opportunities for both to develop as effective teachers in a reciprocal relationship. This epitomizes the best in professional improvement efforts by physical education teachers.

The scenario characterizes two teachers who have a strong and positive working relationship; that fact should not be overlooked or minimized. Surely, developing the relationship depicted in the scenario—two teachers who agree to such an arrangement and trust each other's professional expertise—would require some time. In that sense, the scenario is somewhat idealized, and it needs to be; if the teachers were not cooperative and sharing, there would be no supervisory scenario to present! One of the underlying points in this scenario is that current patterns of collegial interaction must be changed to allow peer supervision to take place and work.

■ *Scenario:* **Peer supervision for a veteran teacher** ■

Cheryl, the veteran teacher in this scenario, has been a high school physical educator at the same school for all of her 13 years of service. Laura, in the role of peer supervisor, has been teaching physical education for 9 years, most of them at the current school. Both teachers work in the same department in a small rural high school and share assignments for students in grades 10 through 12. While they frequently discuss curricular and organizational matters about their program, Laura and Cheryl periodically help each other at their teaching. Both teachers have completed training in the delivery of supervisory functions and use that training with student teachers and for each other's benefit. The first part of the scenario takes place just before school begins, as Laura tries to help Cheryl isolate a recent problem in her classes.

Laura: A few days ago I heard you say you were having difficulty getting students on task and keeping them that way during skill practice time. Are you still having that problem?

Cheryl: Yes, and I think it might be getting even a little worse.

Laura: Are you having trouble in all of your classes, or just certain ones?

Cheryl: Most classes are going quite well except for my two gymnastics classes.

Laura: Can you pinpoint the problem? What about those gymnastics classes isn't going as well as you'd like?

Cheryl: As you know, both are advanced gymnastics classes; students can get into them only after passing beginning gymnastics. We covered all of the Olympic apparatus and events in the first 3 weeks of the term. Now they have the option of working on any two apparatus or events during each class. After warm ups I divide the class into two equal practice segments and they are supposed to choose one station for each half of the period.

Laura: That sounds OK. What is the problem?

Cheryl: It seems that they work hard for the first few minutes of each segment, then slack off for the rest of the time. After those initial minutes of each segment I see lots of standing around, lots of conversing, and lots of what Tousignant and Siedentop [1983] called competent bystanding. Because I need to spot students some of the time, I can't pay attention to everything that's going on in the gymnastics room at all times. I guess they use my focused attention in one place to detach themselves from practice on their apparatus or event.

Laura: What do you do when you see them not working?

Cheryl: I've tried lots of things. At first I ignored some of it, because they were getting reacquainted with some of the stations. I then asked them quietly and calmly to get back to work. Eventually that failed, so I resorted to scolding and nagging them periodically to keep them practicing. That strategy backfired, sad to say.

Laura: What happened?

Cheryl: My public, negative approach caused them to become uncomfortable and defensive.

Laura: Uh oh, I think I know what's coming next!

Cheryl: I'm sure you guessed it. The responded to my hard approach with one of their own, eventually talking back to me. After a while I was forced into even harder responses, like giving class conduct point deductions and in-school suspension for the most serious offenders. I'm now afraid that my original problem of low engagement time has become a full-blown discipline problem! What can I do?

Laura: The first thing I need to do is see one of these classes in person. It's difficult to say from your description what the problem, or problems, might be. Can I sit in on your gymnastics classes tomorrow?

Cheryl: Sure. I have one third period and one seventh period.

Laura: How about if I come into the third period class and just make some general observations? I'll stay way out of the way and won't bother you or the students. If they ask, just tell them I'm sitting in to brush up on my own gymnastics teaching. I'm sure they won't mind or change their behavior on my account. If I get a lead on something, we can check it out more closely during your seventh period class. Sound OK?

Cheryl: Sure. See you third period tomorrow.

Cheryl's third period class is made up of 18 tenth graders, 12 girls and 6 boys. The class meets in a utility room temporarily converted for gymnastics with a floor exercise mat, two uneven parallel bars, two vaulting horses, one regulation balance beam, four low balance beams, and one high bar. Cheryl has set up all the equipment according to safety standards, with plenty of room at and between each separate station. The class has 50 minutes of instruction time. The first 10 minutes are spent completing a warm up routine to the sound of popular music; one student is designated to bring the day's music to class. All seems to be going well during these preliminary activities, with Cheryl conversing freely among the students. With 40 minutes left for practicing, Cheryl informs the class that they will have two 20-minute time segments. For each segment they are to select one station (apparatus, event, or tumbling) and to work on whatever they wish during that time. Cheryl asks them to stay on task and tells them she will be around to help students individually.

Laura sees no cause for alarm in her observation of the warm up period. In fact, she is quite impressed by the relaxed atmosphere in those early minutes. She writes that in her notes and begins to observe students as they select and proceed to their first practice stations. The students all begin working diligently at their respective stations, just as Cheryl predicted they would. All of them start by doing simple stunts and adjusting the apparatus for their own use. The room contains only the sounds of students exerting themselves and Cheryl interacting occasionally with individual students. After about 5 minutes, the room gets somewhat louder, as students begin to disengage from their practice stations and start conversing among themselves. At all of the disengaged stations the students are discussing what they want to practice next and how to set up for spotting, stunts, and sharing of the apparatus. It becomes apparent to Laura that the students have been given no specific instructions for structuring their time within the practice segment.

On further observation Laura notes that the students have been provided with no task cues, no task progressions, and no direction for task accountability from Cheryl; in effect, they are truly on their own during the practice segment, with no expectations other than to stay busy for the 20 minutes. Once they exhaust their limited repertoire of stunts at each station, they don't know where or how to proceed for continued skill development. With Cheryl attending to other students across the room, they lack direction and soon disengage from their practice. Quite naturally, many of them lose interest in their stations and begin to socialize or misbehave with their partners. Once Cheryl notices this off-task activity, she then initiates disciplinary action, setting off the familiar pattern of teacher and student confrontation described previously to Laura.

The class atmosphere has now changed noticeably and rather quickly. What began as a relaxed class with much promise for teacher and students has deteriorated into an unpleasant series of behavior management episodes. After a brief respite during the first minutes of the second practice segment, the pattern continues until the end of class. As in recent days, Cheryl is left wondering what went wrong and turns to Laura after the class for her observations and comments. She has taken lots of notes during the class and seems to have some notion of why Cheryl is experiencing these consistent problems.

Laura: That class had the same pattern you described to me earlier; lots of engagement in the beginning, then a steady dropping off as the class progressed. The atmosphere at the start was very upbeat and enthusiastic for you and the students. I really like your idea of letting one student bring in the day's music; I'm going to try that myself. The students obviously enjoyed that part of the class.

Cheryl: Yes, that seems to go over well. It's the rest of the class that troubles me.

Laura: Well, I may have a handle on the problem but would like to check it further in your seventh period class. Do you mind if I come in again later today?

Cheryl: Of course not. Can you share with me your thoughts so far?

Laura: If you can wait just one more class period, I'd like to confirm some of the things I noted this past period and get some measures of engagement and motor appropriate practicing. I'm afraid of jumping to conclusions right now. I'd like to monitor the seventh period class with the ALT-PEP recording system. Do you remember it from our supervision training workshops?

Cheryl: Yes. Doesn't it monitor how many students are actually practicing and having success at learning tasks during class? But I already know that not enough students are practicing their skills in those gymnastics classes.

Laura: That's true, but along with hopefully confirming some of my observations from the past period, I'll be able to get a picture of the extent of the problem. That will help us see how well you improve after we discuss some solutions and courses of action. I realize I'm putting you off a bit, but it will be for just one more gymnastics class. We can get together after seventh period to discuss some things we might do to help the situation.

Cheryl: OK. See you seventh period.

Cheryl has 20 students in her seventh period class, 12 girls and 8 boys. She has planned a lesson identical to third period, as both classes are in the same part of their respective gymnastics units. Laura once again observes the class, this time using the ALT-PEP recording system. She makes four series of PLACHECK scans in the class, one near the beginning and one near the end of each 20-minute practice segment. The resulting data are shown on page 231. As before, Laura meets with Cheryl after the class, this time more certain about the source of Cheryl's problem. Laura also has some possible solutions in mind but hopes to let Cheryl propose them in the course of their discussions.

Cheryl: Well, the same thing happened again! I hope you have a handle on this, because it's getting me very worried. The gymnastics units are falling apart, and I'm losing the students' respect quickly; they seem to sense that lately I'm not very comfortable or in control.

Laura: Let me show you the PLACHECK data and describe a series of events that might be contributing to the problem. This class did confirm my observations from third period, and those initial observations seem to be reflected in the data from this period.

Cheryl: What do you mean?

Laura: I was struck during the third period by the way things changed from the great beginning—your warm-up segment—to the two practice segments. It seemed clear to me that your students really want to learn better gymnastics skills; they appear quite anxious and enthusiastic going into the first practice segment. When the students in seventh period got to their first station, they went right to work going through some preliminary routines. Notice that in the first PLACHECK series 67% of the students were practicing and succeeding. They practiced those things they knew how to do well for the first few minutes. Once those familiar routines were completed, they had no direction for what to do next. Remember, you told them only to stay busy for those 20 minutes but never really told them what to work on or designed any way for them to be challenged to extend their skills. So . . .

Academic Learning Time—Physical Education PLACHECK Recording System
(ALT-PEP)

Date __4-5-89__   Teacher __CheryL__

Grade __10__   School __Price's Fork HS__

Observer __Laura__   Content __Gymnastics/Stations__

Time Begin __1:15__   Time End __2:03__

Elapsed Time __48 mins.__ # Students __20__

Task	STATIONS - START OF FIRST SEGMENT		Time	1:30
	# Scanned	Relevant Motor Engaged		Appropriate
Scan: 1	20	13		13
2	20	15		15
3	20	13		13
4	20	13		13
5	20	14		14
6	20	12		12
Totals	120	80 = 67 %		80 = 67 %

Task	STATIONS - END OF FIRST SEGMENT		Time	1:42
	# Scanned	Relevant Motor Engaged		Appropriate
Scan: 1	20	7		7
2	20	9		9
3	20	10		10
4	20	10		10
5	20	9		9
6	20	9		9
Totals	120	54 = 45 %		54 = 45 %

Task	STATIONS - START OF SECOND SEGMENT		Time	1:47
	# Scanned	Relevant Motor Engaged		Appropriate
Scan: 1	20	12		12
2	20	13		13
3	20	10		10
4	20	14		14
5	20	10		10
6	20	14		14
Totals	120	73 = 61 %		73 = 61 %

Task	STATIONS - END OF SECOND SEGMENT		Time	2:00
	# Scanned	Relevant Motor Engaged		Appropriate
Scan: 1	20	6		6
2	20	4		4
3	20	3		3
4	20	7		7
5	20	5		5
6	20	5		5
Totals	120	30 = 25 %		30 = 25 %

Cheryl: I see. So, they become bored and restless, resulting in the socializing with their partners or doing some other tasks. Both options resulted in my telling them to get back to work at a task they didn't understand to begin with!

Laura: Exactly. You can see the steady decline in the engagement percentage near the end of the first segment, which showed 45%, a slight increase to 61% to begin the second segment, and then the inevitable reversion to misbehavior near the end of class, with only 25% engaged.

Cheryl: But at least they were doing appropriate tasks! All of the motor appropriate scans match their corresponding motor engagement scans.

Laura: Yes, but only because they chose to do those stunts they were familiar with! Otherwise, they didn't even attempt to practice. The only task accountability they were under was your general statement to stay busy and your regular scolding.

Cheryl: But these are advanced gymnastics classes. They should be able to motivate themselves and not depend on me to be right with them for every attempt.

Laura: That's not fair to the students, Cheryl. They have indicated a willingness to practice their routines; the initial PLACHECK series shows that. What they need is some form of explicit and continuing accountability messages from you, some direction on what to do next at each station.

Cheryl: I see what you mean. They need to have some expectations and challenges set out for their practice segments. Maybe I perceived these classes as being already advanced when I should have focused on how to advance them. Does that make any sense to you?

Laura: You assumed they had advanced skills and that you could just let them go off on their own, rather than trying to keep them advancing to higher levels.

Cheryl: Boy, did I miss the boat on this one! But, I think I can turn it around rather easily.

Laura: How so?

Cheryl: Well, if they need to be challenged and guided in their practice, I just need to look for some ways to do that. For starters, I have several gymnastics skill progression books and some videotapes that show good gymnasts in action. You know, the ones with the narrator and the neat slow motion pictures?

Laura: Sure, but what's your plan?

Cheryl: I can do two things at each station. First, I can post the progressions from the books to let my students know what and how to perform more advanced stunts. The illustrations should give them a good idea of what the stunts look like and how to practice them. I can rotate the video equipment around to different stations each day to supplement the suggestions from the photo illustrations. So, they can get ideas from two sources. They can also use the video camera to record their own stunts and then compare them to the models.

Laura: That lets them know what and how to practice. How do you keep them practicing?

Cheryl: That's the second part of my plan. I can make a personal progress chart for every student and ask them to record how many times they practice each stunt and how many times their partners judged it to be near the desired technique. At each station I can post the number of trials they should get in that 20-minute segment and then monitor how many students are meeting those expectations. I'll probably need to adjust my targets a few times, but eventually I should arrive at numbers that are fair to students at all stations.

Laura: Sounds great! How about if I come back into your third period class tomorrow, to do another ALT-PEP recording? If your plans work, we should see immediate improvements in the engagement and motor appropriate percentages.

Cheryl: OK. See you then, I'm looking forward to it!

Laura observes the next day's third period class with the ALT-PEP system. The class again consists of 18 students. Cheryl has made her new plans for the class and spends a few minutes at the beginning explaining the procedures to the students. They look around the room to see the posted illustrations and video viewing apparatus Cheryl has prepared for them. Cheryl gives each student an index card for recording practice trials; she explains the purpose of the cards and points out the number of expected target trials for each station. She is careful to point out that the target numbers are suggestions for the first few classes and that she will adjust them later as needed.

Following her explanations, the students have their usual warm-up period with music. And, as always, the atmosphere is positive and energetic during this segment. After the warm-up routine, Cheryl directs the students to begin the 17-minute practice segments. The class goes smoothly, with only a few students needing comments from Cheryl to keep on task. The reduced frequency of students off task cues her that they are in fact behaving better today, so she uses a soft voice to redirect these students. The students respond to Cheryl's new approach, and the positive atmosphere in the early part of the class is maintained throughout the whole period. During the class, Laura overhears several students comment about how well today's class is going and how fast the two practice segments have gone by. Cheryl continues to monitor student engagement periodically in the class but is clearly pleased with how seldom she finds students off task. At the end of class she brings the students together to ask them how they like the new arrangement. The response is nearly unanimous: today's class was the best they've had in physical education in some time. Cheryl agrees and thanks them for their cooperation before dismissing them.

Laura and Cheryl meet once again for a postteaching conference. Laura shares with Cheryl the latest motor engagement and motor appropriate data from the PLACHECK scans. The ALT-PEP data sheet is shown on page 235.

Laura: No doubt, that class went much better than either of the ones I monitored before. The improvement shows, any way you look at it!

Cheryl: I agree! That was one of the most enjoyable and productive classes I've had in a long while. I can't tell you how good it felt to see things go that well! What do you have for me?

Laura (showing Cheryl the data sheet): Well, I did PLACHECK scans at about the same four times as yesterday's seventh period class. As you can see, the pattern is very different. The first scans for motor engagement were 83%, about the same as yesterday, but we expected that. The students have been doing well at the start all along. Notice that the motor appropriate percentage dropped off a little to 72% as they began to work on new and harder stunts than before.

Cheryl: That's not bad, though, is it?

Laura: Not at all. The first series indicates that they were about to be challenged throughout the period. But, notice that the second series of scans showed no drop off at all in motor engagement, 83% again. That tells me that they stayed working throughout the time at the first station. That's in direct contrast to previous observations; and their motor appropriate percentage stayed high as well, 67%.

Cheryl: You know, in the first segment of the class I looked around frequently, trying to catch them misbehaving, really thinking that I would! Later on, I looked around for a different reason, to watch them practice their skills! What a difference that makes to a teacher's attitude in class!

Laura: Well, the news gets better. Rather than the usual slight decrease in engagement at the start of the second segment, the students actually maintained their high level of practicing, 89%, but did show a small decrease in motor appropriate responding, down to 61%. I think this reflects their tendency to get right into new tasks even if they couldn't master them right away. But they were trying new and harder stunts, and that was a noticeable improvement.

Cheryl: Yes, it was about then that I thought this new approach would work.

Laura: The final series of PLACHECKs is really impressive, 89% motor engagement and 83% motor appropriate! They responded to their new and more challenging tasks by staying with them and showing fast improvement. They are now ready to really take off in this class and progress the way you have hoped for all along. I should also tell you that I heard several enthusiastic comments by students throughout the class; they were really excited with your new lesson structure.

Cheryl: I can't wait to try this again with my seventh period class this afternoon. I'm confident we'll see the same thing happen.

Academic Learning Time—Physical Education PLACHECK Recording System (ALT-PEP)

Date __4-6-89__   Teacher __CHERYL__

Grade __10__   School __PRICE'S FORK HS__

Observer __LAURA__   Content __GYMNASTICS/STATIONS__

Time Begin __10:30__   Time End __11:20__

Elapsed Time __50 MINS.__   # Students __18__

Task __STATIONS- START OF FIRST SEGMENT__   Time __10:47__

Scan:	# Scanned	Relevant Motor Engaged	Appropriate
1	18	15	13
2	18	14	12
3	18	16	14
4	18	14	11
5	18	18	15
6	18		
Totals	108	$90 \frac{13}{} = 83$ %	$78 \frac{13}{} = 72$ %

Task __STATIONS- END OF FIRST SEGMENT__   Time __10:59__

Scan:	# Scanned	Relevant Motor Engaged	Appropriate
1	18	18	14
2	18	16	10
3	18	13	12
4	18	15	13
5	18	14	13
6	18		
Totals	108	$90 \frac{14}{} = 83$ %	$72 \frac{10}{} = 67$ %

Task __STATIONS- START OF SECOND SEGMENT__   Time __11:05__

Scan:	# Scanned	Relevant Motor Engaged	Appropriate
1	18	18	9
2	18	17	11
3	18	14	10
4	18	16	12
5	18	16	12
6	18		
Totals	108	$96 \frac{15}{} = 89$ %	$66 \frac{12}{} = 61$ %

Task __STATIONS- END OF SECOND SEGMENT__   Time __11:16__

Scan:	# Scanned	Relevant Motor Engaged	Appropriate
1	18	16	14
2	18	16	16
3	18	14	13
4	18	15	15
5	18	17	14
6	18		
Totals	108	$96 \frac{18}{} = 89$ %	$90 \frac{18}{} = 83$ %

THE FINAL SCAN WAS PERFECT, 18-18-18 !

Laura: We? I'm afraid I can't make it, so you'll have to take that one solo. Anyway, I think it'll work with that class as well, and maybe even better, now that you have confidence in these new decisions.

Cheryl: But now I have a new problem.

Laura: What's that?

Cheryl: How to keep up with my classes as they want and can do more advanced skill progressions!

Laura: I'm sure you'll find a way!

Cheryl: Before you ride into the sunset, please know that I appreciate all the help you've given me this week. Even after all these years, I'm amazed at the amount I still need to know and keep in mind in order to be an effective teacher. Your extra eyes and ears were fantastic, and I hope I can return the favor some day. Thanks, Laura.

Summary

Veteran teachers often fall into their instructional patterns for reasons not related to effective practice. Some of those reasons are responses to the realities of working in American schools; often they are asked to assume many more responsibilities than helping students learn. Other reasons for this stagnancy stem from teachers' unfamiliarity with effective teaching practices or a reliance on simple expediency. And for many physical educators, the dual demands of the teaching/coaching roles are another reason for resistance to change. However difficult the task, supervision can be effective in helping experienced teachers continue to improve as long as supervisors first consider how best to approach, communicate, and interact with these teachers. Because such familiarity often comes from being an experienced teacher oneself, peer supervision may be the most promising type of supervision for this stage.

The preceding scenario demonstrates the benefit experienced by both teachers in such a supervision series. Laura probably learned as much about teaching as Cheryl did; a teacher does not have to be on the receiving end of supervision to improve her own instruction.

Both teachers had previous training in supervisory strategies, which certainly facilitated the entire process. The training allowed Laura to make insightful observations and comments about Cheryl's teaching; Cheryl's training, and the fact that her peer was providing the assistance, helped her understand the purpose of the processes they carried out together. This depiction of teachers helping teachers shows the very best that instructional supervision can be when practiced in schools. It demonstrates that trained, informed colleagues can assist each other with actual problems and resolve them within the context of their own school.

Chapter 12

Supervision for Classroom Teachers as Physical Educators

Physical education in American elementary schools holds a unique position on the list of curricular offerings. It is a subject area required in most states (in various ways), yet children are likely to receive a significant amount of their instruction from classroom teachers as well as from certified physical education specialists. The latest report of the National Children and Youth Fitness Study (Ross, Pate, Corbin, Delpy, & Gold, 1987) estimates that classroom teachers provide 20% of all early elementary physical education programming.

The widespread erosion and elimination of physical education programs in recent years, due to budget constraints and calls for more academic work, have left the conduct of some remaining programs to classroom teachers. In an age when curricular programs must often demonstrate tangible outcomes to remain part of the school day, an alarming number of programs are implemented by teachers who are either not specialists or who possess marginally acceptable credentials for teaching children's physical education (Ross, Pate, Corbin, Delpy, & Gold, 1987).

We know little about how classroom teachers approach and implement their physical education instruction in elementary schools. (The terms *elementary physical education* and *children's physical education* are used synonymously in this chapter.) At best we have only hunches about what classroom teachers do during time allocated for physical education. Our lack of adequate knowledge is itself a concern, as more classroom teachers each year become responsible for instructing elementary physical education due to program cutbacks and elimination of specialist positions.

In spite of the largely negative picture painted about physical education taught by classroom teachers, most teachers likely recognize the value and potential for sound programs of motor skills and fitness in our elementary schools. Classroom teachers want to have productive and effective physical education programs; however, many constraints keep them from realizing those goals.

- Most classroom teachers have little if any training as physical educators. Most have taken just one physical education course in their certification programs; the degree to which that course provides meaningful instructional skill development varies across professional preparation programs. Even if such a course does focus on effective teaching skills, one course by itself cannot in any way provide sufficient training for teaching effectiveness.

- Classroom teachers are not likely to keep abreast of curriculum developments in children's physical education.

- Many classroom teachers do not recognize the difference between educational programming and recess, recreation, or youth sports.

- Classroom teachers often view physical education as a contingent part of the school day. That is, they allow students a physical education period only when higher priority academic tasks are completed. From this perspective, physical education is usually squeezed in sometime during the day, without the benefit of prior planning or consideration.

- Physical education holds a low priority with teachers and administrators; many feel it need not be taught very well if taught at all.

- A productive and effective physical education program requires much time and energy from a teacher. The many other demands made of classroom teachers plus physical education's low priority means classroom teachers simply are not able or willing to devote the necessary attention to elementary physical education.

Even with these imposing constraints, classroom teachers can conduct a successful physical education program. Such success, however, happens only when the focus and scope of those programs are in line with contextual factors under which classroom teachers must instruct children's physical education. This can occur most effectively under one of two designs.

With the first design, classroom teachers can work with their school's physical education specialist to provide a supplemental program on the days children do not meet the specialist. Under this scheme, the specialist plans all physical education programming, including enhancement activities implemented by classroom teachers on the days the specialist doesn't meet with the children. This relieves the classroom teacher from needing to keep abreast of curriculum trends and from planning sequenced learning activities for their students' physical education time. In essence, classroom teachers become teaching assistants for the physical education specialist.

The second design is useful when no specialist is assigned to a school. In this case, the classroom teachers should attempt only modest and highly focused curricular goals for physical education. Many of the constraints cited previously are due to classroom teachers trying to conduct comprehensive programming. A classroom teacher who reduces her major physical education goals to just one or two for the school year is more likely to achieve that limited agenda. Classroom teachers cannot be expected to offer the kind of programming possible from certified children's physical education specialists.

If classroom teachers are to succeed at physical education programming and instruction, school administrators must play a central role. The principal is the key person in the overall effectiveness of a school's academic program; that relationship should be no different for speciality programs like physical education. Within reasonable boundaries defined by contextual factors, the principal should expect classroom teachers to pursue a sound program of children's physical education as a regular part of the school day. More importantly, principals should provide supervisory functions to classroom teachers for improving their physical education instructional skills. Ratliffe (1986) showed that principals can be trained to be effective instructional supervisors for physical education specialists; principals can also deliver those same functions to classroom teachers who teach physical education. In most cases, the principal is the only person who can work with classroom teachers to improve their physical education instructional skills; even if a specialist is assigned to a school, that person is not usually available to supervise other teachers as he or she typically teaches 8 to 10 classes a day.

Characteristics of Supervising Classroom Teachers as Physical Educators

Supervisors who want to help classroom teachers improve their physical education instructional skills face a difficult task. But, they can achieve this goal! Classroom teachers can improve their performance in physical education and promote meaningful student achievement in motor skills, concept knowledge, and fitness. Those who supervise classroom teachers must recognize a few characteristics inherent to that task, those teachers, and the delivery of supervisory processes.

Working With a Specialist

A specialist who is assigned to a school should oversee the entire physical education program in a coordinated effort with the classroom teaching staff. All teachers' instructional efforts in physical education should contribute to common goals for a single program, not several independent ones in the same building. If classroom teachers admit to unfamiliarity with children's physical education programming, a trained specialist should plan lessons for those teachers within a school-wide curriculum. This frees the classroom teachers from making difficult programming decisions and simplifies their role as physical education teacher. Supervision in this situation must strive to facilitate communication between the specialist and classroom teacher for improved programming.

Working Without a Specialist

As mentioned before, classroom teachers should not be expected to emulate the scope and breadth of programming provided by certified specialists. These teachers do not have sufficient training, time, or the disposition to implement comprehensive physical education programs. Supervisors should encourage more modest programming goals for these teachers.

Classroom teachers cannot provide wider programming partly because they likely are not abreast of current curriculum trends in children's physical education. Supervisors must assist them in deciding what to teach as well as how to teach it. That means introducing them to new books, new curriculum materials, innovative equipment, and new teaching approaches.

Given the time necessary to learn the content of physical education programming and the severe temporal restrictions within the school day, supervisors should encourage classroom teachers to strive for limited and realistic programmatic outcomes. For example, teachers can repeat lesson content many times to help children master the material. Supervisors should not expect these teachers to effectively cover a comprehensive curriculum plan during the school year; rather, they can focus on only a limited set of curriculum topics.

Because classroom teachers do not have the expertise or time to sufficiently plan comprehensive children's physical education programs, these teachers need general "cook books" and other standardized resources that delineate proper sequencing of curriculum and learning tasks. The supervisor should help teachers locate and understand those resource materials prior to instructional implementation.

Transferring Effective Teaching Into the Gym

The major task for supervision is to help teachers transform effective classroom skills into effective physical education skills. Effective teaching/learning processes in these two settings bear remarkable similarities; their manifestation across the settings merely looks different at times. Trademarks of effective teaching in both settings include efficient use of resources, time management, academic focus, task accountability, and the proper use of instructional information. Strategies for implementing these effective processes change across the settings; however, the need to provide them for students does not. Supervision must help classroom teachers recognize this important feature of effective teaching and must assist them in making that transfer.

A Scenario for Classroom Teacher Supervision

Physical education supervision for classroom teachers cannot be expected to occur often or have a high priority in elementary schools. Teachers and administrators simply have too many other concerns to warrant particular attention to this relatively minor part of a teacher's week. Good physical education programming for children is important, but we must admit that it does not receive much attention from teachers and principals. If supervision for classroom teachers is to be helpful, it must be approached in ways that do not threaten the teacher, and supervisory suggestions should consider the many other priorities that teachers hold above physical education.

The following scenario shows how a teacher and a principal can work together to improve that teacher's physical education instruction. Notice that the scenario focuses on the *planning assistance, monitoring*, and *prescription* functions of supervision rather than the establishment of performance goals. Setting new goals achieves little when opportunities to monitor them are not regular. Instead, the principal provides the teacher with more of a status report and refresher course in physical education instruction.

■ *Scenario:* **A principal supervises a classroom teacher** ■
in physical education

Kathy is a fourth grade teacher at Terrapin Elementary School, located in a small suburban community. She has an intact group of 28 students, all of whom remain with the class for physical education. Her school has no physical education specialist, but she is expected to schedule a 30-minute instructional period each day to implement the district's physical education curriculum.

Kathy has been teaching for 3 years at Terrapin; her only training as a physical education instructor came 6 years ago in the form of one course during her preprofessional program. She recalls very little from that course, and she relies upon her ability to interpret the district's physical education curriculum guide and periodic supervision from her principal for help in conducting her physical education program.

The principal, Doug Scott, takes an active role in the school's entire instructional program; he keeps current in many of the speciality areas through frequent attendance at workshops and professional meetings. He has completed a series of workshops on clinical supervision for physical education and provides his teaching staff with regular assistance in their classroom and speciality instructional skills. His staff considers him to be a model of how administrators can take an active and meaningful role in the improvement of all subjects in the school.

Because he has limited opportunities to observe Kathy teaching physical education, Doug cannot afford to frequently provide her with the following supervisory cycle.

observe → comment → reteach/observe → comment

Therefore, he spends time with Kathy before her physical education period discussing her plans for that lesson, and he offers suggestions for helping lessons go better. Following those preliminary discussions he monitors an aspect of her performance to illustrate the impact their mutual suggestions had on the teaching and learning processes she implemented.

Doug: Kathy, you have your physical education period coming up after this short break. What do you plan to do in that lesson today?

Kathy: In going along with the district curriculum guide, I will have the students work on throwing and catching for the first part of the lesson. Then, to break up this unit a bit, I'll have them work on balance until the end.

Doug: So, you'll have three skill themes in the lesson?

Kathy: That's right. They get bored when I stay on one thing too long.

Doug: But three different skill themes in one 30-minute lesson seems like too much to me, especially when those themes aren't closely related to one another. Would you have them do reading, spelling, and math problems in one 30-minute segment of your classroom schedule?

Kathy: No. They need lots of time for each one of those areas. What is your point?

Doug: Well, just like they need time and proper progressions to master classroom skills, they need the same to learn motor skills, too. I understand that their attention spans are short, but rather than switch activities completely, why not give them several variations of the same skill theme in those 30 minutes? Changing activities does not imply changing skill themes!

Kathy: But if I did that all the time, I'd fall behind the district curriculum guide.

Doug: That's OK with me. I'd rather have you teach them things well than cover every area in the guide superficially. Does that sound reasonable to you?

Kathy: Yes, it does. Now I can slow things down a bit! I've been running full speed to keep up with the suggested schedule. I've also noticed that my students rarely meet the district's stated competencies, most likely because of the lack of time on any one of them. I guess I'll just work on throwing today, then.

Doug: Sounds great. What did you have in mind for the lesson?

Kathy: Well, they know the difference between personal and general space, so I want to do something with both concepts. Once out to the field, I thought I'd have them throw to themselves in their personal spaces, to work on control.

Doug: So, if they can't catch the ball within that space it will mean they don't have sufficient control?

Kathy: Right.

Doug: Great. What will they be throwing?

Kathy: The school has more than 28 balls, but not 28 of any one kind. So, I thought I'd let one group at a time work with the playground balls, then rotate the other students in every few minutes.

Doug: Rather than have all of the children practicing at once, even with different kinds of balls?

Kathy: I sense that you don't agree with that approach!

Doug: Correct. Why not have the lesson focus on throwing different objects and give the children a chance to practice throwing all those different ones? It would be a great way to introduce and familiarize them with the different types of throwing needed for various objects. After all, children do not survive on playground balls alone!

Kathy: Very funny! But, I do like your idea and see a double value to using all the different balls. The children can learn those differences, and we can talk about them before and after class. And all of the children will be able to practice at one time. I can figure out a rotation to make sure all the children get a chance to throw each of the different kinds of balls; all they need to do is switch with someone else until they practice with every kind.

Doug: The idea's fine, but you might want to be a little more systematic about how every child gets to throw each kind of ball. Depending on them to remember those things can cause a lot of confusion and lost time.

Kathy: Good point. They have a hard time keeping track of whose turn it is to be at the computer station in the room; it should take only a few minutes to come up with a rotation scheme for my physical education lesson.

Doug: After throwing in their personal space, then what?

Kathy: The practice in personal space should take about 15 minutes. From then until just before the end of class they will practice throwing in the general space.

Doug: What will that look like?

Kathy: I think I'll have them get with a partner, spread out about 15 feet, and move some distance from their neighbors. The task will be to throw their ball to their partner so that the partner can at least touch it without moving from the spot. This will introduce them to the concept of *accuracy*. I think asking them to make a throw that can be caught is too hard to begin with, so all they need to do is get it within their partner's reach. The target partner will then retrieve the ball, return to his or her original position, and try to throw for the same results.

Doug: I really like that last task. All the children will be getting lots of tries with immediate feedback on how well they've done. You can even ask them to try to get several in a row within their partner's reach; this makes it sort of a game.

Kathy: Good idea. If they can do the task well enough, I'll try that. But I don't want them to be too achievement oriented at the start.

Doug: I understand. We can see how it goes, and you can decide during the lesson. Do you have a lesson review activity planned?

Kathy: I sure do. They really get a lot out of short Q-and-A sessions at the end of classroom lessons, so I thought I'd do the same in my physical education lesson. I can tie together lots of the things we cover during the lesson to see how well they understand the cognitive concepts of the day. That should make for a full 30 minutes, don't you think?

Doug: I agree! Now, what would you like me to focus on while I observe your class?

Kathy: Well, since the children need lots of practice time and help from me to understand *control* and *accuracy*, can you take a look at those two things in class?

Doug: Sure. I have a simple system that monitors how students spend their time in class and analyzes a teacher's verbal statements: cues, guidance, and feedback. That should give us a good picture of just the things you mentioned. I'll come to your room when the period begins and follow you out to the field. Once there, I'll just stay within hearing and watching distance so I won't interfere with you at all. See you then.

Kathy: OK, and thanks for the help so far.

Mr. Scott observes Kathy's physical education lesson with the TA-IIS. He makes some marginal notes on the front of the recording sheet, shown on pages 245 and 246.

A little later in the day, Kathy finds a few minutes to discuss the lesson with Mr. Scott. (They were not able to meet right after her lesson ended.)

Kathy: Thanks again for your help before the class; that really made things go much better. I was really pleased with that lesson; it may be one of my best ever for physical education.

Doug: I agree. The data analyses show that students had only 12% in management, 14% in demonstration (knowledge), and 74% in practice. The low management time is even more impressive when you consider it takes a few minutes to get from your room to the field, which is *transition* time. Your demonstration time was also at a good level, since you took nearly two minutes at the end for your review Q and A. I thought the students needed that little summary to tie things together and prepare them for tomorrow's lesson.

Kathy: Me, too. I could see it clicking for many of them at the end; I plan to repeat the lesson and expect they will do even better on their throwing skills tomorrow.

Doug: Looking at the number of cues and guidance statements you gave, nearly 55, you did a nice job of focusing their attention on the finer points of the tasks. I never knew you knew so much about throwing!

Time Analysis—Instructional Information System for Physical Education
(TA-IIS)

Date __5-19-89__   Teacher __KATHY__

Grade __4__   School __TERRAPIN ELEM.__

Observer __D. SCOTT__ Content __ThROWING__

Time Begin __12:45__   Time End __1:15__

Elapsed Time __30 mins.__   # Students __28__

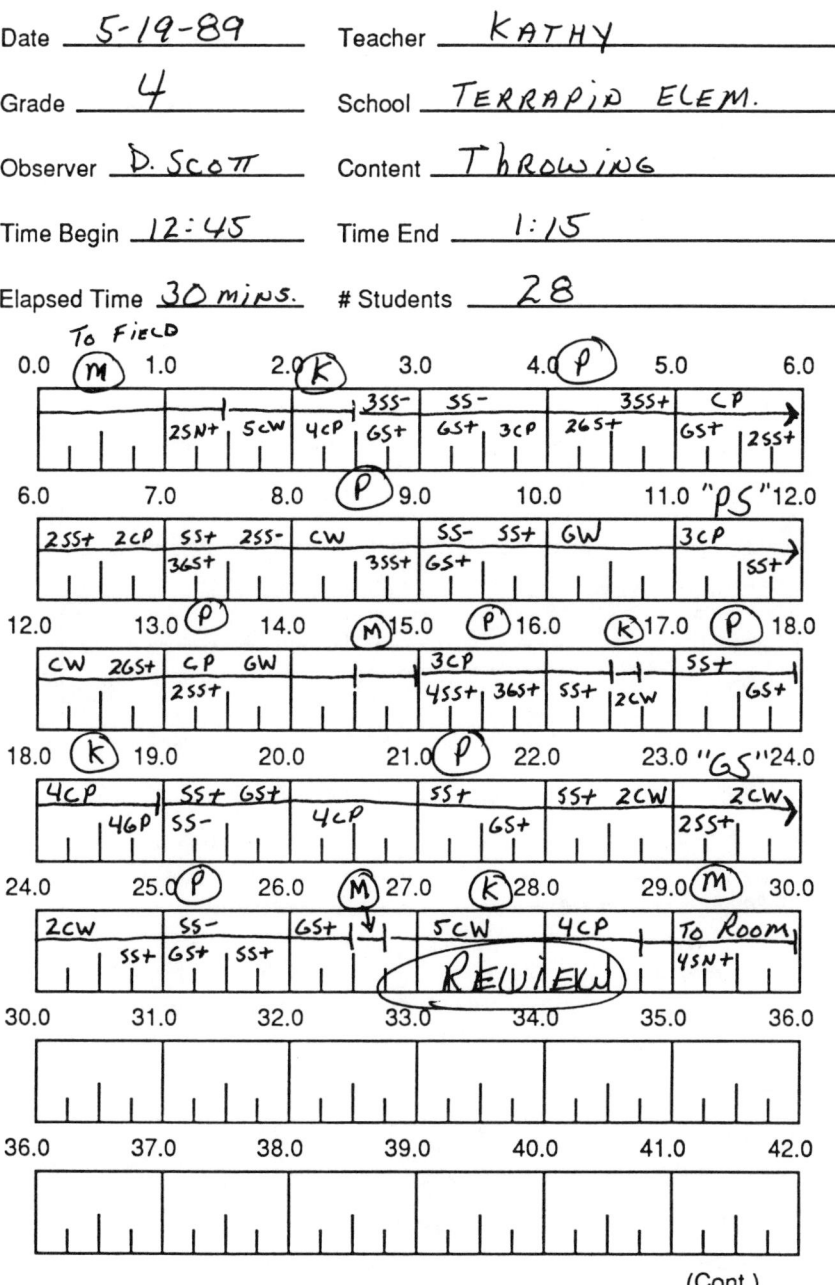

(Cont.)

TA-IIS (Continued)

Time Category (Code)	Feedback Category (Code)
Management (M)	General Skill (GS + or -)
Knowledge (K)	General Non-Skill (GN + or -)
Warm Up/Fitness (WF)	Specific Skill (SS + or -)
Skill Practice (P)	Specific Non-Skill (SN + or -)
Off Task (OT)	Cues and Guidance [(Code)]
Waiting (W)	
Resting/Break (R)	Cue [Whole (CW) or Partial (CP)]
Other/Undefined (O)	Guidance [Whole (GW) or Partial (GP)]

Category Calculations

Time Analysis	Min	%	Instructional Information		
Management (M)	3:30	= 12	+ General Skill (GS +)	= 18	Total
Knowledge (K)	4:15	= 14	+ General Non-Skill (GN +) = ___		Feed-back
Warm Up/Fitness (WF)	___	= ___	+ Specific Skill (SS +)	= 28	60
Skill Practice (P)	22:15	= 74	+ Specific Non-Skill (SN +) = 6		
Off Task (OT)	___	= ___	- General Skill (GS -)	= ___	Rate/min
Waiting (W)	___	= ___	- General Non-Skill (GN -) = ___		2.0
Resting/Break (R)	___	= ___	- Specific Skill (SS -)	= 8	
Other/Undefined (O)	___	= ___	- Specific Non-Skill (SN -) = ___		

FEEDbACK RATE A ND G/S

DISTRibUTioN WAS GooD !

LoTS oF CuES !

Cue—Whole (CW)	= 21	
Cue—Partial (CP)	= 27	Total
Guidance—Whole (GW) = 2		54
Guidance—Partial (GP) = 4		

Notes and Comments

- You WERE WELL PREPARED FOR This LESSON
- The REDUCED ScoPE WORKED WELL, LoTS OF PRACTICE oN JUST TWo Skills
- KEEP UP ThE GooD WoRk ;N PE !

Kathy: Well, right before class I spent a few moments looking at a text-book resource on that skill theme. It gave me a few skill features to look at and some suggestions for explaining them to the children. It had a few creative explanations to use; they seemed to be very effective.

Doug: Yes. The children knew right away what they needed to do for both control and accuracy. As I said, they got progressively better as the lesson went on. So, after 1 or 2 more days of similar skill work they should be ready to move on to something else.

Kathy: I think you're right. I noticed that my feedback rate was nearly 2 per minute. How does that compare to other teachers?

Doug: Because this lesson introduced a new skill theme, you had to spend more time providing students with cues and guidances; they needed some preliminary information before they could even reasonably attempt the tasks. Even though your feedback rate was not bad, as I recall from my PE workshop notes, I think it will get a lot better. When the children understand the tasks completely, you can then shift more of your attention to providing feedback instead of cues and guidance. A rate of nearly 2 per minute is still pretty good, so please don't take that last statement as a criticism.

Kathy: No, I won't. Is there anything else to discuss? I need to get back to my room.

Doug: No, just keep up the good work in your physical education teaching and let me know how I can help at any time.

Kathy: You've already been a big help, but I'll keep that in mind. Thanks.

Summary

In the last 2 decades more teaching positions have been allocated for physical education specialists in elementary schools. Possibly due to this general increase, we have paid less attention to those classroom teachers who still instruct some or all of physical education for young children; they represent a hidden teaching force that continues to provide nearly 20% of children's physical education teaching. Supervision for more effective physical education instruction must also include these teachers and recognize their unique circumstances. These teachers are likely to be undertrained, overburdened with other teaching duties in the day, and unfamiliar with current trends in physical education teaching and programming. These teachers should assume a limited and more realistic role as physical educators, and supervision for them should take on a more general function. Supervisors should spend more time helping these teachers stay abreast in curriculum and promote increased interaction with available physical education specialists.

The single scenario in this chapter highlights one feature of supervision for classroom teachers. It must be simple, help oriented, and brief; many times it must be done on the run or in very short moments during the day. But it can be done in a manner that provides the teacher with useful assistance, commentary, and information about how well he or she instructs during those periods. If physical education is worth including in the school day schedule, it is worth some attention to help teachers implement it more effectively. Only through attention and thought can teachers approach that small part of their curriculum in a manner likely to benefit children.

References

Acheson, K., & Gall, M. (1987). *Techniques in the clinical supervision of teachers* (2nd ed.). White Plains, NY: Longman.

Baer, M. (1977). Reviewer's comment: Just because it's reliable doesn't mean you can use it. *Journal of Applied Behavior Analysis, 10*, 117-119.

Boyan, J., & Copeland, W. (1978). *Instructional supervision training program.* Columbus, OH: Merrill.

Brophy, J., & Evertson, C. (1978). Context variables in teaching. *Educational Psychologist, 12*, 310-316.

Brophy, J., & Good, T. (1986). Teacher behavior and student achievement. In M. Wittrock (Ed.), *Handbook of research on teaching* (3rd ed., pp. 328-375). New York: Macmillan.

Clark, C., & Peterson, P. (1986). Teachers' thought processes. In M. Wittrock (Ed.), *Handbook of research on teaching* (3rd ed., pp. 255-296). New York: Macmillan.

Cogan, M. (1973). *Clinical supervision.* Boston: Houghton Mifflin.

Cooper, J., Heron, T., & Heward, W. (1987). *Applied behavior analysis.* Columbus, OH: Merrill.

Cruickshank, D., & Applegate, J. (1981). Reflective teaching as a strategy for teacher growth. *Educational Leadership, 38*, 553-554.

Darst, P., Mancini, V., & Zakrajsek, D. (Eds.) (1989). *Analyzing physical education and sport instruction* (2nd ed.). Champaign, IL: Human Kinetics.

Dembo, M., & Gibson, S. (1985). Teachers' sense of efficacy: An important factor in school improvement. *The Elementary School Journal, 86*, 173-184.

Dodds, P. (1983). Relationships between academic learning time and teacher behaviors in a physical education majors skills class. In T. Templin & J. Olson (Eds.), *Teaching in physical education* (pp. 173-184). Champaign, IL: Human Kinetics.

Dodds, P., Rife, F., & Metzler, M. (1982). Academic learning time in physical education: Data collection, completed research and future directions. In M. Pieron & J. Cheffers (Eds.), *Studying the teaching in physical education* (pp. 37-52). Liege, Belgium: International Association for Physical Education in Higher Education.

Faucette, N., & Graham, G. (1986). The impact of principals on teachers during in-service education: A qualitative analysis. *Journal of Teaching in Physical Education, 5*, 79-90.

Feiman-Nemser, S. (1983). Learning to teach. In L. Shulman & G. Sykes (Eds.), *Handbook of teaching and policy* (pp. 150-170). New York: Longman.

Feiman-Nemser, S., & Floden, R. (1986). The cultures of teaching. In M. Wittrock (Ed.), *Handbook of research on teaching* (3rd ed., pp. 505-526). New York: Macmillan.

Gitlin, A., Ogawa, R., & Rose, E. (1984). Supervision, reflection, and understanding: A case for horizontal evaluation. *Journal of Teacher Education, 35*(3), 46-52.

Goldhammer, R. (1969). *Clinical supervision: Special methods for the improvement of teachers.* New York: Holt, Rinehart & Winston.

Graham, G., Holt/Hale, S., & Parker, M. (1987). *Children moving: A teacher's guide to developing a successful physical education program* (2nd ed.). Palo Alto, CA: Mayfield.

Griffin, P., & Locke, L. (1986). This is not Palo Alto! *Journal of Physical Education, Recreation and Dance, 54*(4), 38-41.

Hawkins, A., Wiegand, R., & Landin, D. (1985). Cataloguing the collective wisdom of teacher educators. *Journal of Teaching in Physical Education, 4*, 241-255.

Housner, L., & Griffey, D. (1985). Teacher cognition: Differences in planning and interactive decision making between experienced and inexperienced teachers. *Research Quarterly for Exercise and Sport, 56*, 45-53.

Hoy, W., & Forsyth, P. (1986). *Supervision of instruction: Theory into practice.* New York: Random House.

Kounin, J. (1970). *Discipline and group management in classrooms.* New York: Holt, Rinehart & Winston.

Lambdin, D. (1986). Winning battles, losing the war. *Journal of Health, Physical Education, Recreation and Dance, 54*(4), 34-37.

Landin, D., Hawkins, A., & Wiegand, R. (1986). Validating the collective wisdom of teacher educators. *Journal of Teaching in Physical Education, 5*, 252-271.

Lawson, H. (1983). Toward a model of teacher socialization in physical education: The subjective warrant, recruitment, and teacher education (Part 2). *Journal of Teaching in Physical Education, 3*(1), 3-15.

Lawson, H. (1986). Occupational socialization and the design of teacher education programs. *Journal of Teaching in Physical Education, 5*, 107-116.

Locke, L. (1979, April). *Supervision, schools, and student teaching: Why things stay the same*. Paper presented at the American Academy of Physical Education, New Orleans.

Locke, L. (1983). Research on teacher education for physical education in the U.S.A: Part II. Questions and conclusions. In R. Telema (Ed.), *Research in school physical education* (pp. 285-320). Jyvaskyla, Finland: The Foundation for the Promotion of Physical Culture and Health.

Manasse, L. (1985). Improving conditions for principal effectiveness: Policy implications of research. *The Elementary School Journal, 3*, 439-463.

Mancini, V., Wuest, D., Lombardo, B., & van der Mars, H. (1987, March). *Observing behaviors: What have we learned about teachers' and coaches' actions?* Paper presented at the AAHPERD National Convention, Las Vegas.

McGreal, T. (1988). Evaluation for enhancing instruction: Linking teacher evaluation and staff development. In S. Stanley & J. Popham (Eds.), *Teacher evaluation: Six prescriptions for success* (pp. 1-29). Alexandria, VA: Association for Supervision and Curriculum Development.

McKenzie, T., Clark, E., & McKenzie, R. (1984). Instructional strategies: Influence on teacher and student behavior. *Journal of Teaching in Physical Education, 3*(2), 20-28.

Metzler, M. (1981). A multi-observational system for supervising student teachers in physical education. *The Physical Educator, 38*(3), 152-159.

Metzler, M. (1983). ALT-PE for inservice teachers: Questions and insights. *Journal of Teaching in Physical Education Monograph, 1*, 17-21.

Metzler, M. (1989). A review of research on time in sport pedagogy. *Journal of Teaching in Physical Education, 8*, 87-103.

Metzler, M., & Freedman, M. (1985). Here's looking at you, PETE: A profile of physical education teacher education faculty. *Journal of Teaching in Physical Education, 4*, 123-133.

Metzler, M., & Reif, G. (1986, August). *Triangulating teacher efficacy: A pilot study*. Poster presentation at the International Association for Physical Education in Higher Education World Conference, Heidelburg, Germany.

Mosher, R., & Purpel, D. (1972). *Supervision: The reluctant profession*. Boston: Houghton Mifflin.

National Association for Sport and Physical Education. (no date). *Videotape observation systems in physical education programs* [Videotape]. Columbia: University of South Carolina, NASPE Media Center.

Parker, M. (1986a). *Clinical supervision for physical education* [Unpublished videotape]. Blacksburg, VA: HPER Division, Virginia Tech.

Parker, M. (1986b, May). *Training cooperating teachers as clinical supervisors: The University of South Carolina model*. Paper presented at the International Conference on Research on Teaching and Teacher Education, Vancouver, British Columbia, Canada.

Pepin, B., & Sardy, S. (1987, February). *Retired teachers as mentors*. Paper presented at the Eastern Educational Research Association Meeting, Boston.

Placek, J. (1984). A multi-case study of teacher planning in physical education. *Journal of Teaching in Physical Education, 4,* 39-49.

Ratliffe, T. (1986). The influence of school principals on management time and student activity time for two elementary physical education teachers. *Journal of Teaching in Physical Education, 5,* 117-125.

Rink, J. (1985). *Teaching physical education for learning.* St. Louis: Mosby.

Rosenshine, B. (1979). Content, time, and direct instruction. In P. Peterson & H. Walberg (Eds.), *Research on teaching* (pp. 28-56). Berkeley: McCutchan.

Ross, J., Pate, R., Corbin, C., Delpy, L., & Gold, R. (1987). What is going on in the elementary physical education program? *Journal of Physical Education, Recreation and Dance, 58*(9), 78-84.

Siedentop, D. (1981). The Ohio State University supervision research program summary report. *Journal of Teaching in Physical Education,* Introductory Issue, 30-38.

Siedentop, D. (1983). *Developing teaching skills in physical education* (2nd ed.). Palo Alto, CA: Mayfield.

Siedentop, D., Tousignant, M., & Parker, M. (1982). *Academic learning time—physical education 1982 revision coding manual.* Columbus, OH: The Ohio State University.

Sulzer-Azaroff, B., & Reese, E. (1982). *Applying behavior analysis: A program for developing professional competence.* New York: Holt, Rinehart & Winston.

Taggart, A. (1985). Fitness—direct instruction. *Journal of Teaching in Physical Education, 4,* 143-150.

Templin, T. (1979). Occupational socialization and the physical education student teacher. *Research Quarterly, 50,* 482-493.

Templin, T. (1981). Student as socializing agent. *Journal of Teaching in Physical Education.* Introductory Issue, 71-79.

Templin, T. (1987). Some considerations for teaching physical education in the future. In J. Massengale (Ed.), *Trends toward the future in physical education* (pp. 51-67). Champaign, IL: Human Kinetics.

Thies-Sprinthall, L. (1980). Supervision: An educative or miseducative process? *Journal of Teacher Education, 31*(2), 17-30.

Tousignant, M., & Siedentop, D. (1983). A qualitative analysis of task structures in required secondary physical education classes. *Journal of Teaching in Physical Eduction, 3*(1), 47-58.

Verabioff, L. (1983). The five-to-one student teaching experience. *Journal of Teaching in Physical Education, 2*(2), 55-61.

Walberg, H. (1986). Syntheses of research on teaching. In M. Wittrock (Ed.), *Handbook of research on teaching* (3rd ed., pp. 214-229). New York: Macmillan.

Waxman, H., & Walberg, H. (1982). The relation of teaching and learning. *Contemporary Education Review, 2*, 103-120.

Zeichner, K., & Tabachnick, B. (1981). Are the effects of university teacher education "washed out" by school experience? *Journal of Teacher Education, 32*(3), 7-11.

Selected Resources
for Systematic Teaching
Observations

BOOKS

Boyan, N., & Copeland, W. (1978). *Instructional supervision training program*. Columbus, OH: Merrill.

Cooper, J. (1982). *Measuring behavior* (2nd ed.). Columbus, OH: Merrill.

Cooper, J. (Ed.) (1984). *Developing skills for instructional supervision*. New York: Longman.

Darst, P., Mancini, V., & Zakrajsek, D. (Eds.) (1989). *Analyzing physical education and sport instruction* (2nd ed.). Champaign, IL: Human Kinetics.

Good, T., & Brophy, J. (1987). *Looking in classrooms* (4th ed.). New York: Harper & Row.

Medley, D., Coker, H., & Soar, R. (1984). *Measurement-based evaluation of teacher performance: An empirical approach*. New York: Longman.

Rink, J. (1985). *Teaching physical education for learning*. St. Louis: Mosby.

Siedentop, D. (1983). *Developing teaching skills for physical education* (2nd ed.). Palo Alto, CA: Mayfield.

JOURNALS

Educational Technology
720 Palisade Ave.
Englewood Cliffs, NJ 07632

Journal of Classroom Interaction
 c/o H. Jerome Freiberg, Editor
 Farish Hall
 Room 450
 University of Houston
 Houston, TX 77004

Journal of Teaching in Physical Education
 Human Kinetics Publishers, Inc.
 Box 5076
 Champaign, IL 61825-5076

Index